A Matter of Simple Justice

A Matter of Simple Justice

The Untold Story of

BARBARA HACKMAN FRANKLIN

and a Few Good Women

LEE STOUT

This book grew out of the "A Few Good Women" project, which created the oral histories used herein. The funding for this project came from the following sources: Aetna Foundation, Inc., which was the major funder; with additional funding from the foundations of the Dow Chemical Company, TE Connectivity, formerly AMP, Inc., and Milacron, Inc., as well as The Sky Bight Foundation, Inc., and contributions from various individuals. Proceeds from the sale of this book will be used to support the Penn State University Libraries.

Frontispiece: President Nixon greets Barbara Franklin in April 1971. White House Photograph, A Few Good Women Oral History Collection, Penn State University Archives.

Library of Congress Cataloging-in-Publication Data

Stout, Lee.
A matter of simple justice : a few good women / Lee Stout
p.   cm.
Includes bibliographical references and index.
Summary: "Focuses on the major role of Barbara Hackman Franklin, a staff assistant to President Nixon, in expanding opportunities for women in government and in American society in general. Shows how the Nixon administration's achievements reflected the national debate over the role of women"—Provided by publisher.
ISBN 978-0-9839478-0-6 (cloth : alk. paper)
1. Franklin, Barbara Hackman.
2. Nixon, Richard M. (Richard Milhous), 1913–1994—Friends and associates.
3. Women—Government policy—United States.
4. Women's rights—United States.
5. Women—United States—Social conditions—20th century.
6. Women—Employment—United States—History—20th century.
7. Sex role—United States—History—20th century.
8. United States—Politics and government—1969–1974.
9. Women political consultants—United States—Biography.
I. Title.

HQ1236.5.U6S76 2012
305.420973—dc23
2011036981

Published by The Pennsylvania State University Libraries,
University Park, PA 16802-1003

It is the policy of The Pennsylvania State University Libraries to use acid-free paper. Publications on uncoated stock satisfy the minimum requirements of American National Standard for Information Sciences—Permanence of Paper for Printed Library Material, ANSI Z39.48–1992.

To my grandmothers, who in their own distinct ways,
showed me the dignity and strength of women in very
difficult circumstances; to my mother, who showed me the
value of unconditional love and kindness; to my wife, Dee,
who taught me that sharing compassion and wisdom are
just as important as teaching knowledge and skills;
and to Barbara Hackman Franklin and the
"few good women" who demonstrated,
in so many additional ways, that women
can do anything they choose

CONTENTS

ILLUSTRATIONS   *ix*

PREFACE   *xiii*

CHRONOLOGY   *xvii*

INTRODUCTION: *The Question and the Answer*   *xxi*

PART 1   *Advancing Women's Role in Government: Barbara Hackman Franklin*

1. Some Historical Background   *3*

2. Women's Appointments and the President's Task
   Force on Women's Rights and Responsibilities   *14*

3. Setting the Stage for a Program   *35*

4. Calling Barbara Franklin: The Initiative Is Under Way   *57*

5. The Women's Program Meets Its Goals   *77*

PART 2   *A Few Good Women in Their Own Words*

6. Recounting Early Influences and the Special Role of
   Women in the Legal Profession   *103*

7. Recalling Barriers, Appointments, and Family Impact   *132*

8. Considering Networking, the President, and the Impact
   of the Women's Program   *159*

CONCLUSION: *Breaking Barriers and Opening the Floodgates*   *181*

AFTERWORD BY BARBARA HACKMAN FRANKLIN   *189*

APPENDIX: *The "A Few Good Women" Oral History Project*   *195*

NOTES   *201*

BIBLIOGRAPHY   *219*

INDEX   *223*

※

ILLUSTRATIONS

1. Nixon press conference, February 6, 1969
2. Geraldine Ferraro
3. World War II recruiting poster
4. Penn State women debate team members
5. "Mrs. Woodhull Asserting Her Right to Vote"
6. "Packing bacon"
7. Catherine May Bedell at the signing of the Equal Pay Act of 1963
8. Equal Rights Amendment campaign button
9. President Nixon with Pat Hitt
10. Vera Glaser
11. Catherine East
12. President Nixon and Virginia Knauer
13. Virginia Knauer at a 1972 meeting of the Cost of Living Council
14. Pat Nixon campaign button
15. Peter M. Flanigan
16. Meeting of the Citizens' Advisory Council on the Status of Women
17. Dr. Daniel Patrick Moynihan
18. Melvin R. Laird
19. Virginia Allan
20. Elizabeth Athanasakos
21. Rita Hauser
22. Barbara Hackman, Penn State class of 1962
23. Pat Hitt meeting with the president
24. Robert Finch
25. President Nixon with Helen Delich Bentley
26. Representative Catherine May Bedell with Richard Nixon
27. The president with aides Donald Rumsfeld, Leonard Garment, and Charles B. Wilkinson
28. Connie Stuart
29. Mrs. Nixon at the fiftieth anniversary of the Women's Bureau
30. Ethel Bent Walsh with colleagues from the Small Business Administration
31. Bob Haldeman

32. President Richard Nixon
33. Bob Finch takes the oath of office as counselor to the president
34. The president meets with Helen Delich Bentley and other appointees
35. Rose Mary Woods
36. Donald Rumsfeld
37. Carol Marshall
38. The president greets Barbara Franklin
39. Barbara Franklin at her first press briefing
40. Barbara Franklin fields questions
41. Ann Uccello meets with President Nixon
42. Bob Finch
43. The president's directive of April 21, 1971
44. The president with Jayne Spain and Pat Hitt
45. President Nixon with Jayne Spain, announcing appointments for women
46. Judy Cole
47. Virginia Knauer
48. Barbara Franklin played an important role in outreach to women's organizations
49. Al Kaupinen
50. Pendleton James
51. Charls E. Walker
52. Barbara Franklin speaks with representatives of Federally Employed Women
53. Marina Whitman is sworn in as a member of the Council of Economic Advisers
54. Romana Bañuelos
55. Barbara Franklin at her desk
56. First Lady Pat Nixon
57. President Nixon speaking to the National Federation of Republican Women
58. The president delivers the 1972 State of the Union Address
59. Generals Anna Hayes, Mildred Inez C. Bailey, Elizabeth Hoisington, and Jeanne Holm
60. Barbara Franklin in a White House portrait
61. Julie and Tricia Nixon with Catherine Bedell
62. Dixy Lee Ray
63. Barbara Franklin with women appointees
64. Ethel Bent Walsh
65. Frank Herringer
66. Anne Armstrong
67. Connie Newman
68. Nola Smith with Anne Armstrong and the president
69. Jeanne Holm, special assistant on women for President Ford
70. Representatives Martha Griffiths and Catherine Bedell with Generals Anna Hayes and Elizabeth Hoisington
71. Margita White

72. Pat Hitt in her campaign office
73. Marina Whitman
74. Elizabeth Hanford Dole
75. Paula Tennant
76. Bret Sturtevant and Commerce Secretary Maurice Stans
77. Carla A. Hills
78. Bobbie Kilberg and Sallyanne Payton meeting with Barbara Franklin
79. Betty Murphy
80. Marina Whitman with President Nixon and George Shultz
81. Ruth Davis
82. Jeanne Holm
83. Ann McLaughlin Korologos
84. Cynthia H. Hall
85. Carol Marshall meets with the president
86. Virginia H. Knauer
87. Pat Hutar and her husband, Laddie Hutar
88. Patricia Hitt
89. Virginia Allan with William Rogers
90. Julie Nixon Eisenhower
91. Anne Armstrong with President and Mrs. Ford and Henry Kissinger
92. Marguerite Rawalt greets Barbara Franklin
93. Barbara Franklin is sworn in as secretary of commerce
94. Barbara Hackman Franklin
95. Reunion of "A Few Good Women"

The late historian Robert V. Daniels called it the "Gender Revolution"—the march of women to legal, political, and economic equality with men over the last century and a half. With a major acceleration over the last forty years, it has resulted in "the most profound social change that America has ever experienced, certainly since the abolition of slavery, perhaps in all its history."[1] And yet we still have not seen its completion, nor do we know how it will turn out, although a return to past attitudes and practices would seem impossible.

The women's movement has deep roots in our struggles for political and economic equality. By the nineteenth and twentieth centuries, extending equal treatment to women in law and at the ballot box required determined leadership by early feminists as well as fundamental changes in American society. These also inspired women's participation in reform movements such as abolitionism and the increasing presence of women working outside the home and away from the farm. The first and second world wars expanded the economic role of women but also changed women's outlook on life. Women increasingly sensed the value of independence for themselves in terms of family life, sexuality, and work.

Back in 1848, the delegates (both male and female) to the pioneering Seneca Falls Convention on Women's Rights declared that man had "endeavored in every way that he could to destroy [a woman's] confidence in her own powers, to lessen her self-respect, and to make her willing to lead a dependent and abject life."[2] A century later such feelings were still present, but much had changed as well.

The privations of the Great Depression and World War II gave Americans a yearning for "normalcy" and prosperity. By the 1960s, however, an accompanying "sexual counterrevolution," as Betty Friedan put it,[3] had evolved into a conscious antifeminism that disparaged the idea of women's rights. But with the twin earthquakes of the civil rights movement and the Vietnam War, these perceptions could no longer hold. Equality for women in the workplace was no longer just an issue for the factory floor or the secretarial pool. College-educated women increasingly sought entry to management and traditionally male professions.

The oral history project "A Few Good Women: Advancing the Cause of Women in Government, 1969–74" was an archival response to those powerful times. It resulted from my interest in acquiring the papers of Barbara Hackman Franklin, a 1962 graduate of Penn State. At the time, I was the university archivist, and it was my job to preserve the history of Penn State. To do that, we selectively keep the official institutional record, the personal papers of faculty and administrators, and materials from alumni that document student life. In 1992, we decided to expand the idea of alumni collections to more fully record the lives and achievements of our distinguished alumni—those who combine significant service to both Penn State and society at large.

Barbara Hackman Franklin received this award in 1972. Since then she has been a trustee of the university, an active leader in alumni affairs, and a distinguished public servant, most notably as U.S. secretary of commerce from 1992 to 1993. The following year, she launched an international consulting business, and I visited her in her Washington office to discuss her papers. In the course of our conversation, I heard a fascinating story that grew more interesting as Barbara talked about her experiences. It started with a question at a press conference that changed history. As we talked, and later as I read more about it, I realized that this was not an exaggeration.

In 1971, Barbara Franklin was named by President Richard Nixon a special assistant and charged with the responsibility of recruiting women for executive service and leadership in government. This was an extraordinary milestone; there had never been a person specifically tasked with such a role in the entire history of American government. The women she recruited were pioneers who made great advances, but in many cases the beginnings of their careers in the Nixon administration were overlooked. In addition, it struck me at the time that many of these women, whose service in government had started twenty or more years earlier, were advancing in age. It was only a matter of time before we would start to lose them.

I suggested to Barbara that there ought to be an oral history project for these women to record their reminiscences of both the unique journeys they had made and their common experiences in government. Barbara was very interested in this idea, but I set it aside while focusing on bringing her papers to Penn State. She, however, did not let it rest.

One of her first questions, "What is oral history exactly?," prompted this response on my part. Oral history interviewing is a process of collecting evidence. These are people's reflections seen through the lens of time, and one person's perspective may, and likely will, differ from another's on the same events and topics. Historians use this evidence by interweaving a selection of excerpts from interviews in a book or article, while archivists preserve those interviews so that in the future other researchers will also be able to read and evaluate them and possibly reach different conclusions. This is essential to building an evolving historical consensus.

By the end of 1995, we began to focus more on the prospects for an oral history project. We discussed the potential value and significance of these interviews; we talked about the nature of the interview process; and we discussed the logistics of creating and operating an oral history project. I prepared an outline of what we would need, in particular staff—a project manager, an interviewer, and a transcriptionist.

In 1996, Barbara formed an advisory board and launched the project. They decided that the perfect interviewer would be someone with Washington experience, who knew both the women and the era, to serve in the roles of project manager and interviewer. Jean Rainey, a longtime Washington publicist, fit the bill admirably. After discussions at Penn State about the nature of the project, she began interviewing. Eventually, we would have nearly fifty audio recordings with many of the most significant women who took office during the Nixon administration as well as with some of those tough-minded men who worked with Barbara in the White House Personnel Office.

As the project progressed, we created a website for it on the University Libraries webpages (http://www.afgw.libraries.psu.edu/) and began to see research use of the interviews. However, Barbara had more plans for the project. The first was to foster an extension of the project into the schools by sponsoring a women's history curriculum project. Penn State education librarian Karla M. Schmit has developed this curriculum for grades six through twelve in two phases with funding from the Aetna Foundation, and it is available online at http://www.pabook.libraries.psu.edu/afgwcur/home.html. This project has also become the basis for Karla's doctoral dissertation.

A second idea was for a book to describe the history of this experience and to highlight some of the wonderful commentaries that our interview subjects shared with us through their oral histories. That I would have the opportunity to tell this story is both a signal honor and the culmination of more than seventeen years of work with Barbara Hackman Franklin to preserve the recollections and reflections of these amazing women and men.

Many have contributed to this project and deserve acknowledgment. None of this would have happened without the determination and generosity of Barbara Hackman Franklin. Without her, there is no story, no project, and no book. I would also like to thank Wallace Barnes, Barbara's husband, who has encouraged this effort from its inception. I can't count the number of times he's personally flown Barbara back and forth to Penn State for meetings and events. He always has trenchant and useful comments to add to the discussion, and it's always a pleasure to share a Penn State Creamery ice cream cone with him before he leaves campus.

The members of Barbara's staff, present and past, especially Maureen R. Noonan, Mackenzie Burr, and Amy Whiteside, along with Kathy Johnpiere, Susanna Knouse, Susan Thigpen, Elizabeth Denny Haenle, Stacey Neary Normington, and Marlene Lyons, have been loyal friends and indefatigable workers on this project.

At Penn State, I've had the wonderful support of three successive deans of the University Libraries, Nancy Cline, Nancy Eaton, and Barbara Dewey, as well as Acting Dean Gloriana St. Clair and Assistant Dean for Scholarly Communications Mike Furlough, numerous development directors, Libraries Publications Manager Catherine Grigor, and Assistant to the Dean for External Services Shirley J. Davis. At the Penn State University Press, director Patrick Alexander has been a clear guide to the mysteries of publications and marketing at all times, as has the production and marketing staff of the Penn State University Press.

Among my archival and library colleagues at the Penn State University Archives, current archivist Jackie Esposito and archives staff members Paul Dzyak, Robyn Comly, and Alston Turchetta provided invaluable assistance. Past heads of special collections Charles W. Mann Jr. and William L. Joyce were strong advocates for the oral history project and all that has come from it. For their professional contributions, I also thank Martha Sachs and Heidi Abbey at Penn State Harrisburg's Alice Marshall Collection, Pamla Eisenberg, Ira Pemstein, and Ryan Pettigrew at the Richard Nixon Library, and the reference staff, especially Ellen M. Shea and Diana Carey, at the Schlesinger Library of the Radcliffe Institute, Harvard University. In addition, I extend my warmest gratitude to the Schlesinger Library and to the Rev. Carol Barriger, Vera Glaser's daughter, for their permission to quote from and cite her mother's work in this book.

Finally, my wife, Dee, has been my most valuable supporter in this project. She has read every draft of the manuscript, some several times, and is my most helpful critic and editor. This would never have been completed without her encouragement and help.

Lee Stout

CHRONOLOGY

1848   First Women's Rights Convention meets in Seneca Falls, New York, and calls for equal treatment of the sexes under the law and voting rights for women.

1869   The Territory of Wyoming passes the first women's suffrage law and later, in 1890, when it joins the union, is the first state with women's suffrage. Fifteen additional states will legalize the vote for women before 1920.

        Women's suffrage associations form and begin to campaign for constitutional amendments for voting rights for women.

1870   Iowa is the first state to admit a woman to the bar, Arabella Mansfield.

1872   Victoria Woodhull, of the Equal Rights Party, is the first woman to run for U.S. president.

1917   Jeannette Rankin of Montana is the first woman elected to Congress.

1920   Ratification of the Nineteenth Amendment, which says that a U.S. citizen could not be denied the right to vote based on sex.

1923   Equal Rights Amendment (ERA) is introduced in Congress by Senator Charles Curtis and Representative Daniel Anthony, written by Alice Paul, leader of the National Women's Party.

1933   President Franklin D. Roosevelt appoints the first woman U.S. cabinet member, Frances Perkins, secretary of labor.

1941   Seven million women join the work force and 400,000 women join the military in World War II.

1953   President Dwight Eisenhower appoints Oveta Culp Hobby as secretary of health, education, and welfare; she is the second woman to hold a U.S. cabinet position.

1961   President John F. Kennedy establishes the President's Commission on the Status of Women (chaired by Eleanor Roosevelt).

※

President John F. Kennedy stipulates that all women and men in the federal government must receive equal consideration for employment.

1963   Congress passes the Equal Pay Act of 1963, prohibiting discrimination in pay by gender for employees covered under the Fair Labor Standards Act.

Betty Friedan's *The Feminine Mystique* is published and sells five million copies by 1970.

1964   President Johnson signs the Civil Rights Act of 1964. Title VII of the act forbids job discrimination on the basis of race and sex. It also establishes the Equal Employment Opportunity Commission (EEOC) to adjudicate complaints.

1965   Supreme Court issues decision in *Griswold v. Connecticut*, permitting the use of contraceptives by married couples.

1966   Creation of the National Organization for Women.

1967   Executive Order 11375 adds prohibition of sex discrimination by federal contractors or subcontractors, amending Executive Order 11246 of 1965.

1968   EEOC bans sex-segregated help wanted ads in newspapers, a ruling upheld by the Supreme Court in 1973.

1969   At a February 6 press conference held by President Richard Nixon, Vera Glaser asks a key question regarding Nixon's administration appointments of women.

On October 6, Helen Bentley designated chair of the Federal Maritime Commission and the highest ranking woman in the Nixon administration.

"A Matter of Simple Justice," the report of the Task Force on Women's Rights and Responsibilities, is transmitted to President Nixon on December 12; on June 9, 1970, the report is released by the White House.

1971   On April 12, Barbara Hackman Franklin begins work leading the White House's first women recruiting effort.

On April 21, the Presidential Directive to Cabinet Secretaries and Agency Heads requires action plans for appointing and advancing women; plans are due to the White House by May 15.

1972   Senate passes ERA on March 22, 1972 and it is submitted to the states for ratification.

In April, on the one-year anniversary of the presidential directive, the number of women placed in policy-making positions has tripled from 36 to 105, and there are nearly 1,100 women placed in midlevel positions and 339 women appointed to boards and commissions.

On June 23, President Nixon signs the Education Amendments, which includes Title IX, forbidding sex discrimination in educational programs.

In July, *Ms.* magazine is first published.

On August 26, President Nixon issues the first proclamation of Equality Day, celebrating the anniversary of the ratification of the Nineteenth Amendment.

On December 17, Anne Armstrong is named a counselor to the president, with cabinet rank, making her the highest-ranking women in the Nixon administration.

1973   Supreme Court issues decision in *Roe v. Wade*, legalizing abortion.

1974   On August 9, Richard M. Nixon resigns the presidency.

On October 28, President Gerald Ford signs the Equal Credit Opportunity Act, which prohibits discrimination by sex in the granting of consumer credit.

1975   On October 7, President Ford signs legislation directing the military services to admit women to the Army, Navy, and Air Force academies.

Carla Hills is named as secretary of housing and urban development by President Ford.

First World Conference of the International Women's Year is held in Mexico City.

1976–   President Carter names three women to cabinet positions during his
1979   administration: Patricia Roberts Harris, secretary of housing and urban development; Juanita Kreps, secretary of commerce; and Shirley Hufstedler, secretary of education.

1978   The Pregnancy Discrimination Act bans employment discrimination against pregnant women.

1981   In January, President Carter proclaims the first National Women's History Week, incorporating March 8 as International Women's Day.

Sandra Day O'Connor, nominated by President Reagan, is the first woman confirmed as an associate justice of the Supreme Court.

1984   Geraldine Ferraro is the first woman vice presidential candidate of a major political party.

1986   In *Meritor Savings Bank v. Vinson*, the Supreme Court recognizes that sexual harassment is a violation of Title VII of the Civil Rights Act.

1992   "The Year of the Woman." A record number of women run for public office and win. Twenty-four are newly elected to the House of Representatives and six to the Senate. They include the first Mexican American woman and the first Puerto Rican woman in the House, Lucille Roybal-Allard (D-CA) and Nydia Velazquez (D-NY); the first black woman senator, Carole Moseley Braun (D-IL); and both senators from California, Barbara Boxer, Diane Feinstein, who are Democrats.

1993   Family and Medical Leave Act enables both men and women to take up to twelve weeks of unpaid leave if needed to care for a new child or a seriously ill family member, and under several other circumstances.

1994   Violence Against Women Act signed into law in response to the inadequacies of state justice systems in dealing with violent crimes against women.

1995   Lt. Col. Eileen Collins becomes the first American woman to pilot a space shuttle.

2000   Hillary Rodham Clinton elected U.S. senator from New York. She is the only First Lady ever elected to the United States Senate.

2004   Condoleezza Rice becomes the first woman national security advisor to a U.S. president.

2007   Congresswoman Nancy Pelosi (D-CA) becomes the first woman speaker of the U.S. House of Representatives.

2008   Alaska governor Sarah Palin is selected as the first woman Republican candidate for the vice presidency.

        Gen. Ann Dunwoody becomes the first woman to serve as a four-star general in the United States, heading the U.S. Army Materiel Command.

The Question and the Answer

At his February 6, 1969, news conference, President Richard M. Nixon announced details of his upcoming European trip and then proceeded to take questions. Near the end of the news conference, which was dominated largely by foreign and defense issues, Vera Glaser, of the North American Newspaper Alliance, rose and asked, "Mr. President, in staffing your administration, you have so far made about 200 high-level Cabinet and other policy position appointments, and of these only three have gone to women. Can you tell us, sir, whether we can expect a more equitable recognition of women's abilities, or are we going to remain a lost sex?"[1]

The president, in only his second formal press conference, seventeen days after the inauguration, "rolled his eyes upward for a moment in a kind of sighing chagrin," as one reporter put it.[2] He then smiled at Vera Glaser and quipped, "Would you be interested in coming into the Government?" There was some laughter, but apparently realizing that the issue, and the television audience, deserved more, he quickly added, "Very seriously, I had not known that only three had gone to women, and I shall see that we correct that imbalance very promptly."[3]

Vera Glaser later recalled, "I had qualms as a journalist about asking the President the kind of question that I did. And yet in simple justice, you had to ask it."[4]

Like the rest of the women interviewed for the "A Few Good Women" project, Vera Glaser was not afraid to stand up and say what needed to be said. As she later told the Citizens' Advisory Council on the Status of Women, this was "a movement to achieve a fair share of the nation's economic rewards and political leadership—a share to which our numbers, our education, our training, and our capacities as human beings fully entitle us."[5]

Massive changes in American society, such as the women's movement, are woven together from many historical threads. The people, events, and activities this work discusses are but one part of that process. However, their

FIGURE I
President Nixon's second press conference, on February 6, 1969, at which Vera Glaser asked "The Question."
White House Photograph files, Richard Nixon Presidential Library and Museum.

part has largely been forgotten. By capturing these memories in oral history, I have tried to rescue an overlooked but important aspect of those developments. Vera Glaser was just one catalyst for this change; she was not alone.

Barbara Hackman Franklin became the key White House figure in recruiting women for executive positions in the federal government in the administration of Richard M. Nixon. In her two years as staff assistant to the president, she was responsible for recruiting more than three times as many women executives for the government as in any previous administration. The story of these "few, good women" is to a great extent her story as well. Thus, this book is organized in two parts: the first provides a narrative overview of the evolution of the "women's program" and Barbara Franklin's leadership of it, the second tells us more about those "few good women" as they speak out on a variety of topics including their backgrounds, recruitment, and experiences in government.

But before we turn to the Nixon administration and the remarkable experiences Barbara Franklin had there, we should consider several historical threads that led us to that significant but little known early point in President Nixon's first term.

PART ONE

Advancing Women's Role in Government: Barbara Hackman Franklin

CHAPTER ONE

Some Historical Background

Today we rarely give the gender of a working person a second thought. We are as accustomed to seeing female police officers as we are to seeing male nurses, female doctors, and male elementary school teachers. This is not to say that the old traditions of certain jobs being predominantly male or female have completely disappeared; women still fill the majority of positions in teaching, nursing, and libraries, for example. Rather, it is the certainty that most jobs will be composed exclusively of men or women that has disappeared. There are still some glass ceilings, but in the 2008 election, we almost had a woman as a major party candidate for president and, for the second time, we did have a woman as a major party candidate for vice president.

Other benchmarks have also been reached: women now constitute more than half of the American workforce. They are the majority of university graduates and the majority of professional workers in the United States. There are now women CEOs in many important companies. It could well be that the growing economic power of women is the biggest social change of the last half century. Nevertheless, the advancement of women and the concerns of the American women's movement have focused as much on the achievement of civil rights for women as they have on equal participation in the economy and the job market.

*

The evolving role of American women in our society has a fascinating history, but it is generally accepted that World War II marked a turning point. Some 350,000 to 400,000 women eventually served in uniform during the war as nurses, in communications, in staff positions, and, on the home front, in all manner of jobs, as well as in the Women Airforce Service Pilots, who

FIGURE 2
In 1984, Geraldine Ferraro became the first woman candidate for vice president from a major party. Alice Marshall Women's History Collection, Penn State Harrisburg Library.

FIGURE 3
A World War II army recruiting poster for women focused on the many roles they could fill. Alice Marshall Women's History Collection, Penn State Harrisburg Library.

despite their high-risk duties were recognized as official veterans only in 1977. Several million more women joined the workforce to help support the war effort. "Rosie the Riveter" is their symbol, but women served in many other roles in manufacturing, farm labor, and office work as well as in traditional female-dominated professions, such as nursing and teaching. Compared with these millions, however, few women had cracked the barriers to enter business management and other professions.

From 1940 to 1945, women as a percentage of the workforce grew from 26 percent to 36 percent; in real numbers, this meant an increase from 13 million to 19.3 million women. By the end of 1946, however, more than half of those 6.3 million additional women had left the workforce, largely because of the men returning from the war. Some had taken jobs out of patriotism, others because they needed the money or wanted something interesting to do. Now many were happily returning to their families and homes, although some did not leave voluntarily. Although the culture still saw women's primary role as wife and mother, women had changed; the idea of the working mother, either out of necessity or preference, would increasingly become commonplace and gradually be accepted as normal over the next thirty years.

In that great resumption of prewar normalcy, between 1945 and 1950, women as a portion of the workforce fell back from 36 percent to 29 percent, but in the 1950s it would gradually begin to climb again, reaching 35 percent in 1960 and 42 percent in 1970. However, women were still consigned, because of sex segregation or stereotyping, to lower paying positions—one study found three-quarters of all women even in the late 1950s working in "women only," low-wage jobs.

Although more women than men completed high school, college attendance on the part of women lagged behind. In 1951, women made up only a third of all college students, but from 1952 on, women's enrollment grew faster than men's. The tipping point was reached in 1979, when, nationally, out of 11.6 million college students, women outnumbered men by more than 200,000. The gap continued to widen, and by 1995, it was nearly 1.6 million.

While more women were earning degrees in the 1950s and 1960s, the concerns of both working women and homemakers were growing as well. The G.I. Bill of Rights, which educated hundreds of thousands of veterans (male and female), also helped those new graduates, now working in America's booming postwar economy, to buy new homes. Some of them were in suburban housing developments, where men would leave, often with the family car, to commute to work. Women stayed home to raise their children, aided by electric and gas appliances in a new world of labor-saving devices. Although wives were more frequently in the job market now to help support the increasing costs of meeting all the family's expectations and desires in this new consumer-driven society, they tended to be looking for a job, rather than a career.

Still, many suburban women found themselves isolated to a degree that was not common before in city or town environments; they began to feel frustrated in their existence as homemaker and mother. Betty Friedan, in a 1960 article in *Good Housekeeping*, found "a strange stirring, a dissatisfied groping, a yearning, a search that is going on in the minds of women," looking

FIGURE 4
*Women student debate team members record speeches to advance their work in forensics,
1948. Penn State University Archives.*

for a "chance for self-fulfillment outside the home." Friedan did not have a
name for this phenomenon yet, but two years later she filled out the picture
in *The Feminine Mystique*, a book that would connect not only with middle-
class women but also with working-class and minority women, who still were
largely stuck with low-wage, sex-segregated jobs, and with those with children and little or no access to affordable day care.

The social milieu was changing as well. The younger sisters and daughters of
the women workers of World War II had seen women in different roles; this
would also lead to changing values. A sexual revolution had been brewing
since the turn of the century. Arguments over birth control, advocated nationally by Margaret Sanger, melded into the liberating days of the 1920s.
In that era, the divorce rate rose, and there was a growing awareness that
premarital sex—always present in the past but furtively hidden—had now
become an open topic of discussion.

After World War II, many of the social trends reverted to earlier norms.
People married at a younger age, and the percentage of single people in the

population declined. Similarly, women had more children and did so at a younger age. Divorce rates declined, as did college attendance rates for women. The long disruptions of the Great Depression and World War II had made the possibility of a secure, "normal" life very attractive once again.

But as it turned out, family life was different: women did more housework (in part because "hiring a girl to help around the house" had become less common than in the past). The new popular culture, as represented in television, film, magazines, and books, generally emphasized the proper role of women as homemakers and mothers. Throughout the 1950s and 1960s, however, women's roles were gradually called into question more often. At the same time, men were periodically jolted into a new consciousness that women were increasingly looking for new opportunities, not just to contribute to the family income but also to both earn a living and achieve the satisfaction of meaningful work. These were times of economic growth and a fondly idealized golden era of placid and orderly life. But it was, of course, the 1960s that was the linchpin of all that would culminate in the modern women's movement. "The Sixties"—love 'em or hate 'em—were a tumultuous time when the cultural, social, and political changes that are now so familiar to us first began to accelerate.

Society had received a wake-up call with the Kinsey Reports on sexual behavior in, first, the human male in 1948 and, then, the human female in 1953. Their "cold" statistics, with "hot" implications, staggered social conservatives. *Playboy* magazine (first published in 1953) and the mega-selling novel *Peyton Place* (1956) further stoked the fires. With the introduction of the birth control pill, approved by the Food and Drug Administration in 1960 and later backed by the 1965 Supreme Court decision in *Griswold v. Connecticut*, which legalized the sale of contraceptives and introduced the constitutional right to privacy, Victorian sexual mores were on the ropes.

This was only one aspect of an increasingly unpredictable and edgy social environment of rock 'n' roll music, liberalized dress and hairstyles, a growing interest in recreational uses of drugs, health warnings against tobacco, concern for the environment, and the youth culture's increasing rejection of adult authority and expertise. Along with these changes came increasingly ambitious government programs to fight poverty, improve life in the cities, enhance healthcare and education and a variety of other initiatives, matched by anxiety over nuclear war and genuine anguish over the country's involvement in Vietnam. As the Woodstock generation confronted the Cold Warriors, the generation gap became absolutely frigid.

Calling for justice for women in a society that barred them from exercising civil rights, the convention adopted a Declaration of Sentiments and twelve resolutions, including one for female suffrage.

After the Civil War, attempts to attach sex to the Fourteenth and Fifteenth Amendments, which had given freed slaves the right of citizenship and the right to vote, failed to gain a hearing. In 1872, Victoria Woodhull of the Equal Rights Party was the first woman nominated as a candidate for president of the United States, and although there may have been votes for her, there is apparently no record of them being counted.[1] An 1875 Supreme Court decision confirmed women as citizens but said that this did not give them the right to vote unless states permitted it. The Wyoming Territory granted women the right to vote in 1869, and by 1900, Colorado, Utah, and Idaho had also granted women suffrage; more western states would follow.

Through the course of the twentieth century, the majority of women labor leaders, settlement house movement reformers, and women political leaders opposed the ERA, fearing that it would lead to the repeal of protective legislation for women workers that had been won through long, hard battles. These included laws restricting the number of hours women were required to work and the physical demands placed on women in a job. Nevertheless, both the Republican and Democratic Parties included some mention of the ERA in their party platforms starting in the early 1940s.

FIGURE 5
"Mrs. Woodhull Asserting Her Right to Vote." Alice Marshall Women's History Collection, Penn State Harrisburg Library.

FIGURE 6

*"Packing bacon": early women factory workers in the food industry. Alice Marshall Women's
History Collection, Penn State Harrisburg Library.*

Actual participation in the government by women, however, was relatively
uncommon. The numbers of female members of Congress who were not
widows of deceased members (who often held the seat for the party until the
next election) was small. The number of women officeholders in the government was equally minute. In many cases, Civil Service regulations specified that
jobs were for men only, regardless of the physical demands of the position.

President Harry Truman was quoted in 1945 as saying that women's rights
were "a lot of hooey." Whereas President Franklin D. Roosevelt had selected
the first woman cabinet member, Frances Perkins as secretary of labor in 1933,
Truman appointed none, and Eisenhower appointed only Oveta Culp Hobby
as secretary of health, education, and welfare in 1953. Truman had appointed
twenty women to positions requiring Senate confirmation; Eisenhower did
slightly better with twenty-eight; Kennedy, slightly worse with twenty-seven.

John F. Kennedy's President's Commission on the Status of Women
(PCSW) was created at the end of 1961 and delivered its report in October
1963 (about seven months after the publication of *The Feminine Mystique*).
Eleanor Roosevelt chaired the commission until her death in 1962. The
PCSW was a pathbreaking exercise, but it also had to balance feminists' demands with a political desire to placate the labor movement, which wanted
to preserve women's protective legislation. Proclaiming motherhood to be
the major role of America's women, the commission report was less than
feminist, but at the same time, it resulted in the creation of state commissions
on the status of women across the country, which contributed to grassroots

CHAPTER TWO

Women's Appointments and the President's Task Force on Women's Rights and Responsibilities

Vera Glaser's February 6, 1969, press conference question focused attention on the uncomfortable truth that only three of the first two hundred policy position appointments in the new Nixon administration had gone to women: Pat Hitt, assistant secretary for health, education, and welfare; Elizabeth Koontz, director of the Women's Bureau in the Labor Department; and Rita Hauser, U.S. representative to the U.N. Commission on Human Rights and delegate to the General Assembly. Not that there hadn't been pressure for more. The White House began receiving letters almost immediately after the inauguration urging more women appointees and action on women's issues.[1]

Within the White House, there were staff members who saw potential advantages to supporting women's rights. Tom Cole, an assistant to Dr. Arthur Burns, counselor to the president, suggested that "one of those matters we can pursue expeditiously and with minimum of cost is the proposal calling for equal rights for women."[2] This question of administration support for the ERA was to be a topic of continuous staff debate over the next four years. It would often be linked to calls for appointing more women to high-level positions and for a special assistant or office for women's affairs in the White House.

Florence Dwyer, Republican U.S. representative for New Jersey, first broached these issues in a February 26, 1969, letter to the president. She urged concrete steps toward "the expansion of women's opportunities and responsibilities, the protection of women's equal rights, and the elimination of all forms of discrimination based on sex." She suggested as alternative strategies either a presidential commission or the creation of an Office of Women's Rights and Responsibilities and the appointment of a special assistant to the president to head it. The White House's answers were polite but perfunctory.[3]

FIGURE 9

President Nixon greets Pat Hill in January 1969 after her appoint-ment as assistant secretary for community and field services in the Department of Health, Education, and Welfare. A Few Good Women Oral History Collection, Penn State University Archives.

FIGURE 10

Vera Glaser, reporter for the North American Newspaper Alliance and a member of the Task Force on Women's Rights and Responsibilities in 1970. A Few Good Women Oral History Collection, Penn State University Archives.

Clearly, simple confidence on the part of advocates for women's rights would not be enough to bring about change. Vera Glaser's question set off a series of events that led to a dramatic transformation in the role of women in government service. Then a reporter for the North American Newspaper Alliance, she began to write a five-part series on the status of women in government entitled "The Female Revolt," which appeared in mid-March 1969, eventually seeing print in more than forty newspapers. She had been pleas-antly surprised by all the positive feedback she had received for her question after the news conference, but there was, indeed, one person who contacted her who would make a crucial difference in this effort.

FIGURE II

Catherine East, of the Labor Department, was a key figure in the work of both the Kennedy Commission on the Status of Women and the Nixon Task Force on Women's Rights and Responsibilities. Schlesinger Library, Radcliffe Institute, Harvard University.

Catherine East, then chief of the Career Services Division of the U.S. Civil Service Commission, had been an advocate for women's rights for many years. She had served as technical secretary for the Committee on Federal Employment of the President's Commission on the Status of Women (1961–1963) and was also executive secretary of the Citizens' Advisory Council on the Status of Women. She probably had more facts on women in government at her command than anyone else anywhere.

East sent Glaser a note the next day saying, "Congratulations on asking the President about appointments for women. All women owe you a debt."[4] Glaser recalled that Catherine East later called her, "saying that my question indicated I probably could use some statistics on the status of women. 'Indeed, I can,' I replied."[5] And thus began a very productive alliance.

East began to supply Glaser with information and even suggested questions that would be pertinent to ask administration officials. Glaser in the meantime was working all the angles she could. On March 27, she wrote Presidential Press Secretary Ron Ziegler, sending him her series of articles to place before the president. She told him, "I have no desire to become the permanent floating expert on women's rights. There are too many other subjects I am expected to cover. But I do feel deeply on the subject, as do women throughout the country." She also suggested that she had understated the "seething resentment" of women but that the president had a "magnificent opportunity [to] mend fences with women" and inspire the country.[6]

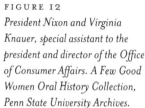

FIGURE 12
President Nixon and Virginia Knauer, special assistant to the president and director of the Office of Consumer Affairs. A Few Good Women Oral History Collection, Penn State University Archives.

In a Rose Garden announcement on April 9, the administration added to its number of women appointees by introducing Virginia Knauer as special assistant to the president for consumer affairs. As Knauer's new Office of Consumer Affairs developed with a staff of 17, it was to coordinate over 900 programs in 413 agencies. Knauer had directed the nationally recognized Pennsylvania Bureau of Consumer Protection. The president noted at her swearing-in ceremony that "her appointment is based solely on merit and qualification for the job. . . . She had the experience, the background, and the dedication in this subject that we thought qualified her for the top position in the Federal Government on consumer affairs."[7] Future senator Elizabeth Hanford Dole and future U.S. representative Tillie Fowler were among the women Knauer mentored in her office.[8] As consumer concerns widened, Knauer acquired more responsibilities, including membership on the Cost of Living Council and U.S. representative to the Organization for Economic Co-operation and Development's Consumer Affairs Subcommittee.

Still the administration moved very slowly for most women. Senator John Tower of Texas, who was known to be a supporter of the ERA, had directed a member of his staff to ask the White House about jobs for women. In response, presidential aide Charles B. Wilkinson reported, "I checked with Harry Fleming in the personnel office. He tells me that at the moment he has no jobs

FIGURE 13
Virginia Knauer was the only woman member of President Nixon's Cost of Living Council, seen here in 1972. A Few Good Women Oral History Collection, Penn State University Archives.

FIGURE 14
Republican campaign button featuring Pat Nixon. Alice Marshall Women's History Collection, Penn State Harrisburg Library.

that could appropriately be reserved for women."[9] This response was an all-too common one; many male staffers did not think that women were qualified for senior positions, or the notion itself simply had not occurred to them.

In April, Vera Glaser sent copies of her series of articles to Bryce Harlow, a Nixon counselor and even sent to Pat Nixon a list of names of women lawyers and jurists who might be qualified to fill a Supreme Court vacancy. The First Lady had requested this when Glaser had talked with her at a White House reception in May.[10]

The day before, Mrs. Nixon was quoted in the *Washington Post* as saying, "I really feel women have equal rights if they want to exercise those rights. The women I know, who are really interested in going out, pitch in and do good. I don't think there is any discrimination. I have not seen it. I know my husband doesn't feel that way."[11] Staff responded to criticisms of the statement by saying the First Lady was misunderstood—obviously, she knew the long struggle for women's rights still had further to go; it was time, now, to enforce existing laws and to adapt those laws and regulations to the new circumstances of today. As there was no infrastructure yet to enforce sex discrimination laws as there was for racial discrimination, the episode was read by many women's rights advocates as another mixed message from an administration that they perceived, fairly or not, to be indifferent to women.

A week later, Glaser had another opportunity to test the Nixon administration. In a May 15 news briefing, presidential counselor Arthur Burns said in response to a Glaser question that he was sure there were women capable of making policy decisions, but "I'm not aware of any discrimination against the better half of mankind. . . . I'm speaking only for myself, and I may be blind." Systemic discrimination would be "abhorrent," he believed.[12] She decided to challenge him on the fairness and equity of Nixon administration policies toward women. She wrote him a letter eight days later saying, "Dr. Burns, I am sure you must know your statement was not true because there are so few women in the administration. Women are being kept out of graduate schools for law and medicine, etc. Meanwhile, the Nixon administration pursues these policies."[13]

Burns called and asked her to come back to see him so that they could resolve these differences. He said, "You are quite right that I have not given this problem any real attention."[14] She asked if she could bring Catherine East and he agreed. Tom Cole's briefing memorandum for the meeting reminded Burns of both the president's campaign endorsement of the ERA and Representative Dwyer's February 26 letter advocating possible courses of presidential action on women's concerns. Cole recommended that Burns consider a presidential directive to agencies urging that "more women be considered for employment, especially high-level jobs."[15]

At their June 2 meeting, Glaser and East provided Burns with information on the inequities to women in government, business, and professional education and also on the potential political advantages to be gained by fair policies. Glaser thought that Burns seemed unconvinced, but he promised to look into it. The two women had pushed, in particular, for an idea first advanced by Representative Dwyer that the president should either name a White House adviser to focus on "making better use of the abilities of the nation's women" or establish "an independent agency to strengthen women's rights and opportunities."[16] Glaser's notes report that Burns commented, "If we put a man in charge of this, he'd probably have to do it along with other things," to which Glaser responded, "then it probably wouldn't get done, needs someone full time, and should be a woman."[17]

Burns was apparently more receptive than Glaser realized. The following day, he met with Peter Flanigan, assistant to the president, and Civil Service

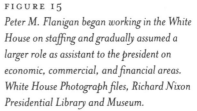

FIGURE 15
Peter M. Flanigan began working in the White House on staffing and gradually assumed a larger role as assistant to the president on economic, commercial, and financial areas. White House Photograph files, Richard Nixon Presidential Library and Museum.

Commission chair Robert Hampton to discuss both placing more women in high-level government jobs and improving the effectiveness of the Civil Service's Federal Women's Program. Cole, in briefing Burns for this second meeting, also suggested that appointing a staff assistant or creating a small office for women's rights and responsibilities could bring positive publicity to the administration as well as helping in efforts to recruit women.[18]

Although visible progress was hard to discern, the drumbeat continued. Throughout the summer, Catherine East continued to send analytical studies and pertinent news articles to Burns, and like others, she was suggesting names for consideration as the possible staff assistant. In June, Letitia Baldrige, a public relations executive and former chief of staff to Jacqueline Kennedy, wrote Peter Flanigan, saying, "I know you are always looking for good women for top government jobs (or at least, you *should* be looking)," and suggested tapping top advertising women. Flanigan responded, "You are quite right, we are on the lookout for qualified women for government posts."[19] The tone seemed to be changing, but results were still modest.

On July 8, Representative Dwyer and three other congresswomen succeeded in getting a meeting with President Nixon for almost an hour and a half. They presented him with an eight-page memo that outlined the problems in depth and delivered a number of recommendations, including, once again, appointment of both a Special Assistant to the President for Women's Rights and Responsibilities and an independent, bipartisan commission to make

FIGURE 16

The Citizens' Advisory Council on the Status of Women, at its second meeting, November 11, 1969. White House Photograph files, Richard Nixon Presidential Library and Museum.

recommendations for executive and legislative action. The memo began: "Our sole purpose is to suggest ways and means by which women's rights as citizens and human beings may be better protected, discrimination against women be eliminated, and women's ability to contribute to the economic, social and political life of the Nation be recognized. None of us are feminists. We do not ask for special privileges. We seek only equal opportunity."[20]

At the next day's cabinet meeting, President Nixon requested those present to place qualified women in high-level positions in the administration as a first step toward correcting the imbalance. Six weeks later, Glaser followed up on the president's instructions with letters to all the cabinet secretaries, most of whom replied but reported little progress.[21] Glaser would finally file the story in October. It began, "On July 10, Nixon gave the word to his cabinet—see that more women in your departments get a better break on jobs and promotions. That was three months ago and . . . the Cabinet's done nothing."[22]

In August, the president announced appointments of a chair and nineteen new members of the Citizens' Advisory Council on the Status of Women, a body for which Catherine East served as executive secretary. A few days later, Daniel Patrick Moynihan, counselor to the president for urban affairs,

FIGURE 17
Dr. Daniel Patrick Moynihan was counselor to the president and assistant to the president for urban affairs from 1969 through December 1970. White House Photograph files, Richard Nixon Presidential Library and Museum.

FIGURE 18
Melvin R. Laird was in his ninth term as a congressman from Wisconsin when President Nixon selected him to be secretary of defense, serving from 1969 to 1973. A Few Good Women Oral History Collection, Penn State University Archives.

created something of a stir with a memo that began with the prediction that "female equality will be a major cultural/political force of the 1970s." He continued, "The essential fact is that we have educated women for equality in America, but have not really given it to them. Not at all. Inequality is so great that the dominant group either doesn't notice it, or assumes the dominated group likes it that way. . . . I would suggest you take advantage of this. In your appointments (as you have begun to do), but perhaps especially in your pronouncements. This is a subject ripe for creative political leadership and initiative."[23]

Moynihan's memo sparked controversy among the staff, but by late September, it had emerged from the domestic affairs arena and went to the president with a cover note from John Ehrlichman, then White House counsel and an adviser on domestic affairs. Ehrlichman's note said that Bryce Harlow and Peter Flanigan, among others, agreed that "politically this is a golden opportunity and that we should, whenever possible, champion female equality."[24] An "OK," presumably the president's, was written next to this final paragraph.

Melvin Laird, then secretary of defense, recalled that Harlow, in particular, strongly backed appointing women. "He built a fire under everybody from Ehrlichman and [H. R.] Haldeman. He built a fire under Arthur Burns. He built a fire under those people so every time they saw Bryce coming, they tried to duck because he wanted more women in top positions. He attributed his call to action as coming directly from the President."[25]

Meanwhile, Glaser had heard nothing from Arthur Burns in the several months since their June meeting when she was contacted by White House Special Assistant Charles Clapp, who worked for Burns. Clapp told her, "President Nixon is preparing his State of the Union message. He and Dr. Burns are setting up a lot of task forces on different subjects to get new ideas for the speech. They're setting up a task force on women and would like to know if you are willing to serve on it."[26] With the permission of her editors, Glaser agreed to serve, and her appointment, along with the rest of the task force members, was announced on October 1, 1969.

※

Charles Clapp, a political science PhD from Berkeley, had been a longtime House and Senate staffer and a Brookings Institute Fellow. He had come to the White House at the invitation of Arthur Burns specifically to work on what eventually became seventeen presidential commissions in the domestic arena. According to Clapp, Burns "liked my background because of the Brookings association and also my association with business groups, really through Brookings. . . . He told me that he wanted task forces to be set up, each of which would have one government representative, a government liaison person. And then they would be composed only of outside people, not government people at all. And he thought that I could do that."[27]

Clapp continued:

> We had a list of task forces . . . [but] the task forces changed somewhat. I mean we were asked to develop some other things and I can't even remember whether the list Burns gave me had women's rights on it or whether it was one of the groups that were added. We

TABLE I

Presidential Task Forces Submitting Final Reports, 1970

Rural Development	Urban Renewal
Improving the Prospects of Small Business	Oceanography
Science Policy	Model Cities
Prisoner Rehabilitation	The Mentally Handicapped
Women's Rights and Responsibilities	Higher Education
The Aging	The Physically Handicapped
Economic Growth	Business Taxation
Low Income Housing	

SOURCE: *Public Papers of the President, Richard Nixon 1970* (Washington, D.C., 1971), p. 1206.

were trying to run the gamut of all sorts of different things. I don't think there was recognition at the time, certainly not in the White House, that this was so important an issue. I don't know whether [Burns's meeting with Glaser and East played a role in the decision to set up the task force]. I can't honestly say. Burns never mentioned that to me.[28]

While Arthur Burns wanted a task force that was made up largely of private citizens, the appointment of a chair would be a critical step. Politics certainly played a role, but Clapp believed that ideology could not be the first consideration. He recalled that the names being suggested by other staff members were too conservative. "For the Chair of the Women's Rights Task Force . . . Virginia Allan's papers were there. I don't know who submitted them really. Her credentials I thought were very good. I checked with a few people I knew. And I talked with her and I came to the conclusion that she would be a good member, a good chair."

"So I went to Burns because the others were pushing hard on a particular person I didn't think would be so good from an administration point of view."[29] Clapp continued:

I said to Burns, look, it's very important if you're going to set this up that you don't make a mistake by your choice of chair. You could ruin everything. It's not going to be accepted by groups in the country if you don't have someone who's respected, and Virginia Allan has the credentials because of her past presidency of the Business and Professional Women, her work with the drug stores and the

---

MEMBERS OF THE TASK FORCE ON WOMEN'S RIGHTS

AND RESPONSIBILITIES

Elizabeth Athanasakos   Dorothy Haener
Ann R. Blackham   Patricia Hutar
P. Dee Boersma   Katherine B. Massenburg
Evelyn Cunningham   William C. Mercer
Ann Ida Gannon, B.V.M.   Alan Simpson
Vera Glaser   Evelyn E. Whitlow

---

college regents and so on. She had the qualifications and the personality and she would be the best one. And Burns went with me. But it was not an automatic thing.[30]

Virginia Allan was named to chair the task force in early September 1969. A Michigan native, educator, and businesswoman, her interest in women's issues developed through her work as president of the National Federation of Business and Professional Women's Clubs (BPW) in the mid-1960s. Allan recalled her preparation for the work of the task force:

> The people in BPW, really we studied discrimination, we had our platform that would correct the situation and so we really had the backing of women across the country. Plus, I had met with many organizations and all of the organizations agreed on what should be done, so we had quite a number of women organized throughout the country. . . . I knew it couldn't be done with just one organization. It had to be across the board. Also, at the same time, some of the newer organizations, we were educating them on what the discrimination was. They had felt it, but they hadn't been in a movement that would do anything about it.[31]

She brought not only knowledge to the work of the task force but patience and leadership skills. Allan recalled, "Well, number one, I like people. I like to work with people. I recognize the ones with ability and try to draw them in. . . . You don't come on aggressively. You get people like we had on the Task Force, we had people who were key to the Republican Party and those people made a difference, ran interference and [showed] that you understood the issues and educated people . . . not scaring or threatening

FIGURE 19
Virginia Allan, a Michigan native, was president of the National Federation of Business and Professional Women when she was selected to chair the President's Task Force on Women's Rights and Responsibilities in 1969. A Few Good Women Oral History Collection, Penn State University Archives.

people. If you in any way show you are belligerent or you don't appreciate what they've done—it is just working with people and doing what you can accomplish."[32] This attitude would prove to be successful.

However, at the same time, she acknowledged that this was a team effort and that Catherine East played a critical role. "She was the key to it. . . . Catherine was the one who had the knowledge. I mean, through BPW and so on, I knew what the problems were, but Catherine knew the people that should be working on this, brought in and recognized. We couldn't have had what we did if it hadn't been for Catherine. She was the center."[33]

The selection of the members for the commission took several months. Clapp recalls:

> We got suggestions from a lot of people, members of Burns' staff went out to their own constituency, so to speak, for suggestions. Some Hill people were approached. It depended, of course, on the task force. . . . But they came from everywhere really. There were far more people suggested than we had places. And the selection was not always easy. My own position was more of a moderate than say Marty Anderson and Dick Burris and Tom Cole . . . on Burns' staff. They were all pretty conservative people. . . . And they didn't hesitate to make suggestions. . . .
>
> Now, on the women's task force, politics played an important role there with me, for example. My feeling was that women's issues had been controlled almost completely by the Democrats; that the

Republicans didn't have anybody with the pedigree or the credentials to lead in these matters. . . . It certainly would give Republicans a larger voice in these issues and more exposure, and it would not be so much the sole province of the Democratic Party. So I did, I have to confess that at least several of these people were selected by me, rightly or wrongly, based on what I regarded as the importance for the Republican Party of having qualified women with a credential who could go out and speak on women's issues.[34]

Clapp noted that almost all of the women selected for the task force were "committed to the development of the importance of women and the necessity of including women in public life. . . . I don't know that these people were so intent on putting the Republican imprint on this as they were in the general philosophy of women needed more exposure, needed more opportunity, that sort of thing."[35] The importance of having a political balance was important to both Clapp and Allan. They worked together on selecting the members.

Allan saw value in having a variety of backgrounds represented. Ann Blackham and William Mercer were business executives, as was Allan. Evelyn Whitlow was a lawyer and Betty Athanasakos a judge, Dorothy Haener of the United Automobile Workers represented labor, and Evelyn Cunningham and Vera Glaser were journalists. Katherine Massenburg was chairing the Maryland Commission on the Status of Women; both she and Pat Hutar had been active with Republican women's groups. Alan Simpson was president of Vassar College, and Sister Ida Gannon was president of Mundelein College, a Catholic women's college in Chicago. Dee Boersma was a graduate student at Ohio State, particularly selected by Allan because she had wanted to bring in young people's views.

Some were active in party politics; Clapp felt that the task force gave women like Pat Hutar, Ann Blackham, Kitty Massenburg, and Virginia Allan a chance to receive more public recognition. Evelyn Cunningham was also a good choice—she "was an assistant to Governor Rockefeller and Black and was very articulate and very useful because New York had accomplished a lot."[36] On the Democratic side, "Dorothy Haener represented the union and she was good. But she kept your feet to the fire, too. . . . [She] was concerned that Nixon might get more credit than he really deserved, something like that."[37]

Of the male contingent on the task force, Simpson probably had the greater appreciation of the issues, but as Clapp recalled, "[the men] had to be

FIGURE 20
Elizabeth Athanasakos, a Florida judge, served on the Task Force on Women's Rights and Responsibilities as well as several other advisory and commission posts in the Nixon and Ford administrations. A Few Good Women Oral History Collection, Penn State University Archives.

led along a little."[38] However, William Mercer, AT&T's vice president for personnel, found his service particularly valuable. Patricia Hutar, native Chicagoan active in Republican politics from her college days, recalls that Mercer "was acutely aware of it because women were raising their voices in companies and expressing themselves very vigorously. . . . He was already recognizing these needs."[39] Mercer was later responsible for adding more programs for women in telephone companies than had existed in the past.

Burns had told Allan that the task force should "appraise the effectiveness of present programs to enhance women's rights, to suggest how such programs might be improved or better coordinated, and to determine what actions might be taken, in light of practical considerations and present budgetary constraints, in this important area." While the work of the task force would look specifically at possible actions to take in 1970, they could determine their scope as they saw fit.[40]

The task force worked through a number of briefing papers and held hearings on a variety of topics. Allan recalled that she and East collaborated on setting the agendas. Pat Hutar described the meetings: "We'd 'chew' over these issues, and there were very, very frank discussions—vigorous pros and cons—we had lively members."[41]

Rita Hauser, a New York lawyer and early Nixon appointee, who had helped to craft the task force's direction and goals and then served as a consultant to it, recalled:

FIGURE 21

An international lawyer, Rita Hauser was a consultant to the Task Force on Women's Rights and Responsibilities and later served as U.S. representative to the U.N. Commission on Human Rights (1969–1972). A Few Good Women Oral History Collection, Penn State University Archives.

We were women who were interested in professions and careers and taking our place. And obviously, there were very few women appointees; it was necessary to get more women. And then there was also a woman's agenda in that at that time there were a lot of state commissions meeting to look at archaic laws. A married woman couldn't get credit by herself. She couldn't open loans or mortgages. In many states, everything she did had to be cosigned by her husband. There were all kinds of restrictions from 19th century law. So we felt this was something the commission ought to take a look at, what we called emancipating women.[42]

Pat Hutar added, "We're talking about rights, but we're also talking about the responsibilities that go along with that. We also said that whatever affected women and was unfavorable to men should be changed,"[43] particularly relating to spousal benefits and pensions of working women.

Evelyn Cunningham, the journalist who was an assistant to Governor Rockefeller and head of the Women's Unit in New York state government, recalled the tenor of the meetings: "We were all so different from each other. We came from different backgrounds. We had different goals. We had different experiences. . . . But all of that had no meaning when we relaxed and just talked and probed each other about what we were doing before we got there. The differences of opinion would emerge, of course. But they were honest differences of opinion. It was just not because somebody did not like somebody and wanted to take another side."[44]

Most recall Allan exercising a calm but determined influence. Clapp noted: "She's got a commitment and she moves toward it. And you know she is pleasant about it, but she is still moving. And it's not easy for people to combat it, because she is so reasonable about it all but there she goes, you've got to keep watching."[45] Hutar concurred: "Virginia is a person of very gentle disposition, but very firm, and could move the agenda along. She's also one of the fairest chairs I've ever seen in that all sides were heard."[46] Thanks to these traits, progress was made.

The task force reached nearly unanimous agreement on its recommendations and, after Vera Glaser did much of the organizing and editing of the justification language, forwarded them to the president on December 15, 1969. The report, with the eloquent title *A Matter of Simple Justice*, was released to the public the following June. The recommendations fell into five basic groups:

1. Create an Office of Women's Rights and Responsibilities headed by a special assistant to the president;

2. Hold a White House conference on women's rights and responsibilities in 1970, the fiftieth anniversary of the ratification of the Nineteenth Amendment and the creation of the Women's Bureau;

3. Send a broad legislative agenda to Congress for women, beginning with a ringing endorsement of the ERA, and for reforms in the areas of enforcement of civil rights; ending discrimination in education, public accommodations, Fair Labor Standards, and Social Security; provisions for child care; equal benefits for the families of working women; and support for state commissions on the status of women;

4. Through cabinet-level action, end discrimination by government contractors and in training and manpower programs; seek legal redress under the Civil Rights Act and the Fifth and Fourteenth Amendments in cases of sex discrimination; collect all social and economic statistics by gender as well as race; establish an office to specifically focus on discrimination in education; support training programs for household employment; and

5. End sex discrimination in the executive branch by appointing more women to positions of top responsibility and ensure that women were treated equitably in all matters of hiring and promotion.[47]

President Nixon's State of the Union Address, on January 22, 1970, focused on peace, the need for a balanced budget, and "quality of life" issues, such as economic growth without inflation, reducing crime, and healing environmental degradation. "New Federalism" at home and the "Nixon Doctrine" abroad were presented. Women were not mentioned explicitly. However, among urgent domestic priorities, he noted: "We must adopt reforms which will expand the range of opportunities for all Americans. We can fulfill the American dream only when each person has a fair chance to fulfill his own dreams. This means equal voting rights, equal employment opportunity, and new opportunities for expanded ownership. Because in order to be secure in their human rights, people need access to property rights."[48]

Task force members and some advocates would read into those remarks with optimism that the concerns of women as expressed in the task force report were heard and would be addressed; many others were more skeptical. White House staffer Charles Clapp, who had worked with the task force throughout its deliberations, assessed the reaction thusly: "I think that within the White House there was opposition to some of the recommendations, because they didn't want anything to happen, you know, the old Ehrlichman crowd, those people. They would come to me occasionally and say, what are these people going to do, where did you find them. So given the state of the art at the time and the situation in which they [the task force] found themselves, I think that they pursued the right path and were more effective because of it."

According to Evelyn Cunningham, there was a unique quality to the task force: "Women's groups during that era—the ones that were trying to get something done were noisy. This was a calmer, cooler kind of modus operandi. And I think the women involved were much respected. Not that other women weren't, but the technique was different. It was something Republican about the technique, about the way it was done. And here again . . . Republican men do things very differently from Republican women."[49]

This sense of the task force bringing something new to the "revolution" could be seen in Ted Lewis's *New York Daily News* column in response to the publication of the report's contents. "Thanks to the Nixon task force report, the view of mature women—the establishment type—is now obtainable and it basically agrees with what the aroused girls of the younger generation have been shouting and screaming about. What this task force has done has set a middle-of-the-road course for the equal rights movement. . . . For too long American males have underestimated the power of women en masse, even though they have never underestimated the power of woman, singularly. For the first time to our knowledge, the danger of such thinking has been pointed out bluntly by a blue-ribbon presidential task force."[50]

Pat Hutar had another perspective: "The task force did [build a foundation], because it certainly motivated President Nixon. . . . But I think the fact that the President did, in his administration, enact some of these things, saw that they were put in place in the White House, made a difference. Because people could see that we were having some movement forward. . . . So I think when women began to see results, that made quite a bit of difference in raising morale."[51]

In fact, virtually all of the legislative and cabinet-level recommendations were eventually enacted. Although a White House Office of Women's Rights and Responsibilities was not created, a significant step forward was achieved. New York business executive Barbara Hackman Franklin was appointed staff assistant to the president in April of 1971. In many ways, she was the model of the very kind of person the administration was looking for.

※

In the fall of 1958, Barbara Ann Hackman left her home in Landisville, in Lancaster County, Pennsylvania, where she had graduated as class valedictorian from Hempfield High School, to attend Pennsylvania State University. Penn State's main campus sits in almost the geographical center of the state, and like her home county, it is a productive farming area and has traditionally been moderately Republican in tone.

During her four years at Penn State, Hackman proved to be an outstanding student and a campus leader. Graduating with honors in political science, she was attracted to activities that developed leadership skills, like student government and women's debate. She was president of her sorority as well as of Mortar Board, the highly selective senior women's honorary society (which would begin admitting men in 1975).

During Barbara Hackman's sophomore year, a new, young dean of women, Dorothy J. Lipp, arrived at Penn State. In one of her first interviews, she told the student newspaper, "We are forcing the present generation to grow up very fast. We must make them responsible and free people, not protect them. The day is passed when we have to protect, with a capital P, women students." In 1962, Dean Lipp had the opportunity to choose a senior woman

FIGURE 22
Barbara Hackman, Penn State graduate, class of 1962, on her way to Harvard Business School. Barbara Hackman Franklin Papers, Penn State University Archives.

to nominate for a full scholarship to the Harvard Business School, whose doors had just opened to women. Recognizing her strength and potential, the dean chose Barbara Hackman.

Although she wasn't awarded the full scholarship, Hackman did receive a combination of a scholarship and loan that made attendance at Harvard possible for her. She headed for Boston and became a pioneer at Harvard, completing her MBA degree in 1964. There, she was one of twelve women in a class of 632, placing her among the first women to graduate from the Harvard Business School.[52] Barbara Hackman Franklin—the surname she acquired after her marriage—went to work initially for Singer Company in New York City. Not only was she the first woman MBA Singer had ever hired; she became a member of the corporate planning staff, where she created their environmental analysis function, to watch trends and analyze competition worldwide.

After four years at Singer, Franklin was recruited to First National City Bank (now Citibank), for another position in corporate planning. As at Singer, she found that "there were some men who just didn't take women seriously. [One] time when I knew I didn't get as much of a salary increase as the guy who worked beside me, I raised that issue and was told, 'You don't need that salary increase. You're doing fine for a girl, and, besides, you have a husband who works.' There was that sort of thinking then at the bank."[53] It was not the first or last example of sex discrimination she would encounter, or the only one she ever questioned.

Franklin's most significant accomplishment at City Bank was creating a government relations department. In 1970, the U.S. Congress passed legislation closing a loophole that had allowed banks to form holding companies, which could add services to the bank's business without violating banking regulations. The banking industry was caught off guard. In a meeting of the planning group with CEO Walter Wriston, Franklin recalled that Wriston said, "Well, we don't want this to ever happen again." He then looked at her and said, "I want you to figure out how we don't get surprised." Her management study of the bank's relationships with government at all levels led to the creation of the government relations department, which she headed. It also later led to the establishment of a Washington office for the bank to track legislation and do lobbying.[54]

In the meantime, Barbara Franklin had joined an informal women's group. Charlotte Browne-Mayers was an executive at Standard Oil Company (now Exxon); they met and became close friends. In 1964 or 1965, they began having get-togethers with some of Barbara's former business school classmates and other women who were working in the city. Franklin recalled: "'The Group' met once a month in someone's apartment, we'd have some glasses of wine and talk about whatever was on our minds. Everyone was in a career, and we shared experiences. It was consciousness-raising and how to get over the obstacles of the workplace, even though we didn't call it that."[55]

At the same time, Franklin was also getting involved in Republican politics in New York City and would eventually be consulted about recruiting new people to work in the White House. Thus began an explicit effort to identify and recruit women for leadership and policy-making positions in the executive branch, an initiative no presidential administration in history had attempted before.

CHAPTER THREE

Setting the Stage for a Program

Patricia Reilly Hitt, longtime Nixon supporter and cochair of the 1968 presidential campaign, was the administration's first female appointment to a high-level, policy-making position after the inauguration in 1969. As assistant secretary for community and field services in health, education, and welfare (HEW), she was the highest-ranking woman in those early days. Three weeks after the president's February 6 press conference, she met with women reporters. Unfortunately, a blunt response to a question about why there were no female cabinet members set back both her cause and the image of the administration with women activists.

Hitt stated, "These cabinet departments are so big and all-encompassing that very few men are capable of administering them and, frankly, I couldn't give you the name of a single solitary woman who has the training, background and ability to fill one of those posts . . . and who also would be free to do the job."[1]

Her afterthought about availability was largely ignored, and the statement was immediately attacked by women's groups. Her boss, HEW Secretary Bob Finch, called her on the phone and said, "My God Pat, what did you really say?"[2] Even Nixon adviser Bryce Harlow disagreed. Citing Carlene Roberts, vice president of American Airlines, as a qualified candidate, Harlow added that he was "sure there must be many, many ladies like this." Hitt was obviously discomfited that her comment had drawn such fire—she later called it "the question that I did such a rotten job of answering."[3] In her 1997 interview for this study, she noted that the crux of the issue was identifying women who were available. "Not every woman could pick up her husband and her family and move to Washington. . . . Two careers was not the question it is now."[4]

FIGURE 23
Pat Hitt meeting with the president in the Oval Office. White House Photograph files, Richard Nixon Presidential Library and Museum.

FIGURE 24
Robert Finch, longtime Nixon supporter, was appointed secretary of health, education, and welfare in 1969. Barbara Hackman Franklin Papers, Penn State University Archives.

Back in 1969, she offered this explanation: "My answer was off the top of my head. . . . I was trying to defend the President but certainly didn't mean to downgrade women. I am still working to find women for sub-cabinet positions. There are lots and lots of women who are capable and willing but I just don't know where they are—maybe somebody else does." Actually, she added, she did have a list of names, but patience was needed.[5]

In her 1997 interview, Hitt identified the list as the members of the Women for Nixon-Agnew Advisory Committee, which she had organized as a part of the 1968 campaign. This was a group of 250 women "who were outstanding in fields that had nothing to do with elections or with politics . . .

very, very prominent women in their own right. . . . What I had hoped is that that list of 250 women would be a list from which Nixon, if elected, could recruit women to advisory commissions and committees and jobs and so on. . . . It never really turned out—it was never used . . . [although] when I had an opportunity to make a suggestion or a decision . . . I did it from there."[6]

A few days after the press debacle, Vera Glaser met Pat Hitt at a party. Glaser's notes quote Hitt as saying, "I'm making sure this time that the list is on the President's desk when he returns." Glaser continued, "She is using all the publicity to show them how important it is. Says she talks about it so much that none of them will talk with her. Insists it's not the President. The obvious implication is that people around him are nixing women."[7]

While Hitt, with the strong backing of HEW Secretary Robert Finch, promoted women in her own department where she could, she actually had no responsibility for identifying women appointees in those early days. However, she was not the only one with a list of names.

✳

The National Federation of Business and Professional Women's Clubs (BPW) had been working on a talent bank for some time. During Virginia Allan's presidency in 1963, BPW assembled the Womanpower Talent Bank, a list of potential women officeholders. Allan recalled that it focused on "people who could be appointed to government positions. And with the backing of BPW it gave it visibility." During the Johnson administration, Allan worked with Liz Carpenter, a former reporter who had been executive assistant to Vice President Johnson and, after 1963, staff director and press secretary for the First Lady, to further circulate the list: "We distributed widely because that was the only way we were going to get appointments, to have enough people putting their stamp of approval on what we were trying to do." Countering the argument that there were not competent women available, "We flooded the opponents, so to speak, with capable women, so we didn't hear much about that after we published all of these names."[8]

Talent banks had been a topic of discussion for the task force at its October 6, 1969, meeting, when the suggestion was advanced for "an inventory of women whose abilities and availability indicate their fitness for appointment to responsible positions."[9] Evelyn Cunningham recalled, "I think all women's groups feel strongly about creating a talent bank, letting powers know wherever they are that there are a lot of useful, productive women to fill these spots. . . . That's why I [still] collect resumes. . . . I have some resumes for anything you want."[10]

the government from discriminating against women, on pain of having their contracts cancelled?

Third, is the Administration willing to use its financial clout as it has done on race—to get universities to remove their unwritten quotas on women entering law and medical schools?

Fourth, and far from last, will the Administration act on the studies or recommendations coming from this advisory council?

How will it respond to the report of our Task Force, which is now on the President's desk, and is to be published around the end of this month?

These things will determine what tomorrow's woman will be like. A conscientious response from the Administration can help remove some of the silly handicaps now operating against her.[20]

The Advisory Council, which was holding only its second meeting of the Nixon administration, would endorse most of Glaser's points and, after listening to Representative Martha Griffiths (D-MI) discuss legislative priorities with them, approve a ringing endorsement of the Equal Rights Amendment. Libby Koontz, director of the Women's Bureau and chair of the Advisory Council, sent the endorsement to George Shultz, secretary of labor, who quickly passed it on to the president, so he would know of it before it leaked to the press.[21]

⁜

While the printed task force report carried a date of April 1970, it was not actually released to the public for two more months, despite Glaser's optimism in her speech. There was ongoing pressure for the administration to release it and say what it was going to do about its recommendations. In February, task force member Ann Blackham had stung Charles Clapp with her impatience over release of the report and action on its recommendations. "Obviously the President should implement, and needs desperately, Recommendation No. 1 of the Task Force, a Director and Office of Women's Rights and Responsibilities and this person serving as a Special Assistant to the President." Clapp pleaded for patience, stating that the report was being studied "just as the others are."[22]

Clapp, who was overseeing the reports of all seventeen of the task forces, received a constant stream of inquiries about the women's report. He routinely responded that the White House had promised that all the reports would be made public and that it was just a matter of time. The women's report and related issues were now turned over to Leonard Garment and Charles Colson. Garment sent a series of memos out in early April to cabinet members William P. Rogers (State), John Mitchell (Justice), David M. Kennedy (Treasury), and Melvin Laird (Defense); senior White House staffers Robert Finch, Peter Flanigan, and Donald Rumsfeld; and Commission chairs Robert Merriam (Intergovernmental Relations), Reverend Theodore Hesburgh (Civil Rights), Robert E. Hampton (Civil Service), and William H. Brown III (Equal Employment Opportunity).[23]

While Garment divided up the recommendations by relevance to the recipients' agencies, the White House retained judgment on three: (1) creating an Office of Women's Rights and Responsibilities directed by a special assistant reporting to the president, (2) holding a White House conference on women's rights and responsibilities to coincide with the fiftieth anniversary of the ratification of the Nineteenth Amendment, and (3) calling on the president to hire more women in top positions to achieve an equitable ratio of men and women and to give equal consideration to the hiring and promotion of qualified women in the departments and agencies.[24]

By this point, Garment and Colson were seriously considering recommending the appointment of a special assistant by naming a woman already

FIGURE 27
The president meets with aides Donald Rumsfeld, Leonard Garment, and Charles B. Wilkinson in May 1970. White House Photograph files, Richard Nixon Presidential Library and Museum.

in a job who could add this responsibility, in part to satisfy budgetary constraints on adding new staff. Colson noted, "This is a little bit like the school desegregation issue. It is beginning to build up a real head of steam. I would like to see us leading the parade rather than jumping on the band wagon after it is already well down the road."[25] In early April, staff were still struggling to reach a decision about the release of the report. Feedback to Garment on the various recommendations was trickling in, but the pressure to show action on some part of the recommendations and to release the report was growing. The question became moot, however, on April 21. The substance of the report and the recommendations in detail were leaked to the press (the White House assumed it was Vera Glaser). The following day, the White House released the task force's summary letter to the president and said it would publish the report as soon as it could be printed.[26]

The printed version still took another six weeks, and even though the essence of the report was now on the record, the White House was still debating the release date of the printed version, which now had become entangled with congressional hearings on the ERA, as well as the possible appointment of a special assistant.

The White House, despite President Nixon's endorsement of the ERA during the campaign, was of two minds concerning the amendment. Moderate to liberal Republicans, particularly women, wanted the president to actively support passage, while the more conservative stalwarts, including most male White House staffers, were reluctant to get involved in the debate.

FIGURE 28
Connie Stuart served four years as press secretary and staff director for Mrs. Nixon from 1969 to 1973. A Few Good Women Oral History Collection, Penn State University Archives.

Connie Stuart, Mrs. Nixon's press secretary, had complicated their lives by telling reporters, "I have spoken to Mrs. Nixon about this matter and Mrs. Nixon, of course, supports the Amendment," just as every Republican convention had over the last thirty years and as her husband did as well, she added.[27]

At the Senate hearings in early May, the White House declined to have a representative of the Justice Department testify, saying the administration "has no position on the Amendment."[28] John Mitchell had described it as "window dressing" that did nothing more than current laws already did.[29] The ERA would eventually pass the House in September 1970 but would have to be reintroduced in the Ninety-Second Congress in 1971, and the Nixon White House would continue to debate the tactics and nature of its position on the ERA.

The task force report was finally released by the White House on June 9, 1970, in conjunction with the fiftieth anniversary of the Department of Labor's Women's Bureau and two days before the convening of the bureau's "American Women at the Crossroads: Directions for the Future" anniversary celebration conference. At the same time, the White House issued new, more explicit, guidelines for enforcing Executive Order 11375, on discrimination by federal contractors. In this way, Garment believed, "we should be able to put the emphasis on what the President *has done* rather than on what he is

FIGURE 29

Mrs. Nixon meets guests at the reception marking the fiftieth anniversary of the Women's Bureau, June 13, 1970. White House Photograph files, Richard Nixon Presidential Library and Museum.

being urged to do."[30] This was followed in July by an announcement that the Justice Department had filed suit, for the first time, on a violation of the Equal Employment section of the Civil Rights Act of 1964 in relation to discrimination against women.[31]

To the public, the administration remained silent on the other recommendations, however.[32] While Leonard Garment's office continued collecting feedback, the three recommendations reserved for White House decision making (the special assistant and women's affairs office, the White House conference, and hiring more women) were still under intense debate. By late summer, it appeared that the appointment of a special assistant might be announced for the celebration of the fiftieth anniversary of the ratification of the Nineteenth Amendment on August 26.[33] As earlier suggested, naming a woman already in the administration, such as Pat Hitt or Ethel Bent Walsh, then director for advisory councils in the Small Business Administration, seemed like a foregone conclusion, but nothing happened. Colson would later say, "We were about to name a woman to this position but the idea was killed at the last moment."[34] No record of who killed it has emerged from the White House files.

By September, according to Vera Glaser's notes, the White House was leaning against both the office headed by a special adviser and the general idea of hiring more women. The conference proposal, they felt, had been satisfied by the Women's Bureau conference in June. Glaser's notes tersely recorded the White House position on the conference: "Served this purpose, was activist, made recommendations."[35]

FIGURE 30
Ethel Bent Walsh with colleagues from the Small Business Administration. A Few Good Women Oral History Collection, Penn State University Archives.

FIGURE 31
Bob Haldeman, chief of staff to the president, in a relaxed moment in the Oval Office. White House Photograph files, Richard Nixon Presidential Library and Museum.

Yet, as she discovered, the White House was not so black and white on the other issues. On September 28, Glaser talked to White House aide Harry Fleming, who told her that the subject of a special assistant had been under almost constant discussion and that they were waiting for H. R. Haldeman to reach a decision on it. Glaser's notes record Fleming in almost a stream-of-consciousness style: "There is a definite recommendation on it. Very good idea. I think it may be a politically good idea. I am not positive it is the way to accomplish the objective here. There has been too much of a tendency to move to the W.H. to solve every problem when in fact it can't."[36]

In the meantime, BPW and its allied organizations supporting the Talent Bank for Promotion of Women to Policy-Making Positions were continuing to push for the appointment of a special assistant. On October 6, Leonard Garment responded to them by letter with a treatise on what he termed "formally-delineated White House Staff monitorship" of women's concerns. Speaking as "public administrator rather than politician," he cited several precedents for not creating such a position, including inviting the inevitable proliferation of such positions, having too much overlap between assignments, and the likelihood of the position becoming a high-profile advocate when the president ought to have quiet, impartial advice. A dedicated staff assistant was not what the president needed; and just to make sure everyone understood, he concluded: "I repeat: President Nixon is going to continue to use the powers of his office, together with that of the Courts, to take out after any institutional or governmental discrimination which he can constitutionally reach, specifically including demeaning discrimination on the basis of sex. This is the important issue—and you and your colleagues should hold our feet to the fire if we do less than our best. But, with respect to the organization of the President's

FIGURE 36
Donald Rumsfeld resigned from his House seat after seven years to become director of the Office of Economic Opportunity and later counselor to the president. Barbara Hackman Franklin Papers, Penn State University Archives.

Glaser, interviewing Malek on January 6, 1971, found that he still wasn't ready to give her specifics, other than to reassure her that things were on the move. However, he apparently told her that there would probably be forty important positions likely to turn over and that the thinking was that 10 percent would go to women.[57]

In February, almost two years since President Nixon's press conference response to Vera Glaser's question, Glaser published a story toting up the score; she gave the administration a ".333 batting average with feminists." Two-thirds of the task force recommendations had not been implemented, but there had been signs of progress. Glaser enumerated these:

- The Justice Department had begun to file cases for sex discrimination in the workplace under Title VII of the Civil Rights Act of 1964;

- HEW had moved to cancel federal grants to universities whose hiring and salary policies discriminated, leading to the beginnings of institutional affirmative action plans for women;

- Labor had issued guidelines on dealing with sex discrimination by government contractors, although implementation was lagging;

- federal aid for day care centers would be part of the Administration's Family Assistance Plan then before Congress; and

- fringe and pension benefits for husbands and children of female federal employees were equalized with those for male employees.[58]

Inside the White House, Finch was continuing work on these issues and convened several meetings to discuss both the development of the recruiting program and the White House position on the ERA. Included in this ad hoc group were Pat Hitt, Helen Delich Bentley, Catherine Bedell, Carol Khosrovi of the Office of Economic Opportunity, and Cynthia Newman, secretary of the Commonwealth of Virginia whom Finch had invited in as a consultant; as well as Rumsfeld, Malek, Dan Kingsley of the White House Personnel Office, who had formerly served as a commissioner of the General Services Administration; and James McLane, a staff assistant and member of the Domestic Affairs Council.

A March 10 news story in the *Washington Star* reported that announcements on the appointment of several women to important positions would

FIGURE 37

Carol Marshall (then Khosrovi) was a Senate aide when she became director of congressional relations for the Office of Economic Opportunity in 1969. A Few Good Women Oral History Collection, Penn State University Archives.

come in the next month or two. It also noted, "As a part of the effort, Malek plans to add a woman to his staff soon to work full time on trying to find women well qualified for key spots."[59] On the same day, Vera Glaser interviewed Pat Hitt, who confirmed that Bob Finch was also working on these appointments and that a number of women in the administration were being consulted. Finch was apparently concerned that this not be seen as cosmetic, Hitt observed; there had been continuing quiet work and interest in this effort, including interest by the president, who "says often why aren't we doing something." Glaser's notes record that Hitt had been told, "You know there are people on the President's staff who are just plain against this." She said, "Yes, that's part of the problem . . . it has taken a lot of perseverance."

Hitt also noted that while the 1970 midterm election may have opened a few eyes, there were growing indications of the likely independence of women in the upcoming 1972 election. "She doesn't vote like her husband votes. She is voting on issues on her own," Hitt noted. While middle American wives were anti–women's lib, the young women and men on college campuses were a "new breed." These women were expecting two careers, home and business, and they were strongly interested in women's political issues. They wanted to make a difference, and young men agreed—they were "not going to throw roadblocks in [women's] way."[60] These comments appeared in substantial detail in a story Glaser published on March 28.[61] She would soon have more substantive news to report.

CHAPTER FOUR

Calling Barbara Franklin

The Initiative Is Under Way

On April 9, 1971, Vera Glaser announced the news: "The White House is borrowing a pint-sized junior official from a New York bank to bolster the Administration's sagging image on the female front. . . . Barbara Ann Hackman Franklin . . . will begin work Monday (April 12) as a recruiter of female talent for high-level administration jobs. . . . She is apparently expected to succeed where others have failed, in breaking down the 'women's place is in the home' philosophy of presidential advisers, which appears to have held down the number of female policy-level appointments."[1]

Glaser did not seem to have a lot of hope for Barbara Franklin in the beginning. While discussing her background and qualifications, Glaser reported that several older, more experienced women had been passed over for the job. She added that Franklin was thirty-one years old, about five feet tall, and, according to a leading New York City woman Republican, a "very pale, delicate-looking little thing, but an excellent worker and a very bright girl."[2] Glaser noted that Franklin was on a six-month leave from First National City Bank, although Anne Armstrong, cochair of the Republican National Committee, believed the appointment would be a permanent one.[3] Despite the disparaging comments, Barbara Franklin would quickly prove she had tougher mettle than Glaser's report suggested.

Her new boss, Fred Malek, already knew that. He recalled:

> I was given the task by the President of locating and bringing on board a woman who would spearhead the effort to recruit other women in the government. I did not mount a nationwide search. I sat back and said I know just the person for this job. It was my old classmate, Barbara Hackman, I think was her name then, that I had

FIGURE 38
The president greets Barbara Franklin in the Oval Office as she joins the White House staff in April 1971. White House Photograph, A Few Good Women Oral History Collection, Penn State University Archives.

been impressed with at Harvard and who had a solid, substantive career following Harvard Business School and who I had stayed in touch with. I thought she was smart, assertive, articulate, attractive, a go-getter, who could adapt to this kind of environment and do a good job, and so I called Barbara and asked her if she would talk about this. I don't recall actively considering anybody else. . . . I thought she was ideally suited for it and that I would be lucky if I could get her.[4]

Barbara Hackman Franklin, who had earned a master of business administration in 1964 from Harvard, had worked first for Singer Company and then for First National City Bank as an assistant vice president for corporate planning. She had volunteered on the 1968 Nixon campaign in New York and in fall 1970 had been contacted by Richard Ferry to help identify women for potential appointments to the administration. "Another [White House Personnel Office] recruiter, John Clark called to set up a date with Fred Malek and said 'You've got to come and do this job.' I went to Washington, talked with Fred and agreed to do the job. That was probably February of 1971."[5]

The official press release from the White House did not come until April 22, when Franklin was announced as a "Staff Assistant to the President for Executive Manpower."[6] This unfortunate turn of phrase became an immediate issue. Margita White, then an assistant to Communications Director Herb Klein, set up one of the regular background briefings she often arranged, this time for Barbara Franklin to meet with the women members of the press. The gathering, in the Roosevelt Room of the White House, was described by Glaser as "disastrous."[7] Franklin recalled, "This whole set-up was bad. The women of the press were angry. They grumbled, 'Why wasn't this held in the White House Briefing Room like everything else? You're treating us differently.' And they were kind of mad at the President in general. So the first question was, 'You're recruiting women. How can you have a "Manpower" title?' This is a good question with no good answer." The press conference didn't get any easier after that and probably went on longer than it should have, given the circumstances. White was distracted, feeling ill with an as-yet unannounced pregnancy, and as she put it, "Once I introduced her and sat down, the world started spinning and I could never interject

FIGURE 39
Barbara Franklin chats with women members of the press at her first press briefing in April 1971. Helen Thomas, longtime White House reporter, is third from the left. Barbara Hackman Franklin Papers, Penn State University Archives.

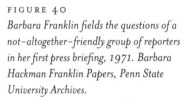

FIGURE 40
Barbara Franklin fields the questions of a
not-altogether-friendly group of reporters
in her first press briefing, 1971. Barbara
Hackman Franklin Papers, Penn State
University Archives.

myself to stop the questioning or do anything else."[8] But as Franklin noted, "We got through this. . . . This effort showed that something was happening, and the press reports were OK, even though the reporters took me apart." Her title was quickly shortened after the press conference to staff assistant to the president. [9]

✳

Even before Barbara Franklin's appointment, the strategy that she would implement had been carefully crafted. The initial goals were explicit:

- double the number of women in policy-making jobs, GS-16 and above on the government pay scale, from twenty-six to fifty-two;[10]

- appoint women to 25 percent of posts on presidential and departmental advisory boards and commissions;

- significantly increase the number of women in midlevel positions (GS-13 to 15) in departments and agencies; and

- require each department and agency to come up with a plan for increasing women's roles through civil service.

Fred Malek would have direct responsibility for implementation of these goals, and the woman recruiter to be hired would also develop a talent bank, work with liaison staff on placements, and track developments. A presidential directive would go to all departments and agencies announcing this initiative. There would be targets, regular reports, and continuous monitoring of progress over the remainder of 1971. As the planning document stated, "It is clear that our efforts to date have not resulted in sufficient high-level women appointments, and this record must be significantly improved if we are to make full use of an important source of talent and gain an election advantage in 1972."[11]

By the end of March, Malek reported to Finch and Rumsfeld that Franklin was on board and that they had several notable appointments ready to announce: Jayne Spain, president and CEO of Alvey-Ferguson, a conveyor manufacturing company in Cincinnati, to be commissioner and vice-chair of the Civil Service Commission; former mayor of Hartford, Connecticut, Ann Uccello to be director of consumer safety for transportation; former Representative Catherine May Bedell to chair the Tariff Commission; and Charlotte Reid, who would resign her seat in the House at midterm to become the first woman member of the Federal Communications Commission since 1948. The only questions were the timing of the president's directive, whether it would be paired with a similar one dealing with minority recruiting, and the need for a stronger and more imaginative communications plan to strike the correct tone in publicizing the program and the individual appointments.[12]

Two weeks later, in mid-April, Bob Finch briefed the president on Franklin's progress, the four upcoming women's appointments, and presenting the draft directive to the departments and agencies. He also commented that while their achievements on presidential appointments were only marginally better than the Kennedy-Johnson record at two years, their greatest achievement so far had been in appointing 216 women, or 16 percent of over 1,300 openings, to advisory boards and commissions. Finch was also optimistic

FIGURE 41
Ann Uccello, left, the former mayor of Hartford, Connecticut, joined the Department of Transportation as a senior staff member in April 1971. Here she is greeted by the president with Mary Lou Grier, a member of the National Advisory Council of the Small Business Administration. White House Photograph files, Richard Nixon Presidential Library and Museum.

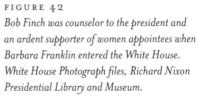

FIGURE 42
Bob Finch was counselor to the president and an ardent supporter of women appointees when Barbara Franklin entered the White House. White House Photograph files, Richard Nixon Presidential Library and Museum.

about the opportunity to significantly increase the number of women in GS-12 government jobs and above from the then-current level of 1,100 out of 78,000 positions nationwide.[13]

On April 21, the president announced the women's initiative at a cabinet meeting and issued the directive to the departments and independent agencies to create action plans for (1) appointing more women to top-level positions, (2) increasing the number of women in midlevel positions (GS-13 to 15), and (3) increasing the number of women on advisory boards and committees. To coordinate the program in each agency, an official would be designated to work with Malek's office on implementation. Fred Malek would follow up two weeks later with more detailed guidelines for developing and implementing the action plans. All plans were due back to the White House by May 15.[14] The directive was released to the press, but the plans remained confidential while they were being finalized. Barbara Franklin spent a great deal of time working with the departments to bring them to a suitable and productive form. After much carping by the press and a Freedom of Information Act request by a very persistent editor of a women's magazine, final versions of the plans were cleared through Associate White House Counsel Fred Fielding's office and released.

Barbara Franklin worked with Herb Klein's office on press briefings and began making contacts with women's organizations throughout the country. At the same time, Anne Armstrong, from the Republican National Committee

THE WHITE HOUSE

MEMORANDUM FOR THE HEADS OF
EXECUTIVE DEPARTMENTS AND AGENCIES

As you know, it has been my desire to attract the ablest and most talented people in the country to join this Administration and assist in the achievement of our far-reaching goals. The Nation's many highly qualified women represent an important reservoir of ability and talent that we must draw on to a greater degree. In this Administration we have firmly espoused the rights of women, and we must now clearly demonstrate our recognition of the equality of women by making greater use of their skills in high level positions.

Our efforts to date in appointing women have offered some encouragement. I have appointed a number of women to top posts and have named more than 200 to Presidential Advisory Boards and Commissions. However, I am convinced that we can and must do better.

To this end, I am now directing that you take the following actions:

-- Develop and put into action a plan for attracting more qualified women to top appointive positions (GS-16 and up through Presidential appointees) in your Department or Agency by the end of this calendar year. This plan should be submitted to me by May 15.

-- Develop and put into action by May 15 a plan for significantly increasing the number of women, career and appointive, in mid-level positions (GS-13 to 15). This plan should directly involve your top personnel official.

-- Ensure that substantial numbers of the vacancies on your Advisory Boards and Committees are filled with well-qualified women.

-- Designate an overall coordinator who will be held responsible for the success of this project. Please provide this name to me by May 15.

I have asked my Special Assistant, Fred Malek, to meet with each of you individually to review further the requirements of this project and to offer his assistance in locating highly qualified women candidates for top positions.

I intend to follow personally the results of this project; I look forward to your giving it the fullest degree of cooperation. It is important not only in terms of opening new opportunities for women, but also as a means of making the fullest possible use of talents that are needed in the Nation's service.

RICHARD NIXON

#   #   #

FIGURE 43
The president's directive of April 21, 1971. Barbara Hackman Franklin Papers, Penn State University Archives.

FIGURE 44
The president has an informal chat with Civil Service Commissioner Jayne Spain and Health, Education, and Welfare Assistant Secretary Pat Hitt about revising regulations on appointments for women. Barbara Hackman Franklin Papers, Penn State University Archives.

(RNC), was mailing announcements of Franklin's hiring and the program to women's publications and organizations.[15] She would later be actively involved in suggesting women to Franklin for appointments, generally improving communication between the White House and the RNC.

On April 29, the first real event in the program's publicity campaign took place as the president met with Jayne Spain to announce her appointment as vice-chair of the Civil Service Commission. He also introduced Dr. Valerija Raulinaitis, a career civil servant who was being appointed as the first woman director of a Veterans Administration Hospital; along with Vicki L. Keller, a consultant from McKinsey & Co., and Sallyanne Payton, a black Washington attorney, both being named as associates of the White House Domestic Council. They joined Bobbie Greene Kilberg, a White House fellow, who was already on the Council staff. Malek, Franklin, and Robert Hampton, the chair of the Civil Service Commission, were also in attendance. The "photo op" included regular pool reporters, and the president was able to reemphasize the commitment to appointing more women to high-level positions by commenting on his directive to the cabinet secretaries and agency heads and the appointment of Barbara Franklin.[16]

As Franklin recalled, the strategy was a "three-part thrust to advance women. I used to talk about this: (1) that I was brought in to recruit women

FIGURE 45
President Nixon meets with Jayne Spain and hosts one of the first press gatherings announcing appointments for women in the administration, April 21, 1971. Left to right: Vicki Keller, Dr. Valerija Raulinaitis, Jayne Spain, President Nixon, Barbara Franklin, and Sallyanne Payton. A Few Good Women Oral History Collection, Penn State University Archives.

at the Presidential appointee level, (2) Jayne Spain was put at that Civil Service position to watch over the advancement of women in the Career Services, and, of course, (3) the linchpin was that the President asked every department head and agency head for Action Plans indicating how they were going to appoint, promote and train women, and for a key official to be in charge."[17]

Franklin's position was unique from the beginning, however. Although her specific mission was recruiting, it was also thought necessary that she become "visible" as a way of demonstrating the administration's commitment to women. Franklin often traveled the country, speaking to large groups and giving print and television interviews, not only about the program to recruit women, but also about the Nixon administration's larger initiatives to address women's issues. She met frequently with women's organizations and often had to respond to questions about the administration's positions on ERA, child care policy, and other women's issues. Although there had been no "special assistant" for women's affairs appointed, as originally envisioned by the task force report, Barbara Franklin increasingly, by default, found herself functioning as an advocate within the White House, as well as a spokesperson outside, on women's concerns. As she put it, "the heat is off for everybody else," and it seemed that many in the White House were relieved to have her play this role for the public. She maintained the delicate balance of presenting the administration's accomplishments without appearing to be pressuring the White House to go beyond existing policies. Actually, she would have to be successful in both aspects of her job, inside and out, to be truly effective and have an impact on the situation.

Clearly Franklin had a full plate—in fact, it quickly began to overflow, and she realized she needed help. About mid-July, Franklin detailed in a memo her progress and how her position had evolved. There was increasing political pressure to show that the program was being effective; however, more than 900 letters and résumés had arrived since her appointment, and around 100 resumes and 200 letters were still coming in every week. She was now also working through the action plans and advising the departments and agencies on strategies for hiring and promoting women.

As she detailed in a July 15 memo to Fred Malek, she was spending only a third of her time on recruiting, and as initially set up, the procedures were not working as well as they had hoped. They had made ten placements to that point, but they were already falling behind their projected rate of progress. Franklin realized they needed to target specific positions; otherwise the other personnel staff members would tend to take the easy way out and just recruit men as a way of getting through the workload. They could not take the time to find potential women candidates for every job.

Franklin realized she needed to restructure her position so that she would be putting the majority of her time into recruiting for targeted positions and focusing on getting women appointed to these important jobs, thus meeting the president's goals. She had to spend less time on managing the process and responding to the public on both recruitment and larger issues. In short, she needed a staff to help make all this happen.[18]

Franklin recalled, "I pointed out that I was a one-man, or one-woman band. . . . There was no structure there, not even a secretary. I brought a secretary from City Bank on loan [briefly] just to help me sort the mail. . . . I did not think we could go public and say, 'We're looking for women,' be outreaching and then not answer the mail."[19] She continued: "When I had no secretary, I was at wit's end. There was no one even to answer the phone, and we needed to start getting out some letters and memos. Helen [Bentley] loaned me this dinosaur-like . . . dictating machine. It took the space of an entire small table, and I would dictate, and she would get her staff to produce it."[20] As a result of her "restructuring memo," Franklin was able to build a staff: Sharon Shay as secretary, Judy Cole as staff assistant in charge of recruiting, and Judy Kaufman as staff assistant for communications and event planning.

Judy Cole helped in contacting candidates, setting up appointments, and checking references. She was according to Franklin, "ever efficient and unflappable, had political sense, and could always be counted on to deliver." Franklin noted that Cole later went on to obtain a law degree and served as a staff lawyer at the Federal Trade Commission for eighteen years.[21]

FIGURE 46
Judy Cole became a key assistant in Barbara Franklin's office in what is now the Eisenhower Executive Office Building. A Few Good Women Oral History Collection, Penn State University Archives.

FIGURE 47
Virginia Knauer at her desk. White House Photograph files, Richard Nixon Presidential Library and Museum.

Judy Kaufman had previously served as communications director for BPW and knew the various women's groups and the talent bank that BPW had organized. According to Franklin, "Judy was creative. One example—it was she who came up with the idea for a Presidential proclamation honoring 'Equality Day,' August 26, the anniversary of the ratification of the 19th Amendment. President Nixon issued the first proclamation in 1972 and every president has continued the practice since then. Judy was always enthusiastic and upbeat."[22]

Franklin also made arrangements with the White House Correspondence Office to develop a system of form letters to respond to the more routine mail (however, presidential secretary Rose Mary Woods corrected Franklin when the latter expressed a preference for "Ms." in correspondence, informing her that the White House only used "Mrs." or "Miss"). All in all, it proved to be an exciting beginning, but without the help of Helen Delich Bentley, Catherine Bedell, and Virginia Knauer, all of whom supported her in various ways, it would have been an impossible job.[23]

※

Central to all the work that Barbara Franklin needed to accomplish was the development of the talent bank. Here she was able to take advantage of the efforts of external organizations, like BPW, supplemented by a continuous flow of suggestions from others, along with unsolicited letters and résumés coming in "over the transom." Her recruiting plan also listed her sources for possible names. It included women already in high-level federal positions; female White House fellows past and present; governors, senators, congresswomen, and other Capitol Hill contacts; department and agency contacts; the Citizens' Advisory Council on the Status of Women and similar entities; Republican National Committeewomen; women's professional groups; and personal contacts in national search firms. There were also lists of selected women from a Civil Service Commission computer search of women holding GS-16 positions and above as well as other existing lists. Considering the huge pool of women to draw from, the plan concluded, "This effort will be continuous."[24]

Franklin's external responsibilities not only provided publicity for the effort but also helped generate more names for the talent bank. Franklin divided the country into ten regions, making sure to visit a "hub state" in each region and then fanning out to create a "source network" of organizations and individuals across the region to provide names. In a letter to a member of the Governor's Commission on Women in Vermont who wanted to set up her own talent bank for state positions, Franklin explained her strategy: "I have developed my talent bank . . . [by] establishing personal contacts with people in a position to know who the outstanding women are. You might set up that sort of source network in Vermont, using not only individuals, but also organizations such as the American Association of University Women, Business and Professional Women, General Federation of Women's Clubs,

FIGURE 48
Barbara Franklin played an important role externally as a spokeswoman for the president in outreach to women's organizations. A Few Good Women Oral History Collection, Penn State University Archives.

and any others which want to help. The original sources will undoubtedly lead to others, and by asking them all to identify outstanding women in any field, you should begin to get some good recommendations."[25]

All of these names needed to be vetted, biographies created, political checks done, and evaluations recorded. Those who seemed promising would be interviewed. Pen James recalled, "She had a parade of women come in and out of that office every day. And I was just astounded at this parade that I would see coming down the hall for an appointment with this Barbara Franklin. She really did a very large outreach, I think with a minimum of staff, really did develop a huge talent bank."[26]

Developing lists of potential women appointees was only half the battle, however. The other necessary component was identifying vacancies and matching possible candidates to them. This began with the liaison staff, the recruiters' opposite numbers on Malek's staff. Jerry Jones, a former Harvard classmate of both Fred Malek and Barbara Franklin, was on the liaison staff.[27] He recalled, "The resignation letters come to the White House. We process them, so we know exactly at all times what positions are open.[28]

As Stan Anderson, a lawyer and member of the liaison staff recalled, once a vacancy was known, "I'd give my evaluation of what kinds of requirements that job should have, what kind of experience, what the responsibilities were, what the subject matter of the job was, and then Fred would assign it to a recruiter who would try to go out and recruit the best possible person for that job. That had never happened before, that was what was unique about this process. . . . Then once a candidate was identified and approved, then it was our job to sell the candidate to the senior people in whatever

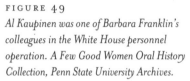

FIGURE 49

Al Kaupinen was one of Barbara Franklin's colleagues in the White House personnel operation. A Few Good Women Oral History Collection, Penn State University Archives.

department we were talking about."[29] Frank Herringer, another member of the liaison staff, described another part of the process that, in higher-level positions required further checking: "You needed clearance from the state Republican Party, the Congresspeople from that state or district . . . where the applicant came from. So we were responsible for the process that got those sign-offs."[30]

Ultimately, however, the choice was approved by the president, and his preferences set the ground rules. Jerry Jones recalled, "Unlike other administrations, President Nixon believed that being able to do the job was really important. So his instruction was to 'Find the best person that you can to do this job who agrees with me philosophically.' It was not 'I want the cousin of a Senator here.' . . . There was absolutely none of that. It was the best guy for the job who agreed with us philosophically. It helped to be a Republican, but it wasn't necessary."[31]

Al Kaupinen, another member of the liaison staff put it simply: "the best politics is the best selection on a merit basis of people. . . . We were looking for the best people because that was the best politics. The best management is the best politics. The best ethics is the best politics. The best all of these things is the way to gain a political advantage."[32]

In addition to this normal recruiting process, Stan Anderson recalled, "Barbara had a dual responsibility. She got assignments to find the best person for job 'A,' but also to find women for senior jobs. There had never been this outreach effort to find qualified women for senior jobs."[33]

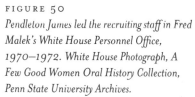

FIGURE 50
*Pendleton James led the recruiting staff in Fred
Malek's White House Personnel Office,
1970–1972. White House Photograph, A
Few Good Women Oral History Collection,
Penn State University Archives.*

As always, work in the White House was pressurized, with long hours in the evening and on weekends. In that kind of environment, adding the "women's issue" to the mix brought fireworks on occasion. Jones noted,

> As you can imagine this was quite a cultural clash. All the liaison officers and the recruiters but one . . . were males, most under 40. I was 33, 34, I mean quite young. . . . The cultural change was quite severe—"these come-uppity women and what in the hell are they thinking? What's enough here? Nothing's ever enough." . . . So this office culture sort of reflected that. . . . But there are two determinants. The first determinant was that it began to be a political necessity and so a political organism responds to that. . . . The second thing is that it wasn't "those silly women up on the West Side of New York." It was now Republican women.[34]

Pen James also reflected on the challenge Barbara Franklin faced in her responsibilities:

> That's tough because the government is full of male chauvinists, as we all were at that time, many of us were. . . . Barbara had to be an advocate. She had to go up against us and fight against us, because we would have candidates of the male gender for these posts. . . . She's undaunted; . . . she has the courage of her convictions. And it took somebody like that to . . . take on this charge against all types of male

chauvinist opposition, overt or subtle, and really battle her way against us. I mean, we weren't against this, we just hadn't given it that much thought. And so I think whatever success the women's movement had in identifying and bringing women into the government in that time really was due to, not only obviously Barbara Franklin's capability, but her personality and her doggedness to get the job done.[35]

Esther Lawton, deputy director of personnel at the Treasury Department was also a beneficiary of Barbara Franklin's work. She "was always very gracious. . . . She was wonderful because she didn't yell at you or point out that something was a very stupid mistake. She never said anything like that. She said I think maybe what was wrong was you were not given all the facts . . . or something happened where you forgot essential matters that could have affected the whole change."[36]

Barbara Franklin also remembered struggling through these battles. Her "outside" role of speaking to women for the administration often transposed into speaking for women inside the administration. She would circulate memos and create discussion papers on issues like the ERA and other women's concerns for staff. Being in personnel, she was under Chief of Staff Bob Haldeman's side of the White House, but with these efforts, she often crossed over into the domestic affairs side that was the purview of John Ehrlichman. Although this was not usually done, Franklin said she did it because she believed it needed to be done, and Malek supported her as long as she met her recruiting goals.

This was not always appreciated, however. "One time, I do remember that Chuck Colson wrote a memo to Fred Malek saying that he thought Barbara Franklin was getting a little out of hand and why didn't he shut her up. Fred, to his credit, didn't respond to it. He just sent it along to me with an 'FYI.' So in effect, I was doing my job better than some people wanted it done."[37]

Franklin did have a secret weapon. In fact, it was Susan B. Anthony—or rather, a bronze bust of the great suffragette. Created for the White House as a symbol of progress at Franklin's instigation and paid for by contributions from members of the Task Force on Women's Rights and Responsibilities and the Citizens' Advisory Council on the Status of Women, it was presented to Mrs. Nixon in early 1973.[38] The statue resided for some time, beforehand, in Franklin's office closet. Franklin recalled, "If someone said something that was derogatory about women, Susan B. would steal out of my closet in the dead of night and appear the next morning in the office of the guilty party to underscore her point. Then of course, I had to come and rescue her and bring her back to the closet. She was heavy. But it was known that the bust and the spirit of Susan B. Anthony roamed the White House on occasion at night."[39]

As she grew into her position and reflected on the dimensions of her task, however, Franklin realized she needed more time: "There were times when I just wasn't quite sure of my own survival. As it was, I was planning to go back to [First National City Bank] in six months. That was the original agreement. I took a six-month leave of absence. Well, after I became visible and started to do this job, I realized I couldn't do this in six months. I was going to have to stay and see it through. So I went back to the bank and negotiated a longer leave of absence and stayed for two years."[40]

❋

The action plans of the departments and agencies, as required under the president's directive of April 21, 1971, were one of the key tools for the recruitment and placement of women into high-level positions. Barbara Franklin recalled, "These plans were not the greatest because no one had ever done this before. . . . It took us a couple of iterations with most departments to get the plans to make sense, but once we had them, my office monitored progress."[41]

The State Department plan, for example, included various procedural measures for increasing women appointees and promotions and listed the numbers of women of GS-13 or equivalent grades or higher employed by the department, a total of 306, heavily slanted toward the midlevel grades.[42] A list of "Departmental Vacancies Targeted for Women," generated by Barbara Franklin's office, included six positions at State, headed by the director of the Office of Public Services in the Bureau of Public Affairs, which was a top-level foreign service reserve officer position, a grade at which there were only twenty-one women serving, according to Secretary William P. Rogers's document.[43] At that point, there were no higher vacancies at the State Department; however, in March 1972, Virginia Allan was named deputy assistant secretary of state for public affairs (a Schedule C noncareer executive appointment).

According to Franklin, "a standout among the Departments in terms of implementing their plans was Treasury . . . perhaps because the designed responsible person was Charls Walker, the Deputy Secretary, a very high level official, and the head of personnel was a superb career professional, Esther Lawton, who was a knowledgeable and effective advocate for women. They really made it work." Deputy Secretary Charls Walker recalled, "Until Barbara started working on it there wasn't any real focus. Our standards at Treasury so far as I knew were balanced, but . . . we didn't go in there with a

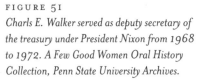

FIGURE 51
Charls E. Walker served as deputy secretary of the treasury under President Nixon from 1968 to 1972. A Few Good Women Oral History Collection, Penn State University Archives.

strong sense of priority. I knew some areas where we could do some shaking up, particularly the IRS, and we did personnel-wise. And in the process some women came out very well."[44]

The plans opened up the opportunities for women candidates. But there were some fundamental problems that Barbara Franklin had to grapple with at this time. One related to competition with minority men in recruiting; the other was the more basic issue of qualifications. In initiating the women's program, the administration had also resolved to enlarge job opportunities for minorities, and another recruiter in the office, Bill Marumoto, focused on that. Although there was sometimes tension over recruiting for jobs with minority men, Franklin was trying to find minority women to hire as well.

On the second issue, she was always struck by the numbers of women who contacted her and needed jobs but did not have the skills. At the same time, there was never a doubt that there were qualified and capable women available. Unfortunately, the reality was that "women were expected to be over-qualified to be considered qualified for a given job . . . that would be more qualifications than a man would have had before people were willing to risk putting him in this job."[45] At the end of June, Franklin had her first meeting with representatives of the group Federally Employed Women. There, one woman gave an example of this: a male lawyer, thirty-four, with limited relevant experience, had been named to the number two spot in a new regulatory agency. What were the chances that a woman with those qualifications would have gotten that job? None, she said; any woman would have to be twice as qualified to even be considered.[46] Franklin recalled that women "were generally undertitled and underpaid and were doing more than they were recognized for. . . . So the women who were appointed were really good. They had already over-achieved."[47]

Not surprisingly, the men of the office had differing perceptions about women's managerial qualifications. Frank Herringer recalled that "a lot of the most senior [women] were on boards or commissions or judges, things that require sort of a professional background. Economists—Marina Whitman on the Council of Economic Advisers . . . as opposed to an executive job, which are the Cabinet officers and the deputies. . . . There weren't a lot of

FIGURE 52
Barbara Franklin speaks with representatives of Federally Employed Women in June 1971. A Few Good Women Oral History Collection, Penn State University Archives.

FIGURE 53
Marina Whitman is sworn in as a member of the Council of Economic Advisers. Barbara Hackman Franklin Papers, Penn State University Archives.

them. There were some assistant secretaries who were again policy-oriented . . . as opposed to the hard executive jobs where you find a lot of [women] today."[48] At the same time, Herringer noted, "We did a pretty good job of getting younger women into jobs, particularly in the White House, who later developed into very senior accomplished women." He mentioned Elizabeth Hanford Dole, Kay Bailey Hutchinson, Diane Sawyer, Sallyanne Payton, and Ann McLaughlin Korologos, noting, "A lot of these women who were there in their twenties and early thirties, who were working in and around the White House, emerged to be sources to fill the pipeline later on. . . . It was an environment that apparently fostered that sort of growth."[49]

CHAPTER FIVE

The Women's Program Meets Its Goals

By the fall of 1971, the "women's program" was making good progress. Barbara Franklin was able to report to Fred Malek, Bob Finch, and Don Rumsfeld that all of the action plans were in place and functioning. Two departments, Interior and HEW, had actually hired their own women recruiters to enable the departments to reach their targets, while the State, Defense, and Treasury Departments had changed antiquated rules. The talent bank had more than 300 women in it, and Barbara Franklin had visited eight states to recruit and give speeches about the initiative.

The first goal set by the president had actually been achieved early. Thirty-five women had been placed in high-level positions since April 3, thus exceeding the goal of doubling the number from twenty-six to fifty-two. In addition, 624 women had been placed in midlevel (GS-13 to 15) positions since April 3, which was approximately 54 percent of the goal, and over 250 women had been appointed to boards and commissions, which was also significant progress. A policy had been established that was helping to boost the recruitment numbers for high-level positions, to target women in 20 percent of the searches. Among the women appointed by that time were Romana Bañuelos, the first Hispanic to be U.S. treasurer; Betty Southard Murphy as general counsel of the National Labor Relations Board; attorney Brereton Sturtevant as the first woman on the Board of Patent Appeals of the U.S. Patent Office; and Bethel O. Cook, the first woman as head of the Treasury's Securities Division.

Press coverage was also judged to be much improved. A lengthy story in the Sunday *Washington Star*, entitled "Top Women Talent 'Breakthrough,'" particularly impressed White House staff. The press was generally positive about Franklin's efforts, although it appeared that there was still skepticism

FIGURE 54
*Romana Bañuelos. A Few Good Women Oral
History Collection, Penn State University
Archives.*

concerning the president's interest and commitment to the program.[1] Franklin believed this article was a turning point in establishing the credibility of these efforts.

These concerns had been reinforced by the failure of the president to appoint a woman to either of the Supreme Court vacancies that occurred when Associate Justices Hugo Black and John M. Harlan announced their retirements, both due to illness, on September 17 and September 23, 1971, respectively. At the time of the Abe Fortas resignation from the court in May 1969 and the almost yearlong saga of the failed Haynsworth and Carswell nominations, which was resolved with the swearing in of Justice Harry Blackmun in May 1970, there had been excitement and discussion about the possible nomination of a woman. But no viable candidates emerged. Women advocates had resolved to be better prepared next time, and they went to work to develop lists of possible women candidates. Barbara Franklin was also actively working on this, inside the White House, creating and submitting lists of possible candidates. She was even visited by Lady Bird Johnson's former chief of staff, Liz Carpenter, who provided a list of names that had been compiled by women's groups. As Franklin recalled,

> I began to look for women to fill these vacancies, thinking that, "Wouldn't it be great if at least one of them could be a woman," but of course, I would have liked to have had two. There were not a lot of women in the judiciary at that point. We could pull out a

FIGURE 55
*Barbara Franklin at her desk in the White
House Personnel Office. Barbara Hackman
Franklin Papers, Penn State University
Archives.*

half dozen who were the right level, including Shirley Hufstedtler
[a federal appeals court judge] being a key one. . . . The problem
was that there just weren't enough to choose from, and there were
many men lobbying for this. . . . The crucial thing was that Nixon
wanted someone who was philosophically compatible with his
point of view. And many of the women in the judiciary were Democrats and/or were not strict constructionists. Finding candidates
became a problem.[2]

In mid-October 1971, the administration released a list, developed by
the Justice Department, of six potential candidates, which included a woman,
Mildred Lillie, a state appellate court judge from California. She was even
identified as the likely nominee to succeed John Harlan. But both Lillie and
Herschel Friday, who was slated for the black seat, were rated as "unqualified" by an American Bar Association (ABA) committee, and the president
withdrew them from contention. Attorney Lewis Powell and Justice Department official William Rehnquist were eventually nominated and confirmed.
Later observers suggested that by labeling Mildred Lillie as "unqualified," the
ABA panel was simply masking its "discomfort with the notion of a woman
on the high court."[3]

Although the outcome was disappointing, at least the administration
had presented a woman as a possible nominee. Skeptics might have questioned the sincerity of the Lillie candidacy, but it is generally accepted today

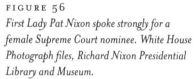

FIGURE 56
First Lady Pat Nixon spoke strongly for a female Supreme Court nominee. White House Photograph files, Richard Nixon Presidential Library and Museum.

that even Mrs. Nixon had lobbied her husband on this. Julie Nixon Eisenhower recalled this as well:

> One thing she felt strongly about is that . . . a woman should have been appointed to the Supreme Court. As you know, my mother's style was not confrontational. She did things in a quiet way. She tended to be very supportive of my father and she really didn't think it was her role to argue policy with him, but I remember she was very strong about a woman on the court. This was one instance where she really spoke up. I remember a family dinner where she didn't tell him off, but she said I think there should have been a woman and I'm very disappointed, etc. My father, as you know, he did have John Mitchell prepare a list of women, but there just wasn't anyone conservative enough for his taste.[4]

In the wake of the action, Fred Malek sent a memo to H. R. Haldeman, noting that although the ABA would "receive some of the heat," there would be "some political cost to the President." In response, Haldeman approved an increase in the drive for more public relations attention to the ongoing successes of the recruitment program, specifically tasking Barbara Franklin to work with presidential counsel John Dean to develop a list of top women attorneys to "provide a talent bank for future court appointments."[5]

FIGURE 57
*President Nixon spoke to the
National Federation of Republican
Women on October 22, 1971,
about the attempt to appoint a
woman to the Supreme Court.
White House Photograph files,
Richard Nixon Presidential Library
and Museum.*

In fact, the president acknowledged these concerns the day after the Powell-Rehnquist announcement. Speaking at a meeting of the National Federation of Republican Women, he quipped, "I feel somewhat lonely here, in one sense. I am the only man on the platform. I must say, that is a better break than a woman gets when she goes before the American Bar Association." However, he continued, "While I know that a great number in this audience, including my wife, felt very strongly that not only should a woman be considered but that a woman should be appointed, let me say that at least we have made a beginning, and there will be a woman on the Supreme Court in time."[6]

In retrospect, despite this failure in 1971, the appointment of a woman to the most senior position in one of the three branches of American government was now, for the first time, a topic for serious public discussion. It would take women two more vacancies over a decade, but Sandra Day O'Connor, an Arizona state appeals court judge and former state senate majority leader, was finally nominated by President Ronald Reagan and confirmed as an associate justice of the Supreme Court in 1981.

✳

Concern over the reelection had long been evident in the White House. However, in April 1971, Rita Hauser had circulated a memo in which she described what she called "Emergent Responsible Feminism—Why We Are Missing the Boat for 1972." Looking forward to the reelection campaign, she cautioned that the administration had "missed virtually every opportunity" so far to take advantage of a social-political phenomenon that she believed would be a major factor in the election. Women, she noted, had coalesced across party, social, and economic lines in support of the quest for equal rights. The president had to take them seriously and approach them "on the same level of intelligence and comprehension as men." She suggested he have a "rap session" with a cross-section of women and that he appoint a White House adviser on women's affairs, not as a political post for the election, but as a counselor on the more fundamental issues facing women. "I believe the moment is here to grasp the Emergent Feminism," she concluded. "We can speak to the New Woman, whatever her age, who is appearing all over America. Not to reach out for her would, truly, be 'missing the boat' in 1972."[7]

The memo raised quite a ruckus among the male staffers. Leonard Garment wrote to Haldeman that it "makes a great deal of sense to me, particularly her suggestion that the President would profit politically from the kind of meeting she describes."[8] Colson thought such a meeting would be a no-win for the president, while others advised holding the meeting only if they could make sure that none of the participants would come out of it criticizing the president. Hauser's second point about a presidential adviser was essentially ignored.[9]

However, Barbara Franklin and the other women around the White House took particular notice. In October 1971, Franklin prepared a lengthy report entitled "The Women's Vote," which analyzed election prospects in the new era of feminism. Covering voting patterns, attitudes, and positions on issues, the paper's suggested strategies essentially advised that the administration stop saying inappropriate things, do its research on women and the issues, and coordinate its positions. Specific tactics entailed appointing the oft-proposed special adviser on women's issues, having a woman as deputy campaign manager, spreading women throughout the campaign organization rather than isolating them in a traditional women's division, and having both the president and the First Lady speak to both men's and women's groups.[10]

As 1972 arrived, the presidential election began to loom ever larger. Barbara Franklin recalled, "The closer I got to the election of 1972, the more clout I had in terms of getting anything done, be it appointments or be it interjecting into the campaign, saying, 'You don't have any women on the platform or chairing anything, and you need a woman keynoter.' I had more clout than I should have, given the location of my position in the White House hierarchy, but that's politics. Some of my clout began to recede after the election."[11]

Perhaps the first achievement of the New Year came with the president's 1972 State of the Union address. While the address itself highlighted only new program initiatives, it once again did not specifically mention the advancement of women's rights and opportunities. However, Nixon cited civil rights proposals that "represent a spirit of change that is truly renewal." Among time-honored principles, he noted, "We believe in full and equal opportunity for all Americans and in the protection of individual rights and liberties."[12]

FIGURE 58
The president delivers the 1972 State of the Union Address. White House Photograph files, Richard Nixon Presidential Library and Museum.

The president's written message to Congress, however, contained more detailed proposals, and there he turned to initiatives to provide that equal opportunity for the aging, minorities, American Indians, women, veterans, and youth. On "Equal Rights for Women," President Nixon said: "This administration will also continue its strong efforts to open equal opportunities for women, recognizing clearly that women are often denied such opportunities today. While every woman may not want a career outside the home, every woman should have the freedom to choose whatever career she wishes—and an equal chance to pursue it."[13]

Following this statement, the president cited the policy and legislative initiatives for ending discrimination mentioned in earlier documents, like the 1969 task force report, and then specifically noted the achievement of the recruitment targets that Barbara Franklin had been pursuing over the past year. He concluded this section by stating, "Our vigorous program to recruit more women for Federal service will be continued and intensified in the coming year."[14]

Barbara Franklin reflected on his statement, emphasizing that freedom to choose then meant a choice of career. The problem was that in promoting women's liberation, some advocates seemed to be attacking women for choosing to be full-time homemakers. "We were trying to bridge that and be in the middle of the issue, saying, 'it's up to you to choose, but then you ought to have an equal chance to pursue your choice.' It was right then and it's right today. But it was important to say it and to have the President of the United States say it."[15]

However, his failure to mention the Equal Rights Amendment specifically was disappointing for women in the administration. In July of 1971, leading Republican women including Representatives Florence Dwyer, Charlotte

Reid, and Margaret Heckler, plus Carol Khosrovi, Helen Delich Bentley, Catherine Bedell, Pat Hitt, Jayne Spain, and Ethel Walsh sent a joint letter to the president urging him to reaffirm his 1968 endorsement of the ERA. It would be a campaign issue, they argued, and he should take the initiative before debate in the House began. The ERA had passed the House in the Ninety-First Congress in 1970 but not the Senate; it would now be reintroduced in the Ninety-Second. William Rehnquist's Justice Department testimony in April 1971 had ostensibly been in support of the amendment but ended up giving more prominent attention to positions in opposition to the ERA. From September 1971 through March 1972, when the Senate followed the House's October 1971 example and passed the ERA, Leonard Garment led the White House effort to create a statement the president could issue on the ERA that would not retract his 1968 endorsement but that also did not significantly influence the outcome of the votes. Reflecting in many ways the mixed range of opinions of the White House staff on ERA and women's issues in general, the White House frustrated its women advocates by appearing to straddle both sides of the issue—not wanting to lose face but also not wanting to be seen as pushing the amendment over the top. Ultimately, the House passed the ERA without substantial White House assistance, while the president's letter of endorsement to Minority Leader Hugh Scott came only days before its ultimate passage by the Senate on March 22, 1972.[16]

The president did not join the ERA Jubilee Banquet in May; instead he had Barbara Franklin carry by hand his letter of congratulations to be read to the crowd. In it he said, "I assure you that this Administration will continue in its determined efforts to ensure equal opportunity for women is translated from ideal to reality."[17] Franklin had spent much of the fall of 1971 and winter of 1972 reassuring women that the president was truly serious about the passage of the ERA, appointing more women, and a variety of other positions relating to women's concerns.[18] Although historians often treat the ERA as a discrete and separate issue, the White House staff found the ERA, the White House special assistant on women's affairs position, and other issues such as child care legislation to be interconnected and tenuously balanced. The recruitment program appeared to be the one area where they were most comfortable with publicly giving their wholehearted support.

In April 1972, there was a flurry of publicity to mark the first anniversary of the president's directive and the recruitment program. Barbara Franklin was able to report that the number of women in policy-making positions had tripled from 36 to 105. Even more significantly, at the top level, more than half the appointments were the first women ever to hold those positions.

FIGURE 59

Four women generals, from left to right: General Anna Hayes, Army Nurse Corps; General Mildred Inez C. Bailey, second director, Women's Army Corps; General Elizabeth Hoisington, first director, Women's Army Corps; and General Jeanne Holm, Women in the Air Force. U.S. Army photo, A Few Good Women Oral History Collection, Penn State University Archives.

In addition, nearly 1,100 more women had been placed in midlevel positions and 339 women appointed to boards and commissions.

These numbers included the first six women general officers in the armed forces.[19] Defense Secretary Melvin Laird pushed for women to be promoted to flag rank. "The first thing that I did when I went over to the Department of Defense is I called in the chiefs from all the services and told them that within 18 months I wanted a [woman] flag officer on the list of admirals and generals to be promoted. And if there wasn't one on the list within the next 18 months, there would be no more admirals and generals."[20] Laird also made other female appointments at Defense, including Georgiana Sheldon Sharp, who helped organize and was deputy director of the Defense Civil Preparedness Agency. Midlevel appointments included the first women sky marshals, secret service agents, air traffic controllers, and narcotics agents. All this was accomplished while economic stringency was forcing static or diminished budgets and a reduction in the federal workforce by 5 percent.

Other major achievements included issuing Labor Department guidelines that required government contractors to have action plans for hiring and promoting women; compliance reviews of colleges and universities receiving federal grants, which led to discrimination charges being filed in 350 cases; proposing to Congress that the Commission on Civil Rights' jurisdiction be expanded to include sex-based discrimination; and signing into law an act that gave the Equal Employment Opportunity Commission enforcement powers in cases of sex discrimination.[21] These advances meant court-approved goals in hiring practices, rather than quotas, and enforcement power for civil rights for women through the courts, "based on recommendations of permanent government affirmative agencies in the Executive Branch"—advances that surpassed those of President Nixon's predecessors.[22]

At the same time, there was still a running battle with the more outspoken women's groups. On April 1, Wilma Scott Heide, a former nursing professor at Penn State and president of the National Organization for Women (NOW), sent the president a five-page letter outlining NOW's concerns. These included, as NOW saw it, his late and lukewarm support of ERA; veto of child care legislation; lack of substantial action against discrimination; failure to appoint a woman Supreme Court justice; and insufficient and inadequate appointments of women to policy-making positions in the government. Clearly, NOW doubted the president's commitment but was willing to meet with him to help him see the proper path.[23] Heide received no acknowledgment from the president, and Barbara Franklin later received a letter noting the organization's disappointment.[24] This was symptomatic not only of unforgiving criticism by parts of the women's movement for President Nixon but also of the high expectations those same organizations had for Barbara Franklin and their desire for her to influence administration policies.

Such potential radicalization of the women's vote was part of the concerns Barbara Franklin and others had for the 1972 presidential election. In addition to her regular White House personnel duties, Franklin took the lead in drafting campaign strategy relating to women. Her April 4 document "Plan—to Reach Women" was a lengthy analysis of issues, potential strategies, and action plans, likely an expansion of her 1971 "The Women's Vote" paper. In it she documented decreasing women's support for the president and the Republican Party in general. The targeted demographic were those most sympathetic to the women's movement and most likely to reject Richard Nixon—mostly under-40, unmarried, college-educated, urban, and suburban women. As the overall movement advanced, these women were quickly becoming conscious of their political and economic rights. She contended, "Winning women's votes in November will be an uphill battle." While women identified the war, drugs, and the economy as their top concerns, they tended to feel more strongly about these issues than men. Of the specifically "women's issues," equal opportunity in jobs and education, equal pay for equal work, child care for working women, and placing women on the Supreme Court and in the cabinet were the most strongly supported. However, Franklin noted, "we are not positioned well on several issues of special concern to women, and our general image is one of 'not caring about women.'" Here she was able to use the positions advanced in the NOW letter as a cautionary example for the overall campaign planners.

FIGURE 60
Barbara Franklin in a White House portrait. White House photograph, A Few Good Women Oral History Collection, Penn State University Archives.

The strategy she outlined proposed using a number of key spokeswomen—Bentley, Hauser, Knauer, Armstrong, Spain, Whitman, and Franklin herself—to appeal to various segments of women voters. She felt that these and other women appointees should be out giving speeches and being interviewed by all types of media as often as possible. A communications plan was suggested to place stories in all types of publications and on television and radio. A calendar of events from April through October was proposed, even including appearances for Mrs. Nixon and daughters Tricia and Julie, for whom Franklin had prepared briefing books.[25]

As the August convention in Miami approached, Barbara Franklin was involved in reviewing the plans for it as late as July. "I started to get very upset about the lack of women anywhere and the lack of consciousness about it. . . . And then, when it came down to picking keynote speakers , there were no women anywhere. I did write a strong memo and talked with the men at the campaign [Malek, Anderson, Jones, and Al Kaupinen from the Personnel Office were all then on temporary duty at the Committee to Re-Elect the President]. . . . They sold it and that's how Anne Armstrong came to be the keynote speaker—a first."[26] In fact, Armstrong's keynote was

FIGURE 61
Julie and Tricia Nixon also rode the "Voteswagon" with Representative Catherine Bedell in the 1968 campaign. A Few Good Women Oral History Collection, Penn State University Archives.

the first for a woman at either party's convention and marked a significant achievement.

In a June progress report to Malek, Franklin's activities represented a mix of recruiting and campaign work. She had prepared the briefing materials and held a kickoff meeting for the women appointees who would be out campaigning, and she had helped organize a large media blitz by and about women appointees, including television spots. She even appeared on the TV game show "To Tell the Truth." However, Franklin recalled, "We didn't stop trying to push people through the pipeline." There were also vacancies to fill on commissions and boards as a result of expiring terms, but "the question is always can you get them confirmed at such a late time" before an election.[27] Among the fruits of the recruitment program that did not require Senate confirmation, Libby Koontz's position was upgraded to deputy assistant secretary of labor, five women were appointed as women's action program directors in HEW (including former task force member Elizabeth Athanasakos), and a woman—Vera Hirschberg—was added to the White House speechwriters office.

There were other notable appointments announced. A marine biologist from Seattle, Washington, Dr. Dixy Lee Ray, who was recruited by Franklin, was the first woman to be named a member of the Atomic Energy Commission (AEC) in early August 1972. Ray had a knack for making science understandable to the layman, as demonstrated in past testimony before Congress for the National Science Foundation (NSF). While also working at the NSF, she wrote feasibility studies that resulted in the establishment of the National Center for Atmospheric Research and the National Radio Astronomy Center.[28] Franklin had actually broached the idea to Ray in an airport meeting; Ray thought it was a joke at first, but Franklin was able to persuade Ray she was serious. Although Ray was "quite unconventional . . . she wore blazers and knee socks, had dogs and lived in a trailer when she was in Washington," recalled Franklin, she was also a strong advocate for nuclear power. In February 1973, when James Schlesinger moved from chairing AEC to a short stint as director of the Central Intelligence Agency, Franklin saw an opportunity. She noted that Schlesinger "was very much against [Ray] being made chairman, but he was on his way out, and so, frankly, we just waited until he got out, and then we went through the drill and she became chairman."[29]

A few days after the Ray announcement, on August 11, 1972, the president nominated Cynthia Holcomb Hall to a fifteen-year term as a judge of the United States Tax Court. The Hall appointment was pathbreaking also because, at the same time, Hall's husband, John, was nominated as deputy

FIGURE 62
Dixy Lee Ray. Barbara Hackman Franklin Papers, Penn State University Archives.

assistant secretary of the treasury for tax policy. Both tax lawyers, they would be the first married couple in history to join the government at the same time. Judge Hall was directly recruited by Franklin, but the key to getting her on board was also persuading her husband to leave California for Washington. This was also engineered by Franklin and Stan Anderson, who encouraged a Treasury executive who knew John H. Hall to recruit him as well.

Coups such as these were increasingly recognized in the press, such as in a *Newsweek* story later in August, which credited Franklin with quickening the pace of change in government "quietly with minimum backlash." Although there was still resistance and many battles to fight for equality for women, *Newsweek* could say without sarcasm, "the person in Washington who has

FIGURE 63

Barbara Franklin gathers a number of high-ranking women for this historic first photo of women appointees on the White House lawn, April 28, 1972. Left to right: Sallyanne Payton, Ethel Walsh, Elizabeth Hanford, Jeanne Holm, Georgiana Sheldon, Rose Mary Woods, Virginia Allan, Virginia Knauer, Carol Khosrovi, Helen Delich Bentley, Paula Tennant, Jayne Spain, Brereton Sturtevant, Evelyn Eppley, Gloria Toote, and Barbara Franklin. White House Photograph, A Few Good Women Oral History Collection, Penn State University Archives.

done the most for the women's movement may be Richard Nixon." It was largely due to Franklin's hard work that such a proposition could even be advanced.[30]

✳

Just before the convention, Clark MacGregor, who had taken over as chairman of the Committee to Re-Elect the President after John Mitchell's resignation in July 1972, reviewed and approved Franklin's plan for the Women's Surrogate Program, a concept that Franklin says originated with MacGregor's wife, Barbara. It provided for teams of three women, consisting of an appointee, a cabinet wife, and a White House wife or the spouse of the local congressman, senator, or governor, to go out on speaking events and other appearances and also to have interviews on television, radio, and with newspapers in secondary media markets in key states.[31] These efforts turned out to be fairly innovative and quite well received.

On November 7, 1972, the voters gave Richard Nixon one of the great landslides of American political history. Nixon's margin of victory was almost eighteen million popular votes, and the Electoral College went 520–17 for Nixon. While the president was acknowledged for extricating the United States from Vietnam, opening relations with China, pursuing arms control with the Soviet Union, and a stable economy, he also benefited from a Democratic ticket debacle and a press that constantly questioned the efforts of the McGovern campaign while portraying the Republicans as an efficient organization running a model campaign. The June 17 Watergate break-in at the Democratic National Committee headquarters had been publicized by the McGovern campaign but was dismissed by the media and had little or no impact on the voters.[32]

In the aftermath of the election and planning for the second inauguration, Barbara Franklin again began concentrating her efforts on recruitment and pressing the women's agenda inside the White House. Although there might have been few vacancies to fill in the months immediately before the election, things would now change. On November 22, Franklin wrote to Malek to argue that it was time to make a substantial leap forward. Nixon had won 62 percent of the women's vote, compared with 59 percent of men's votes. "Our actions in placing women in top jobs now is a strategic step toward keeping women voters with us and the Republican Party" as they looked toward 1976. Franklin argued that it was time to target women for at least one cabinet secretary and two undersecretary posts and at least ten agency or commission heads, including some highly visible, important spots. Among the list of thirty top candidates she attached to the memo were some who needed to stay in place, like Helen Delich Bentley and Ethel Bent Walsh, an Equal Employment Opportunity commissioner; and others already in the administration, such as Carla Hills, Jewel Lafontant, and Gloria Toote, who seemed very promising possibilities for new jobs. Sandra Day O'Connor, then a state senator, also appeared on the list as a good prospect for high-level appointment. It did not happen, but eight years later she would be tapped by President Reagan as the first woman to serve on the Supreme Court. However, Malek was, for the moment, on a presidential retreat of sorts, and Franklin was concerned that the recruitment program might lose momentum.[33]

Soon after the election, the president moved with his cabinet members and top staff to Camp David to plan for the second term. He addressed those assembled on November 27: "I find that getting away from the White House . . . gives a sense of perspective that is very, very useful. I developed that pattern early in the Administration and am going to follow it even more during the next four years. . . . I find that here on top of a mountain it is easier for me to get on top of the job, to think in a more certainly relaxed way at times—although the work has been very intensive in the past two weeks."[34]

FIGURE 64
Ethel Bent Walsh moved to the Equal Employment Opportunity Commission and was acting chair twice during the Ford administration. A Few Good Women Oral History Collection, Penn State University Archives.

The long-range planning for federal departments and agencies had been far-reaching, and an overall message came through—the government needed to be downsized, budgets cut, personnel reduced, and power pushed out to the departments and agencies and even to state and local governments. The second term would not be status quo; there would be no loss of vitality; the American people wanted change that builds effectiveness. The president and his top staff would apparently be there for two more weeks working out the details of programs and staffing changes.[35] On December 11, at the end of the Camp David sojourn, the president imposed a hiring and promotion freeze on the executive branch effective until the transmission of the budget in January.

The way the higher-level staffing changes were handled came as something of a surprise. Stan Anderson recalls, "Right after the election, 1973, Nixon decided to do something that nobody else had ever done. I actually drafted the letter that went to all presidential appointees asking . . . everybody to send in a letter of resignation. This would then give the President the opportunity to accept those resignations."[36] This was the final step in a process that had begun during the previous year, to assess the performance of all existing top-level appointees. Anderson continued, "We talked to their supervisors, their employees, their outside interest groups, saying 'do you think these people are good or bad,' and eventually made an evaluation of all those people." This was more than the typical evaluation exercise, however; external groups were asked "was he available to talk, could you access him, could you feel like he was competent. . . . You asked the substantive people in the White House, how did these people do in implementing the President's policies." These evaluations went to the president, and he "decided to accept or not accept [their letter of resignation] based on, in many respects, the analysis we did during the summer of the '72 election." Naturally, this was not a happy exercise. Anderson recalled, "I know I got a ton of calls from my buddies all around, saying 'How could you do this to me,' and I said, 'Look, this was what the President wanted.'"[37]

Frank Herringer also recalled that, as the election outcome was looking very positive in the fall of 1972, "We started turning our attention to this issue of how we were going to run the government after the election." Together with Fred Malek and Larry Higby, a Haldeman assistant, Herringer began working on a series of reorganization papers. Asking for resignations and starting with a clean slate was part of that process. According to Jerry Jones, roughly 555 people received Anderson's letter and the Personnel Office had 350 or 360 vacancies to fill as a result among the cabinet- and

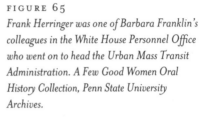

FIGURE 65
Frank Herringer was one of Barbara Franklin's colleagues in the White House Personnel Office who went on to head the Urban Mass Transit Administration. A Few Good Women Oral History Collection, Penn State University Archives.

subcabinet-level offices and agency heads, and other presidentially appointed positions confirmed by the Senate, a task which took more than a year.[38] Herringer noted, "It wasn't the most civil thing to have done, but we did it. Remember, we're 28 or 29 years old. What did we know?"[39]

Among appointees, Franklin recalled, "What rankled some people who felt they had really worked hard for the president and then this edict came, it was very terse . . . it made people mad." Franklin felt frustrated during these weeks: "The appointments process was up there . . . it wasn't as open as it was before, where I could go to talk with various people who might have had an interest in a particular job situation, where I could lobby for various candidates."[40] Once the president and senior staff returned, however, Franklin began forwarding lists of names of women appointees that should be retained or promoted to White House staff making the retention decisions, in an effort to counteract at least some of the negative effects of the resignation letter program.[41]

✳

It was announced on December 17 that Anne Armstrong would be named a counselor to the president, with cabinet rank, making her the highest ranking woman in the administration.[42] The following day, Barbara Franklin sent Fred Malek a memo telling him of an upcoming meeting of a coalition of eighteen women's groups to discuss accelerating the appointment of women.

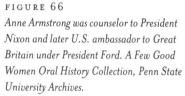

FIGURE 66

Anne Armstrong was counselor to President Nixon and later U.S. ambassador to Great Britain under President Ford. A Few Good Women Oral History Collection, Penn State University Archives.

Though happy with Armstrong's appointment, they felt the administration's investment in this effort was "for appearances and political reasons." She continued, "We need to follow Anne's appointment with additional innovative, substantive, and visible appointments of women in order to preserve [Nixon's] credibility in this area. It would be helpful also if we could announce that some current high-level women were being retained."[43] A week earlier, she had sent John Ehrlichman a similar memo, saying "*Most* outraged are the more conservative women's groups and Republican women. They feel they have supported us and been sold out."[44]

However, the Armstrong appointment might help; in newspaper interviews, she indicated that one of her areas of focus would be women and women's rights.[45] Armstrong would later say that she began with women's rights and set up the White House Office of Women's Programs to act as a liaison with women's groups, among other things, and for which she brought in Jill Ruckelshaus, also from the RNC, as head. Armstrong would serve a number of other roles as well, including liaison to Hispanic Americans, member of the Cost of Living Council, member of the Murphy Commission on foreign policy, first chair of the Federal Property Commission, and liaison to the Bicentennial Program.[46]

Anne Armstrong also continued her advocacy for the ERA. In January 1973, while still officially at the RNC, she sent letters to Republican officials and state legislators in states where ratification was pending. She urged the legislators: "A vote for the Amendment is a vote of confidence in our institutions and their capacity for improvement. On the contrary, the opponents' predictions of dire results for the family are based on the assumption that State Legislatures will act capriciously and without regard to the public welfare. They likewise assume that the Supreme Court, the final arbiter in interpreting the Amendment, will act irresponsibly and without regard to the intent of Congress."[47]

Even with the Office of Women's Programs established, Barbara Franklin continued her advocacy for women's concerns, while still focusing on recruiting and personnel issues. During this time, new appointments continued, including Jewel Lafontant, a black Chicago attorney, named deputy solicitor general in the Justice Department; and Betsy Ancker-Johnson, who became assistant secretary of commerce for science and technology. In March, while speaking to the recipients of the Federal Women's Awards, the president noted that, thanks to the recruitment program, the number of women in top-level positions had "quadrupled in the past 4 years. We think that is quite a record, and if we can, in the next 4 years, quadruple again, that would be by a factor of 16 over the period of 8 years. Now, that is a very, very high goal. The problem we have here is not so much finding the jobs. Many times it is the problem of finding women who are willing to and who want to take the job, because the need for top personnel in the Government is always there for the top people."[48]

But another appointment was also in the works. The Consumer Product Safety Act was passed by Congress and signed by the president in October 1972. It was to begin operating in 1973 as soon as the commissioners were appointed. Its purpose was to protect the public "against unreasonable risks of injuries associated with consumer products."[49] Barbara Franklin would be one of its first commissioners. As Jerry Jones recalled it, "Here is a presidentially-appointed position in a commission on which she is on the ground floor, got to develop it, got to use her skills. . . . Frankly, I have sort of forgotten how that came about, but I think everyone thought it was a great idea, including Barbara. It was a great promotion for her."[50]

In fact, Franklin had not thought about this position for herself. "There were five new seats on that Commission. As was my custom, I would try to go to the powers in charge—meaning Malek and the liaison team—and get a commitment for, in this case, two women. There had never been two women on a five-member commission. I got that commitment and was recruiting for two of those slots. One of those slots would be filled by Connie Newman [a black lawyer who had moved from being a special assistant to Elliott Richardson in

FIGURE 67

Connie Newman has had many government posts in her career and was director of Volunteers in Service to America before joining Barbara Franklin on the Consumer Product Safety Commission. Barbara Hackman Franklin Papers, Penn State University Archives.

HEW to serving as head of VISTA, the "domestic peace corps"], and the other slot was to be someone from the private sector."

At that time, with all the changes Franklin was beginning to consider a change for herself. She had done impressive work for the administration over the previous two years. There was discussion of a senior position in the Environmental Protection Agency (EPA), but she was not strongly interested. Bob Finch, who had resigned from his position as counselor to the president on November 27, 1972, to return to his Southern California law practice and an eventual run for the Senate,[51] called to urge her to stay on and continue the work.[52] But then, "Somewhere in the early part of 1973, February maybe, word came down to me from on high that, 'We want you to go to this commission.' I was not sure whether I wanted to do that."

Having worked in banking, a regulated industry, Franklin had mixed feelings about being a regulator. "I went back to see Walter Wriston, the City Bank CEO, and told him about this. I remember that he looked out the window for what seemed to me a long time and then he said, 'Well, if that's what they want you to do, you better do it or you better get out of the country, because that's just the way the world works down there.'" Franklin felt that Wriston was concerned about the growing political storm that would result from Watergate. It seemed like good advice, and after careful consideration, she took it, ending her leave arrangement with the bank. "That was where I stepped off, without realizing I was stepping off, the corporate career track

I had been planning."[53] This also meant leaving the White House staff where she had focused so much energy on advancing the cause of women, clearly a difficult decision. Nevertheless, on May 14, 1973, Barbara Franklin was sworn in as a commissioner and soon thereafter was named vice-chair of the new Consumer Product Safety Commission.

Before leaving the White House, however, she prepared for Jerry Jones a memo dated May 9, 1973, on the "White House Women Recruiting Function." In it she summarized her achievements over the previous two years. These included creating a network of sources and a talent bank of one thousand women, as well as shaping and monitoring the action plans, all of which had resulted in more than tripling the number of women in high-level jobs paying more than $28,000 per year, from 36 to 130. In addition, she had created a public relations function to communicate these achievements and had provided "substantive input to the Domestic Council on a number of issues of concern to women," preparing fact sheets, briefing books, and related materials. As she put it, "I became involved in the 'other' activities on a rather ad hoc basis—because those things were in [Nixon's] interest and because I was the most logical person to do them."

Since Anne Armstrong would be "taking over and expanding upon" these "other" activities, Franklin's recommendations were limited to the recruiting function. They were to (1) update the departmental action plans and their goals; (2) hire a woman to continue the program for the recruitment of women; (3) keep her visible to ensure that the president got credit for continuing to support this program; and (4) look for someone with professional credentials and a "feminine image," who could handle the visibility, was politically savvy and reliable, could relate to both the women and men she would work with, and who could work well and closely with Anne Armstrong. She concluded, "There is a clear need to hold women's support for [Richard Nixon]. Continuing the momentum of the recruiting and placement of women, spearheaded by a visible woman recruiter, will make a real contribution."[54]

However, as Barbara Franklin had anticipated, she was not replaced in the White House Personnel Office. Anne Armstrong added Nola Smith, former aide to Senator John Tower, to her staff as the White House federal women's recruiter and took on the efforts to have women appointed to positions.[55] Eight days after Franklin's memo to Jerry Jones, on May 17, 1973, the Senate Select Committee on Campaign Activities (the "Ervin Committee") began its hearings. The following day, Attorney General Elliott Richardson named Archibald Cox as special prosecutor to investigate the Watergate break-in and any involvement by President Nixon's staff or the Committee to

FIGURE 68
*Nola Smith, center,
former aide to Senator
John Tower, joined Anne
Armstrong, right, in the
new Office of Women's
Programs in the White
House. White House
Photograph files,
Richard Nixon
Presidential Library
and Museum.*

FIGURE 69
*Jeanne Holm served as a special assistant on women for President Ford after her retirement
from the air force. Left to right: Jill Ruckelshaus, President Ford, Senator Charles Percy
(R–IL), Jeanne Holm, and Betty Athanasakos. A Few Good Women Oral History Collection,
Penn State University Archives.*

Re-Elect the President. Almost fifteen months later, on August 9, 1974, the
president resigned from office.

Yet the "genie was out of the bottle." A fundamental change had occurred
in not only the work of government but also the attitudes of those who prac-
ticed those skills of both public administration and politics. The women's
movement continued to push for equality, and both the "din" of the crowd
outside and quiet work by women like Barbara Franklin inside were necessary

to move forward. In the Ford administration, 14 percent of all new appointments were women, and the activism persisted. The Equal Credit Opportunity Act of 1974 was a landmark law that prohibited discrimination by sex in the granting of consumer credit. New legislation admitting women to the military service academies passed in 1975. That year was also designated by the United Nations as International Women's Year, and the United States sent a delegation to the first World Women's Conference in Mexico City. Both President and Mrs. Ford remained strong supporters of ratification of the ERA, as did President and Mrs. Carter. The Pregnancy Discrimination Act, passed in 1978, banned employment discrimination against pregnant women. In January 1981, at the request of women's organizations, President Carter proclaimed the first National Women's History Week, incorporating March 8 as International Women's Day. The listing of achievements could continue indefinitely. What is most significant here is that many of the women leaders who played instrumental roles in effecting these changes first came on the stage during the Nixon administration, and many owe that initial opportunity to the work that Barbara Franklin began.

PART TWO

A Few Good Women in Their Own Words

Recounting Early Influences and the Special Role of Women in the Legal Profession

Influences

We are not born knowing what we want to do in life; we are the product of our environment and the families and friends who, consciously or unconsciously, teach and guide us and become our role models. Public service is a calling for some and a career for others. The "few good women" who were recruited into the federal government largely through the efforts of Barbara Franklin, and who were interviewed in this project, are not exceptions. Their backgrounds are as varied as America. Some seemed to take to politics right from the beginning as adolescents, for others developing a profession would become their entrée, while still others made their way in the world of business before hearing the call.

Helen Delich Bentley (1923–) grew up in Nevada mining towns in the most difficult circumstances. She found guidance from her local state senator, Charles Russell, and, surprisingly, through him found a position with a U.S. senatorial candidate of the opposite party. James G. Scrugham had been an engineering professor, governor, and a congressman before running for the Senate in 1942. Bentley worked in his office in Washington for several months before returning to the University of Missouri, where she graduated in journalism soon thereafter. She became a reporter for the United Press in Indiana and for the *Lewiston Tribune* in Lewiston, Idaho, before landing a position with the *Baltimore Sun* in 1945. There she covered maritime, labor, and transportation affairs for almost twenty-five years, a most unusual beat for a woman reporter at that time. She was named chair of the Federal Maritime Commission by President Nixon in 1969.

I guess that I was a pretty strong person, I would say, had to be to make my way from a very small mining town, Ruth, Nevada, and Ely, 8,000 feet above sea level. And I had a wonderful mother—my father died when I was eight. So there was my mother who was keeping boarders and trying to make things go for herself, my two brothers and me.

And in Ely, which was the county seat where we all went to high school, the owner of the weekly newspaper was State Senator Charles Russell who was a good Republican, took me under his wing, along with his wife Marge. And Charlie backed me up a great deal on what I wanted to do.

And then at the same time a Democrat, U.S. Senate candidate was visiting our county. Like so many of the state's sparsely-populated areas, there wasn't that much difference in those days between Republicans and Democrats. They were all basically conservative. This Democrat Senatorial candidate Jim Scrugham called on Charlie Russell for "some help in this county." "I need somebody who can do whatever needs to be done in this county and the next county," Scrugham said. So Charlie pointed to me, "I think Helen can do it."

[I was] 18, 19. That was my first taste of politics, my first taste of going around and holding people's hands and listening to their stories as you were trying to sell your candidate—who won.[1]

Bentley left the Maritime Commission in 1975 and was subsequently elected to Congress, representing Maryland five times (1985–1995), and later ran unsuccessfully for both governor and for another term in the House. During her time in Congress, Bentley was recognized as a leading expert on federal maritime policy and as a strong advocate for U.S. manufacturing. Prior to her election to Congress and since that time, she has been an international trade and business consultant. On the three hundredth anniversary of the founding of the Port of Baltimore in 2006, Maryland Governor Bob Ehrlich named the Port of Baltimore in her honor: the Helen Delich Bentley Port of Baltimore. She is the only living person for whom a port has ever been named.

※

As with Helen Delich Bentley, a rural childhood can sometimes provide strong influences. For Catherine May Bedell (1914–2004), that was certainly also the case. Probably her strongest influence was her grandmother, who, while relatively uneducated, read avidly about current events and had strong convictions on which she did not hesitate to act. Catherine May grew up in the Yakima Valley of south central Washington State, attended college there, and earned a teaching certificate from the University of Washington. After three years as a high school English teacher, she entered the world of radio journalism. She also became involved in Republican politics and was elected to the state legislature. In 1959, she became the first woman elected to Congress from the state of Washington and would serve six terms in the House of Representatives, from 1959 to 1970, when she lost her bid for reelection. She was appointed by President Nixon to the U.S. Tariff Commission in 1971, which subsequently became the U.S. International Trade Commission.

Grandmother's two big causes in life—with as much as she had going on in her personal life and the need to keep her children fed and clothed and the house running—[one was] she went out and marched every chance she could in favor of giving women the vote. She started that as a young woman. And then the second big cause was prohibition. She wanted the United States to go dry. She was

FIGURE 70

Representatives Martha Griffiths and Catherine Bedell chat with army generals Anna Hayes and Elizabeth Hoisington after their promotions were announced, May 1970. A Few Good Women Oral History Collection, Penn State University Archives.

horrified that they were selling liquor, and she took her part at smashing in windows of bars as well as marching. She was very patriotic, too.

I might say that various counties, individually in my state of Washington went dry. And then they began voting themselves wet as prohibition failed. . . . But Whitman County was the last county. It had stayed dry right up to the time I ran for Congress. And I had quite a problem with that. Because I was not a prohibitionist and so they used to just say Catherine May, the granddaughter of Laura Melrose. And boy, to the "dry's," that was enough. I didn't have to say I was a dry.

When I went to college, there was never a week Grandmother didn't write me a letter. She kept up on all her reading magazines, warning me against Communism—not to become a Communist, because she'd heard some pretty distressing stories out of the University of Washington, that there might be a Communist or two around there. And calling my attention to things that were before the legislature and before the Congress, keeping me up on things like that.

And to the day of her death, she gave the graduating class of the Colfax High School, every member of the graduating class a little American flag. And bought them herself and took them to see that each one got one. She had an amazingly clear mind. She used to recite parts of the Constitution to me. I'd be bored, you know, I was a terrible little granddaughter. Because I never got as enthusiastic—none of these causes meant anything to me. But Grandmother said I was late-blooming, and all that effect from her came out later in life. . . .

I can see her now—she was pretty, white-haired, blue, blue eyes, and stood very straight and tall. And boy, she had an opinion on everything . . . though she wasn't an unpleasant person, she didn't push it into you. But she just felt very strongly and not just from a little tiny corner, she read widely. I don't remember when she didn't have a news magazine or a newspaper around her someplace. She used to read to me from the newspaper. Sometimes I had not the faintest idea what she was talking about. Other times she would find things that interested me. But she didn't read Winnie the Pooh to me.[2]

After Bedell completed her term on the Tariff Commission in 1981, she served on President Reagan's Task Force on Legal Equity for Women, the "fifty-state project" that examined state laws for discriminatory language. She died in 2004.

✳

Being an immigrant, Margita E. White (1937–2002) had the barrier of language and culture to overcome in adjusting to life in America as a child. A year back in Sweden with her grandmother proved to be of vital importance to both her self-confidence and approach to school. Returning to America, she eventually became an honor student and graduated from the University of Redlands with a degree in political science. A semester spent in Washington, D.C., and summer job in a senatorial office cemented her interest in public service and politics. Margita White worked on three presidential campaigns, in 1960, 1964, and 1968, after which she became a staff assistant to the White House communications director, Herb Klein.

In 1948, my father was in his early 30s, and as best as I can recall, because he never really spoke about it much, he was dissatisfied with his career in Sweden with the Swedish airline industry and wanted to try something new. And at first, he was going to move to Argentina, and then somehow he changed his mind and took his family, his wife and three children, and moved to California.

FIGURE 71
Margita White, as assistant of Communications Director Herb Klein, introduced Barbara Franklin to the press in 1971. Courtesy Peter Cutts Photography. A Few Good Women Oral History Collection, Penn State University Archives.

As a ten year old child, I was miserable to start with. I had only a little bit of English, and I was 5'8" or thereabouts. And initially, my memories are of saying "I'm from Sweden, I don't speak English," and hearing "How's the weather up there?" and comments such as those.

So, my parents sent me back when I was thirteen to live with my grandmother for a year in Stockholm. She was quite an interesting lady—A one room school teacher who went on to become a member of Swedish parliament in the '30s. And my staying with her was a very good thing for me. It sort of turned me around and made me a good student. And I came back to the United States and started high school. [She became an honors student in both high school and college.] . . .

Grandmother was a part of it. And Barbara Franklin's thesis when she got her MBA at Harvard, was about the first-born daughter. I had that in spades as the immigrant first-born daughter, and I think there is something to that—that determination to succeed.

My career goals varied. At first, I was going to be the best secretary, that was in high school, and I took a lot of typing and shorthand. And then once I realized that I had an opportunity to win scholarships to go to college, I was going to be a teacher. And then I expanded my horizons, I wanted to be a foreign service officer, and then I found out that required that you had to be an American citizen for so many years. So then I had a wonderful political science teacher who inspired me, my interest in government, and that led to my coming to Washington in my junior year for one semester to participate in the Washington Semester at American University. And then that led to my contracting "Potomac Fever." . . . Actually, when I was here, not only did I attend school, but I ran out of money and ended up with my first government job filing letters in the basement of the Russell Senate Office Building for Senator Knowland, who was the minority leader of the U.S. Senate, and I stayed through the summer to work there.

So then I did return to the University of Redlands, determined to make public service a career. As I used to tell young people not to give up hope, because six years later, I had worked for seven elected officials who managed to lose a total of eight elections between them.[3]

Margita White moved to the U.S. Information Agency in 1973, where she became the assistant director for public information. Two years later, she was back in the White House, first as assistant press secretary and then as director of the Office of Communications for President Ford. In 1976, she was appointed to a two-year term on the Federal Communications Commission. After the expiration of her term, she served as a director and then vice-chair of Radio Free Europe/Radio Liberty, Inc., as well as on a number of other corporate boards. Between 1988 and her retirement in 2001, she was president of the Association for Maximum Service Television, Inc., an industry group working on technology policy issues and the primary advocates for high-definition initiatives in broadcast television.

✳

Patricia Reilly Hitt (1918–2006) spent her childhood in the same Southern California area as Richard Nixon and grew up in a family that supported him from his earliest campaigns. As a young mother, she began campaign work in Nixon's congressional contests. Pat Hitt was a lifelong advocate for women in politics, and she chaired many campaigns for other politicians. In 1964, she gave the opening speech at the Republican National Convention, and she was a cochair of the 1968 Nixon campaign, the first time a senior leadership

FIGURE 72
Pat Hitt in her campaign office. A Few Good Women Oral History Collection, Penn State University Archives.

position in a major party campaign had been occupied by a woman. She was one of President Nixon's first woman appointees; in her HEW post, she had responsibility for ten regional field offices across the country.

I got into politics to begin with because of Richard Nixon. I worked in every one of his campaigns from 1946, right straight on up through 1972, as a matter of fact.

I was raised in Whittier, and so was he. And there was a connection there. My father was one of the Whittier men, very instrumental and very excited about him as a candidate for Congress in 1946 from that district. They wanted a Republican, and he was fresh back out of the Navy. And in my family, whenever my father got involved, he dragged the whole family along. But I think I must have wanted to, anyway.

I never did know either Dick or Pat Nixon when I was in school, because they were ahead of me. Pat came to Whittier High School a year after I graduated, and Dick was in Whittier College when I was in Whittier High School. But, we knew the family. We knew the [Nixon family] market and knew the family.

So I started out, and the first time I was ringing doorbells in his district, which was near, not in Whittier, near South Pasadena. I had two children. The boys were little, and I had one of them in a Taylor Tot, we called it, I think they call them a walker, now. And the other one was walking beside me, because the boys were four and a half years apart. But I didn't realize 'til years after what a dramatic impact that must have had on the people when the doorbell would ring and they would come to the door, and here was this young mother with two little kids and a sack full of political flyers that she wanted to give to you and ask you to vote for her candidate. And I did that precinct work in '46, again in '48.[4]

Pat Hitt also served as an official emissary of the president on state visits to China, the Soviet Union, Ethiopia, and South America. She retired from government in 1973 and continued to be active in California politics.

❊

Marina von Neumann Whitman (1935–) was born after her father and mother emigrated to America in 1930. Her parents divorced in 1937, and she lived with her mother in Hungary for a time. After her mother's remarriage, she moved to Washington and then to Cambridge, Massachusetts, with her

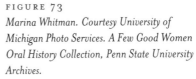

FIGURE 73
Marina Whitman. Courtesy University of Michigan Photo Services. A Few Good Women Oral History Collection, Penn State University Archives.

mother and stepfather. Later, she spent her teenage years back with her father, as he worked among the country's scientific elite at the Institute for Advanced Study in Princeton, New Jersey. She recounts her family's influence on her as well as her father's particular expectations. Marina Whitman graduated from Radcliffe and earned her PhD in economics from Columbia University in 1962. She was a professor at the University of Pittsburgh when she came to Washington as a senior staff member on the Council of Economic Advisers.

My parents were both Hungarian, born and grew up in Budapest. They married and came to the United States before I was born. My father, who later became a world-famous mathematician, John von Neumann, started actually I think in the late '20s or maybe 1930 spending half a year teaching at Princeton and half a year teaching in Germany. Then when the Institute for Advanced Study was founded in Princeton, he was one of the five original members along with Einstein and two or three other people. . . . But we basically lived in Princeton from my first couple of years.

Then my parents were divorced, and after spending a year in Hungary while my mother was getting divorced and remarried, I am told that during that year I learned to speak perfect German to the family and perfect Hungarian to the servants, neither of which I can speak a word of now. I then lived with my mother and step-father in

Washington and then Cambridge, Massachusetts, during World War II where both my mother and step-father were at the Radiation Laboratory, which was run by MIT, and which is where radar was developed or at least refined and built. Later I actually spent my high school years living with my father. . . . So it was a pretty driven family intellectually.

In terms of influences, nobody pushed me to go into any particular field, but my father made it clear to me that he believed it was every person's sort of moral obligation to make use of whatever intellectual capacities you had been given. He wasn't so concerned about whether you did it for pay or not, but simply that you don't let intellectual assets be wasted.[5]

In January 1972, after a year on the Council staff and three months on the Price Commission, Marina Whitman was named a member of the Council of Economic Advisers, the first woman to be so honored. She returned to Pitt in 1973 and served on several corporate boards before becoming an executive for General Motors. After her retirement from GM in 1992, she took a half-time appointment teaching in the Gerald R. Ford School of Public Policy at the University of Michigan.

✳

Cynthia Holcomb Hall (1929–2011) credited her father with being the primary influence on her career in the law. She was a Los Angeles native and attended undergraduate and law school at Stanford. She spent a year as an undergraduate at the University of Geneva in Switzerland and later took a master's degree in tax law at New York University. She served as a law clerk to a judge on the Ninth Circuit Court of Appeals, before joining the Justice Department in 1960 as a trial lawyer and later the Treasury Department to work on tax policy. She took up private practice in 1966. In 1972, she was nominated by President Nixon to a seat on the Tax Court in Washington.

I hadn't any real idea of what I wanted to do when I was in college. In fact, in those days, I hadn't any idea that I would do anything when I got out of school. Like my mother, I expected to get married and have children and do charity work.

My father was a Naval officer, and he had seen many of his peers killed during World War II, leaving behind widows with small children who did not have the ability to make a living, and he felt that it was important that I learn to make a living, and he stressed that to me, I knew that if not with the first degree, then with a second degree, I was going to have to come out with the ability to carry on a job. I think he thought I would be a teacher and just go on for a teaching credential, but I didn't want to be a French teacher, and so I began looking for some other occupation. It turned out to be law. . . .

In my case, [family influence] was very important. I never would have even considered going to law school without Father. . . . A grade school friend married when she got out of college and had two children and then was divorced, and she had never worked. She was telling me how difficult it had been for her to get any kind of a challenging job. Employers expected her to be a secretary, and even when she became an administrative assistant, they would have her doing things like running the executive dining room or something of that sort, and it wasn't until she had been working for probably 10 or more years that she finally got a job where they actually used her talent as the administrative assistant to the personnel department of a large business. She oversaw budget reductions and personnel reductions and many other crucial aspects of the business, and she was sorry that she had not had a father, as I had, who had taught her early on that she should be able to make a living and get interesting work.

It was understood you were supposed to do well. It was understood you were going to college. It was not whether you go to college, it was which college. There were very high expectations. No question about that.[6]

Judge Cynthia Holcomb Hall served on the Tax Court until 1981. She then moved to the U.S. District Court for the Central District of California and in 1984 was named to the Ninth Circuit of the U.S. Court of Appeals, where she was a highly respected jurist. She later moved to senior status on the court. She died in 2011.

✳

Like those of many good students, the parents of Elizabeth Hanford Dole (1936–) instilled in her the discipline and habits of doing all she could to the best of her ability and then looking for something more to accomplish. Her undergraduate education at Duke was particularly important to the formation of her character. After graduation in 1958 and postgraduate work at Oxford, she received both a master of arts in teaching and a law degree from

Harvard. Elizabeth Dole worked at HEW in the Kennedy-Johnson administrations and did pro bono legal work. She then moved to a job in the
White House Office of Consumer Affairs under Betty Furness, and with the
change of administrations, she stayed from 1969 to 1973 as Virginia Knauer's
deputy in that office.

> I grew up in a wonderful little town, Salisbury [North Carolina]—
> it's about 22,000 people. . . . Mother and Dad certainly didn't have a
> career in mind for me, but I think the values that they instilled in me
> and the fact that they were such encouragers definitely had an im-
> pact on my future career life. I can hear my Dad now, saying, "If it's
> worth doing, it's worth giving it your very best effort." And Mother
> would say, "You're finishing your homework early. Wouldn't you like
> to enter that essay contest?" It's the little extras, just being motivated
> by wonderful parents who gave me every sort of support and love but
> had no idea of a career in my future. I finished high school in 1954
> and college was a given. Then they assumed for me, like most *south-
> ern* girls of that era, marriage and settling down raising a family.
>
> I applied only to Duke . . . and finished there in 1958. I found
> that political science was fascinating, using your interpersonal skills
> to promote ideas and programs that would make a difference, a posi-
> tive difference in the quality of people's lives. I became involved in
> student government in high school as well as at Duke. I think it's a
> great education in itself, student government. I ran for freshman class
> president at Duke and lost. There's a lot you learn in losing, no ques-
> tion. Then, my junior year I ran for student government president
> and I was elected. At my first town hall monthly assembly, the editor
> of the student newspaper, the *Duke Chronicle*, criticized me for an
> error in parliamentary procedure. I studied *Robert's Rules of Order*
> all summer. I would have been ready for the state legislature I think
> by the fall! And I'll always remember my dad's delight, when he
> opened up the *Duke Chronicle* during my graduation weekend and
> discovered that the same editor, and his staff, had named me the stu-
> dent "Leader of the Year."
>
> They were wonderful days at Duke, and a great education not
> only academically but mediating between the needs of the students,
> faculty, administration and trustees through my student govern-
> ment.[7]

FIGURE 74
*The Honorable Elizabeth Hanford Dole. A Few
Good Women Oral History Collection, Penn
State University Archives.*

In 1973, President Nixon nominated Elizabeth Hanford to a term on the Federal Trade Commission, where she served until 1979. She married Senator Robert Dole in 1975. Under President Reagan, she served as a staff assistant for public liaison from 1981 to 1983. She was nominated, confirmed, and served as U.S. secretary of transportation from 1983 to 1987 and, under President George H. W. Bush, as secretary of labor from 1989 to 1990. She left government in 1990 to become president of the American Red Cross, a position she held for ten years. After her unsuccessful bid for the Republican presidential nomination in 2000, she was elected to the U.S. Senate as Republican senator from North Carolina in 2002 and served from January 2003 to 2009.

※

Growing up in a political family can produce mixed feelings about campaigning but often a positive feeling toward public service. Carol Mayer Marshall (formerly Khosrovi) (1935–) had her first "hands-on" campaign experience at the tender age of twelve. Later, in 1955, while a student at Mount Holyoke, she served as a congressional intern. She was married, had a daughter soon thereafter, and completed her degree in political science at George Washington University by attending night classes. Graduating in 1960, she went to work for the RNC as a researcher during the Nixon presidential campaign. She then moved to Capitol Hill as a staff assistant to Representative Richard Schweiker (R-PA), eventually working with Senators Robert Griffin (R-MI) and Charles Percy (R-IL) as legislative assistant. She was recruited to the Office of Economic Opportunity (OEO) in 1969.

I grew up in a very political family. My father was the youngest member of the Ohio legislature prior to my birth and was Chair of the Cincinnati Republican Party for many years. He was a good friend of Senator Robert Taft, Sr. All dinner conversations were political in nature. I was raised to believe that I could have any opinion I wanted, but that I needed to be prepared to debate and defend my position. So I was tested early in that regard and it's just been in my blood ever since.

I became a volunteer when I was 12 because there was a campaign at that time going on for Senator Taft and my father allowed me to go downtown to Republican headquarters, all by myself, and to lick stamps and envelopes for the Senator. And I remember it being so exciting. There I was with all of these adults and listening to their political discussions while they were handling various campaign tasks for the Senator Taft campaign. It was a very exciting evening for me and I have never forgotten it.[8]

Carol Mayer Marshall remained with OEO in various roles, including director of Volunteers in Service to America (VISTA), until 1973, when she resigned and moved to Berkeley to attend law school. Upon her graduation, she worked in a variety of consulting and real estate positions, most relating to policy issues in poverty and economic development. She ran unsuccessfully for the California State Senate, and in 1989, President Bush appointed her the superintendent of the San Francisco Mint. She was the first woman to hold that position. She is now retired and resides in the Bay Area.

Women in the Law

In a talk at Harvard in 2009, Justice Sandra Day O'Connor said, "It's been an amazing century for us. . . . It was not that long ago that the only relevant statistic regarding women in the legal profession was zero percent—as in zero associates, zero equity partners, and zero judges."[9] Five years earlier, Justice Ruth Bader Ginsburg recalled the story of women being denied admission to Columbia's law school in 1890 and quoted one of the board members as saying, "No woman shall degrade herself by practicing law in New York especially if I can save her."[10] The first American women to pass bar examinations and practice law fought bitterly for these privileges in the 1870s. Most law schools at the time denied women entry. By the turn of the twentieth century, there were perhaps five hundred women lawyers in the entire country, less than 1 percent of all lawyers. These women almost always worked outside of the male-dominated legal establishment and frequently in battles for women's rights. Into the 1950s, women still composed only 1 to 3 percent of the law profession, and many law schools still barred women from entry. In 1968, this started to change almost overnight as male law students lost their Vietnam War draft deferments and places for women quickly opened. Over the next decade, the number of women entering law school rose from 1,200 in 1967 to almost 12,000 in 1977.[11] Nevertheless, acceptance and equality was slower to come.

�֍

Rita E. Hauser (1934–) is an international lawyer and holds advanced degrees from the University of Strasbourg in France, Harvard and New York University law schools, and the University of Paris Law Faculty. She chaired the 1968 campaign for Richard Nixon in New York and in 1969 served as a consultant to the Task Force on Women's Rights and Responsibilities.

There were very few women then going into law altogether and certainly into the major law schools. Harvard was very late in the day in admitting women. It only admitted them in the class of '53 which was my husband's class. And by the time I got there five years later, we were only one percent—one percent—of the class. We were something like 14 women out of 400 plus. And only about half the women graduated. The rest dropped out. It was difficult. It was very painful. A lot of the men didn't want you there. Some of the professors were positively hostile.

Now, of course, it's 50/50 in all the law schools. So often when I address women at Harvard Law School on their careers and prospects or women in the bar in general, I try to tell them about this. They think you're talking about ancient times. And this was just a short period ago. There were very few women who made it to the major law firms. There were very few women who became partners and certainly very few women became, as I did, a managing partner and a major figure in a large law firm, which is still the case. Very few women do that.

We all had the problem [of getting a job after graduation]. I remember Ruth Bader Ginsburg, who's a friend of mine, she's a little bit older, and she went to Columbia Law School. But the reason she became a professor of law was that she couldn't get a job anywhere. So she gravitated to the university, and even then couldn't get a place at a major university. She started at Rutgers and eventually got to Columbia Law School. The same was true for most women. I was a very strong student and I already had a French law degree and I spoke several languages and I was admitted to the French bar. It was a fairly unique background. I was interested in international law and I interviewed in many of the major firms here in New York. And either they said, "Well, you're very exceptional, but we don't take women." Or, "We'll only take you and put you in estates and wills which is where women were generally put." And I kept saying "I'm interested in the international practice. This is my area. This is my field." And you just didn't get the time of day.

So I went a circuitous route with a smaller firm that did a great deal of international work, represented Volkswagen and other companies like that. And I built up very quickly a sizeable clientele. When I had the real clientele, then the law firms were interested. So that turned out to be my avenue. But everybody struggled very hard.[12]

Interested in world peace, security, and human rights, Rita Hauser was appointed U.S. representative to the U.N. Commission on Human Rights and served on commissions affiliated with the U.S. Department of State. In 1972, she cochaired President Nixon's national campaign. Dr. Hauser presently chairs the International Peace Academy and the Advisory Board of the RAND Center for Middle East Public Policy. She has served as a director for a number of organizations, is on the Visiting Committee of the John F. Kennedy School at Harvard University and the Dean's Advisory Board of Harvard Law School, and is chair of the Advisory Board of the Hauser Center for Nonprofit Organizations at Harvard University. She is also president of the Hauser Foundation.

※

Gloria E. A. Toote (1931–) graduated from Howard University and both the Howard and Columbia University law schools. She joined the law firm of Greenbaum, Wolff, and Ernst in 1957 and from 1957 to 1958 was a member of *Time* magazine's editorial staff. Governor Nelson Rockefeller appointed her assistant general counsel to the New York State Workmen's Compensation Board (1958–circa 1962). She was president of Toote Town Publishing Company and Town Sound Studios (1966–1970). In 1971, President Nixon appointed her assistant director of ACTION, a new agency that oversaw the Peace Corps, VISTA, and other federal volunteer programs.

> Because of my youth, I had difficulty finding a job, period. When I passed the bar, I wasn't 21, so I had to wait to be admitted. When appearing in court, the judge would say we don't take secretaries. Even when my case was number one on the calendar he would invariably ask the clerk to ascertain whether I was a secretary or an attorney. By this time my poor clients were sitting there all day. And it reached the point that I knew that if I did not find a way to control the anxiety that was building up in me, I wouldn't be a lawyer for long because I would be disbarred. And that is why I went to Columbia graduate law school [for the master of laws (LL.M.) degree in constitutional law].
>
> Women were not respected. It was thought, "We didn't have the ability to be lawyers." So it was very, very difficult. A very prejudiced situation for any woman who was a lawyer, but for a Black woman, impossible.[13]

Leaving ACTION in 1973, Gloria Toote then served as assistant secretary in the U.S. Department of Housing and Urban Development until 1975. Under President Reagan, she was appointed vice-chair of the President's Advisory Council on Private Sector Initiatives from 1983 to 1985. Besides serving on numerous boards, from 1984 to 1992 she was vice-chair of the National Political Congress of Black Women and a member of the RNC's Council of Economic Affairs. She was a national board member of the American Association and the Hoover Institution at Stanford University and appointed by President George Bush in 1992 with U.S. Senate confirmation to the national board of directors of the Federal National Mortgage Association. She is also a real estate developer in New York City.

✳

For Paula Adams Tennant (1913–2010), achieving her lifelong goal of becoming a lawyer came the hard way. Following military service in World War II, she embarked on a law degree without a college education, a not uncommon practice many years before when most law schools discriminated against women. Nevertheless she persevered and after passing the bar served as assistant U.S. attorney for the Territory of Alaska in Fairbanks. She then became a district attorney in California and was twice appointed by Governor

Ronald Reagan to the California Youth Authority Board, the state's parole body for juveniles. In 1970, President Richard M. Nixon appointed Tennant to the U.S. Board of Parole.

It was just my idea in high school. I wanted to be an attorney. And, of course, I graduated from high school in the depression, so college was out. [With World War II service in the Navy] I had to wait for quite a while until I was able to go to law school.

I'd always wanted to be a lawyer, and never had the opportunity to go to school. Then, of course, the G.I. Bill of Rights was available, and I took advantage of it. . . . There were a lot of women that I knew who benefited from the G.I. Bill.

I didn't go to college. . . . I went to this law school in San Francisco. We were living in San Francisco at the time. And it was an unaccredited law school, but that had nothing to do with taking the bar. As long as you could pass the bar, you could be admitted to practice law. And so I went to that school. And then I passed the bar. . . .

I was the only woman in the class, for quite some time. And then another woman came in . . . but she did not graduate with me. I was the only woman who graduated.

I don't think I remember anything special about [the attitude of the men in the class toward me]. . . . Most of the men were working, and so we were all working very hard to master the very difficult business of being a lawyer.

[Then] I worked briefly in Alameda County . . . social services. I guess it must have been a family support division, because I remember interviewing some absent fathers. It was called a legal assistant, but it really wasn't legal. It was more caseworker type of thing. I think there were some law firms that were taking graduates, but none of them appealed to me for what they had to offer.

My husband was traveling. He [was an insurance adjuster and] had offices from Alaska down to San Diego. When he was in Alaska, in Fairbanks, he read in the paper or heard that the U.S. Attorney was desperately looking for an assistant. He called him up and told the U.S. Attorney that his wife had just graduated from law school . . . had been admitted to the bar, and was looking for a job. The U.S. Attorney was traveling down to the Bay Area, and I met him. And he asked me to go to work for him.[14]

FIGURE 75
Paula Tennant. A Few Good Women Oral History Collection, Penn State University Archives.

Paula Tennant, in her term on the U.S. Board of Parole, played a significant role over a number of years in reforming the federal parole process. In 1983, President Reagan appointed her to the U.S. Parole Commission. After her retirement, she continued to write and publish poetry, was a volunteer for the SETI Institute, and was involved in a variety of community projects where she resided in northern California.

✦

Brereton (Bret) Sturtevant graduated from Wellesley in chemistry in 1942 and then worked as a research chemist for DuPont in Wilmington, Delaware, until 1950. She commuted evenings to Temple University in Philadelphia to earn her law degree. She then became the first woman law clerk for the Delaware Supreme Court, went into private practice, and later became a partner in the firm of Connolly, Bove & Lodge, a Wilmington firm specializing in patent law. In 1971, she was appointed by President Nixon as examiner-in-chief for the U.S. Patent and Trademark Office Board of Appeals, the first woman to hold such a position.

> My class graduated in early June [1942]. . . . I was a chemistry major, and the big chemical companies came, after Pearl Harbor, recruiting. . . . I went with DuPont. . . . We all had only bachelor's degrees. When the war was ending, DuPont . . . said, "The Ph.D.'s are coming back, go and get an advanced degree, . . . [otherwise] you're going to be out of a job."
>
> I decided that I wanted law instead of any more chemistry, and the bosses in my research department said, "Fine. Of course we'll be

FIGURE 76

Bret Sturtevant receives her appointment as examiner-in-chief of the U.S. Patent Office from Commerce Secretary Maurice Stans. A Few Good Women Oral History Collection, Penn State University Archives.

grooming you—if we help with tuition, we'll be grooming you not for us, but for the legal department because you will be able to go in the legal department." So they gave me the same big raise they gave anyone who was going on to get an advanced degree in chemistry, and it was four years law school, five nights a week. It was not really much worse than the three years that the day law school took. The place that had night law school, and it was a very good law school, was Temple University in Philadelphia. So for four years I commuted five nights a week doing most of the studying on the train going to and from. When I finished, I applied for a transfer to the legal department. The legal department told my research bosses, "Oh, we don't take women."

My department bosses were a whole lot—well, they were angry, and I think rightly. They moved heaven and earth but the head of the legal department said, "Oh, we'll take you alright to stay in the library and do legal research for the other lawyers, but we don't think that the head of a manufacturing department of DuPont will ever obey a woman lawyer's opinion that tells him he cannot do something, so we don't think a woman can really be a lawyer in a corporate setup such as we have." [This] became one of my favorite stories to tell some of my clients like Charles Pfizer Company, Esso, two or three others, over the years.[15]

Bret Sturtevant remained in office through the presidencies of Gerald Ford, Jimmy Carter, and Ronald Reagan, retiring in 1988. She resides in Alexandria, Virginia.

❋

Carla Anderson Hills (1934–), a native Californian, decided very early that she wanted to be a lawyer, and she pursued her goal with tenacity. She earned her BA at Stanford and graduated from Yale Law School in 1958. After passing the bar exam, she became an assistant U.S. attorney in Los Angeles and later entered private practice. In 1974, she became assistant U.S. attorney general for the Civil Division of the Justice Department. She was initially offered the position in October 1973 by Elliott Richardson, but immediately after her interview visit, Richardson and his deputy, William Ruckelshaus, resigned rather than fire Watergate Special Prosecutor Archibald Cox—in what was called the "Saturday Night Massacre." She put off accepting the position until she could meet with the new attorney general. Senator William

FIGURE 77
The Honorable Carla A. Hills. A Few Good Women Oral History Collection, Penn State University Archives.

B. Saxbe assumed the post in January 1974, and after meeting with him and other staff in the Justice Department, Carla Hills accepted the position and moved to Washington.

When I grew up, I didn't know any lawyers, but in my readings it seemed to me that all the people who had made a contribution to our history were lawyers. I say the word "all." That's from the vantage point of a 10-year-old. So I declared early on that I was going to be one, and my parents had no objection.

I went to Stanford University as an undergraduate. I actually was so anxious to be a lawyer I enrolled in their 3–3 program which is three years of undergraduate, followed by three years of law school with the result that your undergraduate degree is in "pre-law." But one day when I was a junior, I walked by a bulletin board and saw that there was an opportunity to go to Oxford for a semester abroad. I applied, and lo and behold I was accepted.

So I went to Oxford knowing I had enough units to graduate in "pre-law" and continue on the 3–3 program, but when I came back, I went in to see the Dean, then Dean Carl Spade. I said, "Will you still let me in on the 3–3 program?" And he said, "Young lady, what's your hurry?" It set me back, because here was a plan I had in my head from age 10 to age 17. In addition he said, "Why do you want to go to the Stanford Law School?" I thought it was really amazing for the Stanford Dean to be saying that to me. I said, "Well, where would you go?" And he said, "Well, my son is at Harvard." I think he said that he went to Harvard, but then he said, "I think I'd go to Yale." And I said, "Why?" And he said, "Because the number of faculty relative to students is much higher at Yale. And it's a wonderful institution." So I went back to my dorm and applied to Yale, which was the only school I applied to, and luckily for me they accepted me. So I went to Yale Law School. These days you wouldn't do that. . . .

Yale at that time did not accept women in its undergraduate programs, but it had for some years accepted women in the law school. I had a wonderful time. It was intellectually stimulating. I had never been on the East Coast. I had never lived in a real winter, with snow, and I made some very good friends there. . . .

The pool of talent grew enormously between my days in law school and today. When I was in law school, we had I think 177 in my law school class. There were about six or seven graduating women out of that class. When I got to the U.S. Attorney's office in Los Angeles, a county of about 10 million people, there wasn't a single woman lawyer who was a partner in any law firm.[16]

Carla Hills had served a little more than a year at the Justice Department when President Ford asked her to become secretary of housing and urban development, making her only the third woman to serve as a cabinet secretary and the first in twenty years. She would later serve as U.S. trade representative, also with cabinet rank, from 1989 to 1993. She has created her own international business consulting firm in Washington and also has served on a variety of corporate boards. In recent years, she has been cochair of the board of directors of the Council on Foreign Relations and also chairs the National Committee on U.S.–China Relations.

❊

Sallyanne Payton, a native Californian, graduated from Stanford University in 1964 and Stanford Law School in 1968, where she had been a member of the *Stanford Law Review*. After graduating, she worked for the law firm Covington and Burling in Washington, D.C., and in 1971 began work on the White House Domestic Council staff.

I had made the *Stanford Law Review* on first-year grades, which placed me in the academic cohort from which large firm associates are drawn. That was my side of it. The more interesting question was why Covington & Burling hired me, of all people, to work for them during the summer after my second year. I knew nothing about the Eastern establishment and so did not understand at the time what an adventurous step this was for them. It was 1967. Covington consisted of seriously powerful Eastern white men in the leadership of the legal profession. I was colored, which was from their point of view good, because they wanted to integrate by race. However, I was a girl, which made me a lot less valuable, and I was from California, which was for easterners a very different and somewhat suspect part of the country. The law firms were not enthusiastic about hiring women; and the Eastern firms were not yet hiring routinely in significant numbers from even midwestern law schools, much less from California schools. So I was under the microscope all summer, the question being whether a person different in so many respects from

C&B's usual profile could actually do the firm's work. The summer turned out well, however, and I was invited back for a permanent job after graduation, by which time the ice had been broken and they had hired other young associates distant from their usual profile, which itself changed remarkably during the time I worked for the firm.

I want to give credit where credit is due, however. The fact that I could deal so easily with being at Covington is without question a result of the devoted mentoring that Associate Dean Bill Keogh of the Stanford Law School provided to me. Although I did not appreciate what kind of environment I was going to work in during my professional life, Bill did, and he took me under his avuncular wing. He made me understand the high calling of the law; he taught me the importance of overcoming preconceptions and intellectual habits and approaching matters with fresh eyes. He taught me the central role in the legal system of the challenger. Knowing how much of an outsider I was, he brought me inside. I still see the world partly through the lenses that Bill gave me.

Covington taught me to be a lawyer. It was Howard Westwood, Bill Allen (the Stanford Law School graduate who recruited me) and Peter Nickles, particularly Peter, who taught me carefully, in the old way, and made me feel at home. Westwood even did me the great honor of swearing at me. I will always be grateful to these guys, and to their families. I am also grateful that they did not subject me to any of the race or gender stereotypes. I was not stuffed into the "female" specialties but was assigned to the transportation regulatory practice, representing airline, railroad and shipping clients; and my pro bono work consisted of building nonprofit subsidized housing and handling governance issues in the nonprofit sector. The combination turned out to be perfect background for my subsequent work in the Nixon administration. In fact, the main reason why I went to work for the Nixon White House was that John Ehrlichman and I found ourselves unexpectedly on the same page with respect to what needed to be done to improve the situation of the District of Columbia.[17]

In 1973, Sallyanne Payton became chief counsel of the Urban Mass Transportation Administration in the Department of Transportation. She joined the faculty of the University of Michigan Law School in 1976 as associate professor of law, where she has specialized in administrative and health law. She served as a public member and senior fellow of the Administrative Conference of the United States, chaired the Section on Administrative Law of the Association of American Law Schools, and is a fellow of the National Academy of Public Administration. She served on the President's Commission on National Health Care Reform during the Clinton administration, was one of the first directors of ERA America, and has cochaired the Michigan Women's Political Caucus.

✳

Bobbie Greene Kilberg (1944–) grew up in New York City and graduated from Vassar in 1965. The following year she received an MA in political science from Columbia but decided to pursue law and graduated from Yale Law School in 1969. She then became a White House fellow for a year and continued working as a staff assistant to the president until 1971. During these two years, before and after the creation of the Domestic Policy Council, she worked for John Ehrlichman and Kenneth Cole on domestic policy issues.

> [After a few months of graduate work in political science] I really didn't think I wanted to be a professor. I wanted to be a lawyer. . . . There was another part to it that relates back to the early women's movement and the workforce back then. I watched young

FIGURE 78
Domestic policy assistants Bobbie Kilberg and Sallyanne Payton meeting with Barbara Franklin (center). White House Photograph, A Few Good Women Oral History Collection, Penn State University Archives.

women who were a little older than I, two or three years older, who graduated from Vassar and a number of whom had even gotten Master's degrees. They came down to Washington to work, which was the place I wanted to be. Washington, in my mind, was the place where all the exciting things were happening. So these women came here to work and they were placed in administrative and secretarial roles while the guys, my friends from Yale, Harvard and Dartmouth whom I dated, were all being hired as professionals, as junior legislative assistants, with just their Bachelor's degrees.

I had also observed from having been an intern in the Senate during the summer before my senior year, that a woman could not be treated that way if she were a lawyer. So I said to myself, well, if I want to spend my career in Washington in the public policy arena, I need to have a law degree so I will have to be treated as a professional. It was as much that analysis and the rigor of a law school education, in the sense of the analytical and intellectual thinking capabilities that you develop, which appealed to me rather than the thought of being a corporate lawyer. I never thought I'd be a corporate lawyer because, really, I wanted the degree for public policy and for the intellectual rigor of it.[18]

From 1971 to 1973, Kilberg worked with the Washington law firm Arnold and Porter, becoming vice president for academic affairs at Mount Vernon College in 1973. She served as associate counsel to the president from 1975 to 1976 under President Gerald Ford and joined the Aspen Institute in 1978. She became the vice president and general counsel of the Roosevelt Center for American Policy Studies in 1982 and ran as the Republican candidate for a Virginia State Senate seat in 1987, losing to a twenty-two-year incumbent by only one percentage point. From 1989 to 1992, she served President George H. W. Bush as deputy assistant to the president for public liaison, directing all policy and event relationships between the White House and American interest groups. In February 1992, she became director of the President's Office of Intergovernmental Affairs. In 1993, she ran unsuccessfully for the Republican nomination for lieutenant governor of Virginia. From the fall of 1993 through the fall of 1998, she stayed at home with her fifth and youngest child, involving herself in community leadership positions. In 2001, she was appointed a member of the President's Committee of Advisors on Science and Technology. Since September 1998, she has been president and CEO of the Northern Virginia Technology Council, the largest technology council in the nation, with one thousand member companies, and has served on a number of advisory and policy bodies for the Commonwealth of Virginia, including as a cochair in 2009 of Virginia Governor McDonnell's transition team.

✳

Betty Southard Murphy (1931–2011) grew up in Atlantic City, New Jersey. Her father died when she was very young, and her mother, who had never worked, urged her to have a profession to support herself in case her husband would die and she had to support her family. She graduated from Ohio State University, then worked as a dishwasher on a Norwegian freighter to Europe. After working and studying in Paris, she then worked her way home traveling through Africa, the Middle East, and Asia by writing two hundred newspaper articles. She obtained her JD from Washington College of Law (WCL) at American University in 1958, by attending at night. After practicing in the court enforcement section of the National Labor Relations Board (NLRB), she entered private practice and was also an adjunct professor of law at WCL. President Nixon appointed her as the general counsel of the NLRB in 1972.

> My mother encouraged me to study law, but she also encouraged me to be whatever I wanted to be. When I was in the seventh or eighth grade, we had to complete a project for school—I went to public school—entitled "My vocation." Mother suggested I ask

FIGURE 79
Betty Murphy. Courtesy Howard Tucker, Mort Tucker Photography Inc. A Few Good Women Oral History Collection, Penn State University Archives.

women lawyers about becoming a lawyer. My mother arranged all the interviews for me. Surprisingly, each of the three women lawyers—all members of the Bar—told me *not* to become a lawyer, that it wasn't worth it. One was a legal secretary. The second lawyer spent her working life in the library, she never dealt with clients. The third woman had a similar story. It was rank discrimination. But I thought, "That's not going to be me." When I became a lawyer, I did not think of discrimination. I believed that the law was the most wonderful profession in the world and that I had as much of a chance as anyone to get to the top.

I really had no difficulty [in getting a job] although I had absolutely no contacts. I came to Washington, D.C., for the first time to go to law school. I had no contacts, not one. I wanted to be an international lawyer. So I looked in Martindale Hubbell [the law directory] and found, maybe 20 or 30 law firms that did some international law and I called them one by one. . . . I thought that if I asked for a job interview over the telephone nobody would want to see me, so I asked for advice. I figured, "I like to give advice, lawyers like to give advice." Another firm was Roberts and McInnis. I called Mr. Roberts, and he took my call. I said, "I graduated from law school. I don't have any contacts. What should I do?" He said, "Well, come on down and we'll talk." I said, "Okay," so I went down and we talked. He said, "Apply everywhere." So I applied everywhere, even to places that I would never consider working. For example, I applied to Social Security in Baltimore. I applied to the Department of State. My friends accused me of always wanting to interview and never wanting to work.

By the time I graduated, I had something like 12 offers in government and 7 or 8 offers in private practice. When you apply everywhere, the law of averages is in your favor. One offer was from Roberts and McInnis. Another was from the National Labor Relations Board. So I went back to Mr. Roberts and said, "What do I do?" He said, "Well, you can stop applying for one thing." And I said, "Okay, what do I do next?" He looked at my offers and he said that he thought I should go to the NLRB because "the NLRB has the best supervisors in town." He told me I "would learn a little bit about labor law, but that doesn't matter. But what is more important is that you will learn how government operates and you'll learn how to write."[19]

Serving as general counsel of the NLRB was the first of seven presidential appointments Betty Southard Murphy received. In 1974 she became administrator of the Wage and Hour Division of the Department of Labor, a position she held until 1975, whereupon she was appointed chair of the NLRB. In 1979, she left the NLRB and reentered private practice and would serve on several presidential commissions afterward. Besides winning many awards, she became the first lawyer to be elected to the National Academy of Human Resources. In 1996, the D.C. Bar named her one of twenty-four "Legends of the Law" for her accomplishments.[20]

CHAPTER SEVEN

Recalling Barriers, Appointments, and Family Impact

Overcoming Barriers

"As women entered the law, the law resisted."[1] This could easily be said of women crossing the threshold of any professional or managerial field or their education to prepare for such a position. Economist Marina Whitman described barriers in both graduate education and employment that many women have faced. She also related her experiences of her own daughter's disbelief at how women of the time reacted to these barriers—another experience that many women who fought the battles for women's liberation in the 1960s and 1970s have shared.

There were all kinds of constraints which, looking back, are absolutely intolerable but which somehow we really didn't notice, or if we noticed, we didn't take them terribly seriously. That seems incredible now, but I guess we hadn't been really sensitized and there were so many things that we could do and did do that it didn't bother us that way, certainly later it seemed appalling. I remember when I was graduating, one of the best employers was IBM which hired young liberal arts graduates for what they called computer engineers. They were really sales people with a little bit of training. It was a great job and the interview was going splendidly. I was first in my class and had this, what was by then, a very famous name in computer circles, von Neumann. Everything was going just great until he looked at my left hand and said, "Oh, I see you're engaged." And I said, "Yes." And he said, "Well, I am sorry. We have a policy. We don't hire engaged girls."

FIGURE 80
*Marina Whitman meets with
President Nixon and Secretary
of the Treasury George Shultz in
the Oval Office, January 29,
1972. Left to right: Barbara
Franklin; Dr. Herbert Stein, chair
of the Council of Economic Affairs;
Marina Whitman; President Nixon;
Secretary Shultz. White House
Photograph files, Richard Nixon
Presidential Library and Museum.*

I was telling that story to my daughter and her best friend when
they had just finished college. And they said, "Then what did you
say, Mom," waiting for some wonderful snappy answer. I said, "Well,
I don't know how to tell you this, but I stood up, smoothed my skirt,
and apologized for taking his time and left." Of course their faces fell
right to their knees. And I said, "You don't understand. At that time,
I could have laid on the floor and kicked my legs and screamed and
it wouldn't have made any difference. There was no EEOC. There
were no rules. He had a perfect right to say it and there wasn't much
I could do about it." ...

Then, the reason I went to Columbia [for graduate work], because I was living in Princeton, my husband was an instructor in the
English Department at Princeton. The Princeton economics department when they learned that I wanted to go and get a Ph.D. in economics said, "Well, why don't you come here?" And they said,
"There's just one little wrinkle, you have to go talk to the president
because we have never had women in graduate school." So I went and
talked to the president, who said essentially, "Oh, Mrs. Whitman, we
feel terrible that we can't take a student of your caliber, but unfortunately we have no housing for women students." And I said, "Well,
that's alright because I already live with my husband, who is an instructor, in the World War II barracks for graduate students and
junior faculty." Then he said, "Oh yes, but we really don't have ..." I
don't know what word he used. It wasn't anything as straightforward
as bathroom facilities for women. Anyway the upshot was that the
answer was no and I commuted right through my graduate school
career from Princeton to Columbia.[2]

After earning her PhD in economics at Columbia University, Marina Whitman became a professor at the University of Pittsburgh. She came to Washington as a senior staff member on the Council of Economic Advisers in 1971.

❊

Ruth M. Davis (1928–) was one of the first women to graduate from the University of Maryland with a PhD in mathematics (in 1955). She helped design some of the earliest computers and satellites and went on to hold many scientific positions in the federal government. During the Nixon administration, she served as director of the Institute for Computer Sciences and Technology at the National Institute for Standards and Technology, as the first director of the National Center for Biomedical Communications at the National Institutes of Health, where she helped create the MEDLARS medical information database system. Nevertheless, she faced many barriers in common with other women in scientific and technical fields at the beginning of her career.

> When I first started out, a woman considered herself lucky if she had a job in the area of science and engineering. I had a Ph.D. from the University of Maryland. I had worked with IBM. . . . I knew a lot of the management. I inquired about getting a job. They said, "We have a policy not to hire women for technical jobs. Do you type?"

FIGURE 81
Ruth Davis. A Few Good Women Oral History Collection, Penn State University Archives.

And I said no, I hadn't taken typing on purpose because I didn't want to end up being a typist. I then went to Johns Hopkins Applied Physics Lab out here . . . and asked them the same question. . . . They said, "Well, we have three pay scales. One is for married men. One is for single men. And the third is for women." I don't remember the actual salaries, but the prices went down. The women got the least and the married men got the most. . . . I thought what the heck am I going to do? Here I have a Ph.D. and I can't even get a job as a typist.

Somebody said, well, you know [the "Father of the Nuclear Navy," Admiral Hyman G.] Rickover is going around the country looking for anyone who knows computers, can set up large networks, can manage the area of computers, why don't you go and talk to him. And I did. I went through his now famous interviewing. I got selected. He found six of us around the country who had Ph.D.'s and some of them had Master's. Getting a Ph.D. in math at that time was not common. He hired me. He was a very interesting guy to work for. I guess I worked for him for maybe five years. That was the first job I had. The reason I went with Rickover was because nobody else would hire me as a mathematician or physicist. So you didn't have much pride. You just wanted to get hired.[3]

Dr. Davis is president and CEO of the Pymatuning Group, a Virginia firm specializing in industrial modernization and technology development, which she founded in 1980. Dr. Davis has held many scientific positions in the federal government, rising to deputy undersecretary of defense for research and advanced technology and, later, assistant secretary of energy for resource applications. She has been elected a member of the National Academy of Public Administration, the National Academy of Engineering, and the American Academy of Arts and Sciences.

✳

Evelyn Cunningham (1916–2010) graduated from Long Island University in 1943 and worked for the *Pittsburgh Courier*, then one of America's leading newspapers serving the African American community across the nation. She covered many of the era's biggest civil rights stories at a time when there were few women reporting hard news. She also produced and hosted for five years a popular radio program that featured interviews with significant figures in New York's African American community. Cunningham had campaigned for Governor Nelson Rockefeller, and in 1968, she accepted a position on his staff as administrative assistant to Jackie Robinson, working on community affairs. After two years, she became director of the Women's Unit of New York State. There, she served as a liaison with women's organizations and mounted the first major conference in New York government on women's issues. She was invited to become a member of the Task Force on Women's Rights and Responsibilities in 1969.

When I went to Long Island University . . . I had my meeting with the vocational guidance person who was a white male. And LIU at the time had a wonderful school of journalism and it still has, and that's why I wanted that school. And this man told me very quickly and very frankly and very coldly that "journalism's not for you. You'll never get a job and on and on and on. Let's get you into social sciences and that will round you out."

As it happened, it wasn't the worst major in the world. And I found the things I learned in the social sciences did help me in my journalism career. I was so pleased to go to that vocational guidance man a week after I graduated from LIU to tell him that hooray, guess what, I got a job on a newspaper. . . .

I got a job with the *Pittsburgh Courier* as a kind of a fluke and I must tell the whole truth about it. The *Courier* was the largest and most powerful black news publication in the world, at the time.

The then editor of the New York edition and my aunt were keeping company, as they said in the old days. On my graduation from LIU, he asked me what I planned to do. I told him I was going to get out here and find myself a job on a newspaper. He said he might be able to fit me into his paper. "Come on over to the *Courier* Monday and let's talk about it," he added.

As I said, it was a kind of fluke, a bit of luck. But it worked out because 24 or 25 years later I was still writing stories. I started out doing rewrites of stories in the *New York Times*. First, I had to read the *Times* and search for little pieces of news that had any relevance to black people. Then I would rewrite it. That was fun. It was easy. I understood exactly what I had to do, and quickly got better, more meaty assignments. And then I was able to initiate stories and finally get to do a column which I kept doing until I got out of the newspaper business.

So it was adventurous. I had assignments all over the world. I've been to Africa. I've been to all the Caribbean islands and was assigned to Fidel Castro, spent a couple of weeks listening to him talk. God, that man could talk. And still does, I'm told.

But most importantly, I think I was the lead reporter on a lot of the horrible things that were happening in the South during the Martin Luther King days, during the bombing of the church where the four kids died, during the time when men and women were killed because they exercised their right to vote. Real bad times, but juicy stories, of course. I had to beg for those assignments. I had to literally beg my *Courier* bosses who were reluctant to send me down into that hot bed.

[They were afraid for my safety] because so many reporters, black reporters, were chased out, threatened and a couple were killed. . . . I chided my editors later, claiming that the only reason I got these assignments down South was because the men get killed—so they said, "Let's send Cunningham."

Those years with the paper exposed me to the cream of black leadership, of black arts, actors, athletes. And it gave me a wonderful sense of pride and also a sense of security, and I think, most importantly, a sense that I had for the rest of my life a responsibility to young black people to let them know what is really happening, what has happened to let them know about the people they never heard about, about the Thurgood Marshalls who I regret some of them have never heard about.[4]

Evelyn Cunningham later served in several positions in the White House. She was the founder of the Coalition of 100 Black Women and was an active supporter and participant in a number of organizations dedicated to the arts in the African American community. In 2002, Mayor Michael Bloomberg appointed her to a New York City commission on women's issues.

✳

Major General Jeanne M. Holm (1921–2010), of the U.S. Air Force, made an extraordinary contribution to bettering the lives of women in the military. She was the first woman in the armed forces to be promoted to the rank of major general (1973), and this was only one of her many firsts. She served in the army from 1942 to 1945 and transferred to the air force in 1948, when

FIGURE 82
Jeanne Holm at her desk in the White House during the Ford administration. A Few Good Women Oral History Collection, Penn State University Archives.

a new law integrated women in the regular armed forces. General Holm served in a variety of personnel assignments, including director of Women in the Air Force from 1965 to 1973. She played a key role in eliminating restrictions on the number of women serving in all ranks, expanding job and duty station assignments for women, opening the Reserve Officers' Training Corps and service academies to women, and changing the policies on the status of women in the armed forces. According to her citation in the National Women's Hall of Fame in 2000, "Major General Jeanne Holm, USAF (Ret.) was a driving force in achieving parity for military women. . . . She worked tenaciously to enhance the status and expand the roles and opportunities for women in the armed services."[5]

Because the military structure was so used to thinking in terms of men, they automatically ignored women. It was very difficult to get policy makers when they made policy, to think in terms of how that policy would affect women. And it wasn't just the men in the power structure who wore these blinders, many women had the same problem. . . .

Society believed married women should not work. So when a military woman got married she was allowed to get out immediately, even encouraged. Even though a man who had had the same training as she was not allowed to. He had to fulfill his contractual obligation. But we would allow her to just leave, just because she was a married woman. If she became pregnant or married a man with children, she was forced out whether she wanted to or not.

Pregnancy had always been grounds for immediate discharge, irrespective of the question of legitimacy. That practice was shot down by the courts in 1972. I played no part in it because, frankly I was very ambivalent to the issue. It was a tough one for the military and still is.

One of my biggest battles was to reverse the practice of involuntary discharge of women (in the military) with minor children by virtue of adoption or marriage. The most frequent cases involved women who married men who had children by a previous marriage and were either widowed or divorced. The children may have been without a mother present for many years but the moment a military woman married their father her career was over no matter how much time she had invested.

This policy made no sense to me but there was great resistance within the Air Staff to discontinuing it. Part of my problem was my counterparts in the other services. The women directors had always tried to have consistency in service policies unique to women. In this instance the Army and Navy directors were dead set against any change and they let the Air Staff know how they felt in an attempt to undercut my efforts. So this was a much more difficult fight than I had ever anticipated but we won, with help from the courts.

I found support from many of the men, but my boss, General Robert Dixon, was the key. He agreed with me and told the personnel staff to change the policy. But, as I said, the directors, my counterparts in the Navy and the Army, fought it all the way because they realized that if the Air Force caved in on these social policies, their service would have to as well. And, in the end, they did.

There was also strong institutional resistance to allowing women to have the same allowances as men when it came to dependents. In other words, it was automatically assumed that any man who was married, his wife was his dependent. She might be a multimillionaire. But it didn't matter. She was assumed to be a dependent with specific rights in terms of medical care and her husband was to receive additional allowances for housing and for food. He was entitled to family quarters, just by virtue of the fact that he was married. It was not true of women. The military regarded them as single. They were not entitled to those benefits unless they could prove that their husbands were dependent upon them for more than 50 percent of their support.

Well, I fought that for many years without success. I had to go through the legal system of the Air Force but they would not support me on it. There is a 1952 decision of the Comptroller General of the U.S. that was against us. Every time I would talk to women in the Air Force during my field trips, they would raise this issue. "Why can't we have the same [military] benefits as men when we marry," they'd ask. If her husband was going to school as a civilian, she could not claim him as a dependent. He couldn't get medical care either. He couldn't go to the base exchanges. They were very upset about this. I would tell them that we're not going to win this until we have some woman or man who's a civilian husband willing to challenge the ruling in a court of law. If we do that, I was convinced we would win. I said if anyone wants to take it upon themselves to fight, either for their benefit or their husband's benefit, be my guest. That I would send them all the information that I had in my files to bolster their case.

Well, fortunately some lady by the name of Frontiero at Maxwell Air Force Base picked up the challenge. Her husband had left the service and was a civilian and going to school. She was told that she could not live in family quarters and could not get family allowances. For all practical purposes, she was single. So she took it to court. My office sent her all the material we had. The case went all the way to the Supreme Court to be resolved. And guess who argued it before the Supreme Court? Ruth Bader Ginsberg. She won.[6]

After her retirement, Holm served as a special assistant on women for President Ford and as a policy consultant for the Carter administration. She was the author of *Women in the Military: An Unfinished Revolution* (Presidio Press, 1986; revised edition, 1993) and editor of *In Defense of a Nation: Servicewomen in World War II* (Military Women's Press, 1998).

Recruitment and Appointments

The stories of how these "few good women" came to join the Nixon administration are as varied at the positions they took. In many cases, Barbara Franklin recruited them for service in the federal government, although other women came through different paths. They shared, however, unique circumstances and challenges. Catherine May Bedell, a former congresswoman, was appointed by the president in 1971 to a ten-year term as chair of the U.S. Tariff Commission, which later became the International Trade Commission.

> [After losing my bid for reelection to the House] I married Don [Bedell] ..., and we went on our honeymoon and I got a call from the White House. ... We were in Morocco where they had the women still walking behind their donkeys. They told me the President wished to talk to me. ...
>
> Anyway, he told me he wanted me to serve on Amtrak, put it together and then take the Commission job, the International Trade Commission. ...
>
> I know I will always remember when Nixon called me in. He said, "Catherine, I want you to get down there and bring that Commission into the Twentieth Century." I really didn't know what he was talking about. Then, he went on to say, "I cannot in clear conscience make these decisions and neither can the Congress who has to back me up or agree with me."
>
> And I talked to the Senators that were on the trade committees. ... When I became Chairman, I had two very capable Republicans on the commission, Joe Parker and George Moore, and they were with me.
>
> The Democrats didn't think too much of some of my modernizing ideas. But I did some terrible things like taking all the major housekeeping decisions out of the attorney's office and running the agency on a day-by-day business day, putting an actual office manager in charge of getting the proper repairs done, ... getting rid of the ants that were running all over the desks down in the basement

driving the secretaries wild, [and] fixing the roofs which had leaked in one of the oldest buildings in Washington. It's really beautiful today. They've saved it, thank goodness. They now have built a whole new building for the International Trade Commission, but in those days it was pretty dreadful, and there was just no management at all, so we did that make-over, but that was aside from the great learning experience for me, too.[7]

Catherine Bedell would later serve on President Reagan's Task Force on Legal Equity for Women before her retirement.

✳

Ann D. McLaughlin Korologos (1941–) received her BA from Marymount College in English literature and history. She also studied at the University of London. After several years working for ABC television in New York, she returned to Marymount as alumnae director. After entering public relations work with Myers InfoPlan, an Interpublic company, she became communications director for the Campaign to Re-Elect the President (CRP) from 1971 to 1972 and spokeswoman for the 1973 Inaugural. Following the re-election campaign, she was appointed director of the Office of Public Affairs at the Environmental Protection Agency under administrator William Ruckelshaus.

FIGURE 83
Ann McLaughlin Korologos. A Few Good Women Oral History Collection, Penn State University Archives.

My first leap into major league politics came in 1971 when my name was floated to the White House Personnel for a position on the 1972 Committee for the Re-election of the President—which later became the more than suitable acronym "CREEP."

A year before the campaign formally began I received a call from Cliff Miller, of Braun & Company, a PR firm in Los Angeles, who was an adviser to Bob Haldeman, Chief of Staff at the White House. Cliff, who was assisting Haldeman in gearing up for the 1972 Presidential Campaign, interviewed me and I eventually was recommended for a communications position at the Committee.

After my initial conversation with Cliff, I found myself in the office of Barbara Franklin, who was at White House Personnel at the time helping to establish the staff for the coming campaign.

Eventually I joined the rather sparse CRP group which was headquartered on Pennsylvania Avenue near the White House. My first assignment there was to begin organizing State Committee operations for "Nixon-Agnew in '72" and later organizing and managing a surrogate program the highlight of which was the women in the administration surrogates.

I was passionate about Nixon and his vision for America at the time. The first time I cast a Presidential vote came in 1964 when I strongly supported Senator Goldwater—and my conservative attitude carried over through the years into the 1972 race and beyond. In fact, in 1989 I learned through some family background research I was a fourth-generation Republican![8]

Ann Korologos left the administration in 1975 and began the communications office in Washington, D.C., for Union Carbide Corporation and then moved to Braun & Company, where she developed the issues management practice. Later, during the Reagan administration, Korologos was called back to politics and joined as the assistant secretary of the treasury for public affairs, where she received the Alexander Hamilton Award for distinguished leadership, and in 1983, she became undersecretary of the Department of the Interior. Ann left the administration to attend the Executive MBA program at the Wharton School of the University of Pennsylvania before becoming secretary of labor for President Reagan from 1987 to 1989. President Reagan awarded her the President's Citizen Medal in recognition of her public service.

After entering the public sector during the George H. W. Bush administration, Korologos was called back once again to government service, this

this was—maybe he'd been "called" at this time. His father was a minister. He was used to the idea of being "called," and I thought that's a very funny way to look at government service. He'd been in the Air Force during the Korean War. Much to my shock and surprise, he said yes, we should go. So that's what happened.

The Assistant Secretary of the Treasury is the one who engineered the deal, because he saw in this problem that the White House was having with me a way to get John to Treasury.[9]

We were the first husband-and-wife team, as far as I know, to go to Washington. I can remember when the appointments were announced, we had been hiking in Glacier Park and had come down to San Francisco to an ABA [American Bar Association] meeting, and we were immediately deluged by the press. I wasn't very interesting to the press, but John was, because, after all, he would deal with tax policy, something that the press is very interested in. I had thought I had made a deal that they would leave us alone until about ten o'clock in the morning, and I had planned to, quick, get to a hairdresser. After all, I had been hiking for a week, before all this hit me. But they found us having breakfast, and they arrived with their photographers, and the picture that hit the front page of the newspaper was of the two of us sitting having breakfast at the hotel in San Francisco.

After that, John was dragged from radio interview to television interviews and so on. One reporter followed me into the hairdresser, and I said I would talk to him as long as he left his photographer outside. So there was a lot of publicity when we went to Washington.

And as you know, all government salaries are public information, so one of the things that they published was our salaries,[10] and that generated a lot of letters saying that no one family should make this much money out of the government. This represented just a fraction of our normal income from private practice, and, in fact, from the day we left Los Angeles we began to go in debt, because most of our capital had gone to pay income taxes (we were on January 31st fiscal year) which were accelerated by our leaving. We paid almost two years of income taxes in one year. So we were in the process of going in debt, which continued as long as we were in Washington. The question was how far, how deep we were willing to go into debt, and that determined how long we stayed.

My confirmation was very smooth, and there was only one question asked that raised an issue and that was raised by Senator

Talmadge of Georgia. He wanted to know if there were a conflict of interest with my being appointed to the Tax Court where one of the two parties in litigation in every case was the Commissioner of Internal Revenue, and my husband being Deputy Assistant Secretary of the Treasury for Tax Policy, recognizing that the Internal Revenue Service is under the Secretary of Treasury. All others on the committee—it was the Finance Committee—and the head of the Joint Committee on Taxation, I think it was called—all said they didn't think there was any problem, and at that I was passed by the committee, and then later unanimously by the Senate.[11]

Cynthia H. Hall served as a judge on the U.S. Tax Court from 1972 to 1979. She was a distinguished senior judge of the U.S. Court of Appeals for the Ninth Circuit before her death in 2011.

❊

Constance Berry Newman (1935–) earned her BS in political science from Bates College in 1956 and her JD from the University of Minnesota Law School in 1959. She had worked in the Department of the Interior and the Office of Economic Development before her position with HEW. She was named director of VISTA by President Nixon in 1971.

My first political position was at a department—it was the Health, Education and Welfare at the time. I was special assistant to the Secretary and to the Deputy Undersecretary. So I was special assistant to Eliot Richardson and to Robert (Bob) Patricelli. That was not a presidential appointment, so I didn't go through the White House for that. But then Barbara Franklin contacted me about the opening as Director of VISTA. And so I became, through her, the Director of the Volunteers in Service to America. That was a presidential appointment. It did not require Senate confirmation. But that was the beginning of my knowing Barbara and working with her.

[I've had seven presidential appointments and] I found interest in all of them. When I stop being interested, I usually leave. I've had the luxury of being able to leave. I mean, that is a luxury. Not everybody can leave when they're ready to leave. But I've had the luxury plus I'm a risk-taker. I'm just basically a risk-taker. And I think for women who are interested in moving up, they have to be risk-takers.[12]

Connie Newman was recruited by Barbara Franklin as one of the founding commissioners of the U.S. Consumer Product Safety Commission in 1973. After another position in the Department of Housing and Urban Development, she left government and cofounded a consulting firm that conducted policy research in international development, regulatory matters, housing, transport, and urban development. She was the president of the Institute for American Business from 1982 to 1984 and was appointed director of the U.S. Office of Personnel Management in 1989, where she served until 1992. From 1992 to 2000, she was undersecretary of the Smithsonian Institution. She was later vice-chair of the District of Columbia Financial Responsibility and Management Assistance Authority. She then served as assistant administrator for Africa for the U.S. Agency for International Development and from 2004 to 2005 was assistant secretary of state for African affairs. She continues in consulting and lobbying work today.

✳

Carol Mayer Marshall (formerly Khosrovi) was a veteran congressional staffer when, in 1969, she was recruited to join the Office of Economic Opportunity. After her long experience on the Hill, she had many concerns about

FIGURE 85
Carol Marshall (then Khosrovi) meets with the president. A Few Good Women Oral History Collection, Penn State University Archives.

the requirements of this new job. However, in offering her the position, Don Rumsfeld persuaded her that she really could do it on terms that were acceptable to her.

> There had never been a woman head of Congressional Relations at any of the departments in government. It was definitely considered a man's job. At that time there were very few women on Capitol Hill and there were even fewer Legislative Assistants. When Don Rumsfeld asked me to take this job [head of Congressional Relations and Intergovernmental Affairs for the Office of Economic Opportunity], I said to him, "Don, you know I can't do that." And he said, "Why can't you?" And I said, "Because I am a woman and a Congressional Relations Director is expected to go and have drinks with the Senators and the Congressmen after work and they often have to hole up the Senator to get his vote in the men's bathroom." I knew how it worked and it didn't work for women. There was no way I could go and have a drink with a Congressman after work. In those days it was considered very inappropriate, besides which I had a family and I had to get home to them.
>
> So I said to him, "I can't really do that." And his reply to me I took as a great compliment. Rumsfeld said, "You're right, Carol, that's the way Congressional Relations people *usually* work. But," he said, "I want a different kind. I want someone who can talk to Fritz Mondale and Al Cranston" (some of the major players at the time who I knew well). And he said, "They all know you and respect you, and they won't expect you to be in the men's bathroom or having a drink after work." And so he said, "You can do the job very well, and I want you to do it." So I accepted the position and, I must say, it caused quite a bit of comment on the Hill at the time.[13]

Carol Mayer Marshall remained with OEO in various roles until 1973. She later moved to California, earned a law degree, and became involved in consulting and real estate. In 1989, President Bush appointed her the superintendent of the San Francisco Mint. She is now retired.

�֍

Sallyanne Payton was in practice with Covington and Burling in Washington, D.C., and also working on the committee on federal legislation of the Health and Welfare Council of the National Capital Area when she was unexpectedly tapped for President Nixon's new Domestic Policy Council.

Ehrlichman was a Stanford grad. . . . [He] had asked the Dean of the Stanford Law School, Bayless Manning, if he had any young people who were in Washington. The President had just formed the Domestic Council in 1971 and had put Ehrlichman in charge of it. They wanted a professional staff that would do disciplined analyses of the President's options on policy matters. So Ehrlichman's assignment was to develop a truly professional staff. He called around and got people from the law firms, the consulting firms, academia, and so forth. He had called, of course, Bayless Manning, who was the Dean at Stanford, and said, "Have you got anybody?" And the Dean put me on the list never thinking that I could ever get picked to work in Mr. Nixon's White House, but it all worked out and I had a great couple of years.

I was assigned to work for Bud Krogh, Egil Krogh, who had a lot of different subject areas, including transportation policy and the District of Columbia. As things settled in, I began to take on the kind of work I had been doing at Covington, which was building things and tending after governance relationships. Rebuilding the city after the 1968 riots was a priority of Mr. Nixon's, and in addition the Washington Metro was being threatened by Congressman Natcher of Kentucky, who was Chair of the subcommittee of the Appropriations Committee that controlled the District's budget. Mr. Natcher had been holding up the District's contribution to the regional transportation authority, demanding that the Three Sisters Bridge highway project be built [across the Potomac River between Arlington County, Virginia, and the District of Columbia]. This dispute had national implications because it was clear to everyone that if the Washington area succeeded in building a transit system rather than a highway then no other highways would be built inside the beltways anywhere in the rest of the country. The White House was squarely on the side of the Metro, and was doing everything it could to keep the project going through all the controversy. In the background of it all was the policy of moving the District toward home rule, and a defeat for the Metro would have been fatal to that objective because it would have been impossible to prevent the federal agencies from moving out to the suburbs. Mr. Nixon ordered the agencies to stay in the city.

I don't have to go into the racial politics of all of this, which were thick: not everyone wanted the nation's capital, which was already majority black, to become prosperous and competently self-governing. The irony was that the Nixon White House, which was not courting the black vote, put more boots on the ground, so to speak, and took more political risks in support of the tangible economic and administrative interests of the city than any presidency before or since.

Let me digress here to talk a little about making presidential leadership effective. People do not realize that the White House does not run the government. Operational control is in the agencies, which have the money and the people needed for achieving presidential goals. The agencies generally interface with the White House through the Office of Management and Budget, which is located in the Executive Office of the President. The OMB people tend to be deep public administration specialists, intimately familiar with agency programs and budgets. By contrast, the White House staff are political appointees of an assortment of backgrounds, who may be involved in numerous different substantive areas as the president directs.

Bud Krogh realized that he could not sit in the White House and issue orders to the agencies; he needed a more collaborative approach. For District of Columbia affairs he put together a team that consisted of both White House and OMB people, with the operational-level OMB people reporting directly to him. That made four of us. Ted Lutz and Mary Graham at OMB handled the money, and Bud and I handled the policy and relationships. The team was accountable to Art Kallen and ultimately to Paul O'Neill at OMB, and to John Ehrlichman in the White House. We had the capacity to stay tuned to developing situations and to act quickly with the backing of the President.

This commitment and capability paid off when Representative Natcher of Kentucky tried to kill the Metro finally by preventing the appropriation of the District of Columbia's share of the financing. This was the showdown. Bud went in and threw himself on the mercy of the President, who personally authorized him to support the District even against the House Republican leadership, in the person of Gerald Ford, who was siding with Mr. Natcher, who was a Democrat. It was a moment of odd alignments and high stakes. If Bud had lost, what remained of the Metro would now be nothing more than a set of unfinished tunnels under downtown streets, as in Cincinnati, and the highway interests would have been encouraged to try to realize their plan to push freeways through the heart of the District and other cities. But he won, and the Metro was saved. Metro's victory was a game-changer. Later, when he became President, Mr. Ford supported funding for the Washington Metro and signed the Urban Mass Transportation Act of 1974, which put $11.8 billion into mass transit, making mass transit his signature urban program.

I am telling you this story because the depth of Mr. Nixon's commitment to the District is difficult to fathom without understanding that he wanted America to have a great capital city as beautiful, prosperous and functional as the capital cities of other great nations. In addition to staying in close touch with the Washington Metropolitan [Area] Transit [Authority], WMATA, and making certain the federal financing for the Metro was supplied, our group also worked with the federal and local transportation and housing and redevelopment agency people and with agencies handling specialized federal initiatives such as the Pennsylvania Avenue redevelopment plan and the building of the Air and Space Museum and the Convention Center and of course the planning for the Bicentennial celebration of the signing of the Declaration of Independence. Both the president and Rep. Ancher Nelsen of Minnesota, who was the ranking Republican on the House District of Columbia Committee, were committed to making the Washington Technical Institute flourish on Connecticut Avenue. This was a time of building: as you move around the city, you see the fruits of this work.

In order to move the District toward home rule, the Congressional leadership formed the Commission on the Organization of the Government of the District of Columbia, chaired by Rep. Ancher Nelsen, to work through the governance design issues. When I came onto the White House staff, the President appointed me to the White House seat on the Commission. This was a wonderful immersion in the complexities of practical metropolitan management. For example, we spent endless hours on the intergovernmental issues involved in sewage disposal. The Congress adopted most of the Commission's recommendations when it enacted the 1973 Home Rule Act.

This was a huge exercise. Self-government is not just voting. Local self-government requires having the capacity to deliver public services, and the most basic of those public services depend on legal and physical infrastructure. You have got to be able to own or regulate your water and sewer systems, your electricity and telephone service. You have got to have streets, roads and mass transportation. You have got to have an adequate tax base. You have got to have the ordinary range of legal authorities—legislative, executive, judicial. All of that, and more. That is what we were working on, putting these powers in the hands of the people of the District.

This was all possible because Mr. Nixon, unlike some others who were involved in District affairs, was supportive of the emerging African American civic leadership. We must remember that Mr. Nixon's position on civil rights had always been impeccable and he had enjoyed the political support and even personal friendship of many middle-class African Americans. Even in 1968, running on a law and order platform, he got 38 percent of the black vote. Recall that at that point in time most of the segregationists were Democrats; the Republican position was mildly progressive on racial matters. Civil rights legislation had always been enacted with bipartisan majorities dependent on the support of centrist Republicans. When he was elected in 1968, Mr. Nixon brought numerous African American executives into his administration, notably in powerful positions not stereotyped as "black," and used his presidential power to open up opportunities for businesses owned by minorities and women. So there was nothing at all out of character in Mr. Nixon's support for the District and its aspirations. All that people now remember of Mr. Nixon's attitudes on race is the Southern Strategy. But it was much more complicated than that. He was also a talented outsider who sympathized with other talented outsiders. . . .

By the time the Congress was enacting District Home Rule, under the leadership of Rep. Charles Diggs of Michigan, the Nixon White House–OMB team had been disbanded: Bud Krogh, Ted Lutz and I had all gone to the Department of Transportation, Bud as Undersecretary, Ted as Deputy Undersecretary, and I as Chief Counsel of the Urban Mass Transportation Administration. So my story about the District ends in the spring of 1973.[14]

After service on the White House Domestic Council staff, Sallyanne Payton became chief counsel of the Urban Mass Transportation Administration in the Department of Transportation in 1973. She has been a member of the faculty of the University of Michigan Law School since 1976.

Supportive Husbands

For women who work, balancing the responsibilities of the job with those of home and family has always been a challenge, and professional and managerial positions exert even more stress. Coping with running a household and raising a family is difficult enough when both partners play active roles, but "trying to have it all," as it came to be described in the 1970s, was a pursuit certainly helped by having a supportive spouse. This was the case for Virginia H. Knauer (1915–2011), a Philadelphia native who served consecutive terms on the Philadelphia City Council and became Governor Raymond Shafer's principal adviser on consumer affairs, a new post. She was named to head the White House Office of Consumer Affairs by President Nixon.

I became Vice Chair of the Republican Party in Philadelphia and was always promoting women. We had a mayoral election coming up in 1959, and also we . . . put up candidates for five slots, council-at-large. I had made a great campaign to choose women, introducing to the party leadership these very attractive and talented young women, and later the Chairman called me in and he said, "Virginia, we have made a selection," and all I could think of, they didn't consult me which of these women I had recommended, and I said, "Who?" And he said, "You." I said, "Oh, don't be silly. I don't want to run. I'm too busy running things. I don't want to run for office." He said, "It's either you or we'll just put a man in that slot." Well, of course, they were fighting words for me, and I said, grudgingly, "Okay," and, of course, with a great deal of push from my husband, who was a con-

FIGURE 86
Virginia H. Knauer. A Few Good Women Oral History Collection, Penn State University Archives.

summate politician, having served three governors of Pennsylvania as Deputy Attorney General, and when I met him, he was in the Mayor's Cabinet in Philadelphia. . . .

Anyway, it came my turn, and he was wonderful, and, of course, I had organized all these women's groups throughout Philadelphia and had worked with all the male party leadership. So, when the votes came in, Philadelphia's Constitution is such that the top two of the minority party, which in Philadelphia was the Republican Party, of these five Councilmen at Large, the top two were the ones elected. I came in second, but only by about 257 votes, and the number three person was the President, then, of the Philadelphia Bar Association, who had fits—public fits. He could never be beaten by a mere housewife, he claimed, and so he got in front of a judge. He said, "It must be massive fraud on her part," me, as if I were tampering with boxes. So we did a massive recount, and the only fraud we found was in his count, and he lost another couple of hundred votes, and I chortled about that. I talked about it publicly! He didn't speak to me for years, of course, because I made so much of the fact that a mere housewife had licked him.

[My husband] loved playing Svengali, and I often teased him. He was perfectly willing to be on the sidelines. Unfortunately, some women have husbands who are rivals, and that's unfortunate or they have to give up what they're doing and move with the husband. That wasn't the way with me. My husband was older. As he said, he had been in the limelight for years and was a very successful lawyer beside his public service—but he thought it was just great pushing a woman.[15]

Virginia Knauer later directed the Office of Consumer Affairs under Presidents Ford and Reagan. Because of her expertise, she also served on the Cost of Living Council and a number of other White House domestic policy committees. When not serving in Washington, she formed her own consulting service on consumer affairs, was chair of the nonpartisan Council for the Advancement of Consumer Policy, and served on a number of other organizational and corporate boards. She had received numerous awards for her public service and work on behalf of the consumer movement. She died in 2011.

※

FIGURE 87
Pat Hutar and her husband,
Laddie Hutar. A Few Good
Women Oral History Collection,
Penn State University Archives.

Chicago native Patricia Hutar (1926–2010) was an early advocate for women's rights in both her professional and political careers. She served as chair of the Young Republican National Federation in 1961–1963 and in 1964–1965 was cochair of the RNC. In 1969, Hutar was appointed to the Task Force on Women's Rights and Responsibilities.

My husband's name is Laddie, and he has always been very supportive of what I've been doing. But of course, we've always discussed things because after all it is a family matter, just as I appreciate when he discusses things with me as to what he is going to be doing in his career. And I think that it's worked out very well. It is a sacrifice really on both sides, because you are separated at times when you might want to be doing something together. And yet you have to both believe that the cause is worth the separation temporarily and have the other person's support in what you are doing, and believe in it. . . .

When I became the co-chair of the Republican National Committee, there were some questions there, about how to handle that with two young children and that sort of thing, and we talked about it. And, of course, it was not a forever deal, so that we were able to work it out. And the other—in addition to having a wonderful husband, you have to have good help at home, and I had that. And that makes a difference, too. And either people have grandparents who can help out or they have very reliable people, and I was able to have people who had gone through nurses training, but decided not to be certified, once certification became a requirement for nursing in hospitals, etc., at the levels that they had been doing their work.

And so they were very, very competent people, wonderful people to help out, but basically it was my husband. He's one of the good guys.[16]

Pat Hutar was later appointed by President Ford to serve as U.S. representative to the U.N. Commission on the Status of Women, and in that capacity was chair of the U.S. delegations to the 1975 International Women's Year Conference in Mexico City. As a result of her interest in international women's affairs, she became the founding president of the United Nations Development Fund for Women (UNIFEM). Later Pat Hutar was elected president of the National Federation of Republican Women. She also served as a consultant on national and international affairs and as the director of the Office of International Medicine for the American Medical Association from 1978 to 1996. In addition, she served as a member of the Washington Roundtable of the Center for Strategic and International Studies and was a founding member and chaired the board of directors of the International Foundation for Election Systems.

＊

Patricia Hitt (1918–2006), a lifelong advocate for women in politics, cochaired President Nixon's 1968 campaign. She was one of the first three women appointed to a high-level position in the Nixon administration, serving as assistant secretary for community and field services in HEW.

FIGURE 88
Patricia Hitt. A Few Good Women Oral History Collection, Penn State University Archives.

Bob Hitt [her husband] . . . had a great deal of confidence in himself. He was a very secure man, so that it didn't intimidate him to be married to "somebody"—it didn't bother him the least bit because I was four or five places ahead of him in the reception line at the White House, because that's a protocol thing. But . . . he was totally supportive of me, even to the extent that when, to stay back there, he sold his part of a company that he had—a public relations management consultant firm that he had. He sold out to his partner and never went back to it, because it would have been a conflict—it was a potential conflict of interest when he went with Rog Morton to Interior. . . . One time, some press woman in Washington once said, well, how do you feel about your wife being so involved in politics and being gone quite a bit and everything. And he grinned and said, well, you know the boys and I think that sometimes it's a good thing to get all that energy out of the house.

Every time a step came, including the invitation of Richard Nixon to go back and help run the campaign of '68, I always felt, no, I don't think I'm ready, I don't think I can do it. I could name you two people that I thought could do a better job. And Bob was always the one that said, honey, they wouldn't ask you if they didn't think you could do it. And he said, of course, you can do it, you can do anything you want to, and I think you should. And so that would kind of more or less settle it.

If [women in politics or in government] have a husband, he's got to support. I don't know how any woman could accomplish very much of anything if she had to fight with her husband over it. They have to be supportive. Even today, when women are much more secure and they're not just half of a combination, you still have to. Because, for one thing, Washington is a graveyard of marriages. And I think it has been for many, many years. . . . It takes a very strong, a very good marriage to weather several years in Washington. And so your husband has to . . . be supportive. You wouldn't get the job in the first place, and you couldn't do it.[17]

Pat Hitt retired from government in 1973 but continued to be active in California politics. She died in 2006.

CHAPTER EIGHT

Considering Networking, the President, and the Impact of the Women's Program

Networking and Executive Women in Government

In the mid-1960s, Barbara Franklin began to meet with some of her Harvard Business School colleagues and other women executives in New York City to share experiences. As for a multitude of other women, these informal groups evolved naturally as women came together to relate their problems and celebrate their successes. In the modern business buzz, they were networking, and so it should come as no surprise that Barbara Franklin played a key role in doing the same thing in Washington for the very women that she had recruited into government. She had meetings of women appointees in the White House, often in the Roosevelt Room, and invited them to lunch in the White House mess and to the president's box at the Kennedy Center. They enjoyed being in the White House and getting to know each other. So it was quite natural that in 1974, the informal get-togethers became a formal organization, the Executive Women in Government (EWG).

Elizabeth Hanford Dole served as deputy director of the White House Office of Consumer Affairs, under Virginia Knauer, until 1973, when President Nixon nominated her to a term on the Federal Trade Commission.

> My career almost parallels this phase of the women's movement because when I started out there were so few women in policy-making positions. Barbara Franklin and I worked with other women to launch Executive Women in Government, an organization which is still thriving today. There were so few women in policy positions that it helped to relate to each other and also we could help those young women coming behind who wanted to follow our footsteps

into public service. We could show them shortcuts along the way or maybe help them avoid a few pitfalls.[1]

Elizabeth Dole later served as secretary of transportation and labor as well as representing North Carolina in the U.S. Senate from 2003 to 2009.

✻

After serving as an assistant U.S. attorney in Alaska and a district attorney in California, Paula Adams Tennant was twice appointed by Governor Ronald Reagan to the California Youth Authority Board, the state's parole body for juveniles. In 1970, President Nixon appointed Tennant to the U.S. Board of Parole.

> The thing that in my mind, started EWG, was . . . a dinner meeting of an organization called the Under Secretaries, which was a male organization. And I can't remember how I got invited to that. It may have been that the Chairman [of the Parole Board] was invited and took me along. But I remember being very surprised that this organization existed, and realized that the women had nothing like that, and that we needed something like that, very much. . . .
>
> We had started [EWG] as a way to compensate for our inability to be part of the Under Secretaries organization, which brought the Under Secretaries together for the purpose of telling them what was going on in government and associating with each other and finding out what other people at their level were doing.
>
> For people who go . . . to Washington for the first time, it's a very traumatic kind of thing. You're so lost; you just don't know anything about the ins and outs of government. And I think we all, probably most of us, shared that kind of feeling and the need to increase our knowledge about each other and about how government was working. . . . And to make it responsive . . . to what we were doing.[2]

In 1983, President Reagan appointed Paula Adams Tennant to the U.S. Parole Commission. She died in 2010.

✻

Sallyanne Payton was appointed an associate on the White House Domestic Council staff in 1971. Two years later, she became chief counsel of the Urban

Mass Transportation Administration in the Department of Transportation.

> [The characteristic these women had in common was] Determination. They were aware that they were pioneers. They were determined to do the best they could not only where they were but for the women that would come behind them. Every one of them was a staunch supporter of women's rights and the advancement of women. It was really thrilling. They were from immensely varied backgrounds, but they all had that in common and nobody ever wavered. They all fought where they were for women's rights.[3]

Sallyanne Payton has been a member of the faculty of the University of Michigan Law School since 1976. She also served on the President's Commission on National Health Care Reform during the Clinton administration.

※

Bret Sturtevant was appointed by President Nixon to be examiner-in-chief for the U.S. Patent and Trademark Office Board of Appeals in 1971.

> That was Barbara Franklin who did the most marvelous job with [EWG]. . . . She started us meeting regularly when we came in government . . . I think in . . . the Indian Treaty Room [in the Eisenhower Executive Office Building]. Anyway we met at various locations in the White House, or in those good old days with traffic not a problem, we could drive our cars in through the gates and park within the White House grounds. That would be unbelievable today.
>
> A lot of things she did and we always had a great time with her. She had speakers very often for us, and if we said we wanted information, for instance, about the next campaign for Nixon's re-election, she would arrange the proper speakers. She was absolutely great. Of course, we always had snacks and very often we wound up after the meetings either a couple of blocks over in the . . . Hay Adams Hotel . . . or . . . The National Press Club . . . for drinks and dinner.[4]

Continuing on the U.S. Patent and Trademark Office Board of Appeals, Bret Sturtevant remained in office through the presidencies of Gerald Ford, Jimmy Carter, and Ronald Reagan, retiring in 1988.

❉

Jeanne Holm was the first woman to reach the rank of brigadier general in the U.S. Air Force and the first woman to become a major general in all of the U.S. Armed Forces.

About 1972, the senior women appointees were all invited over to the White House as kind of a show-and-tell for President Nixon. It had to have been sometime after he met with the female generals.

On this occasion, at Barbara's instigation, the women who had been appointed to high level positions in the Nixon Administration were invited over. So we met with the press and described what was going on in terms of identifying women for top level jobs.

Then we posed for a photograph in the Rose Garden. I've forgotten how many of us there were, but there couldn't have been more than about 30 or 35. That included Elizabeth Hanford, later Dole, Barbara of course, who was organizing this thing, Virginia Allan, Jewel LaFontant, and Catherine Bedell. It's a wonderful photograph.

But that was all there were in positions of government that could be classified at that level at that time. Except there were some other generals who were not there that day for some reason. . . . They were all political appointees except for me.

It was a wonderful gathering of great women and it was the beginning of an important network. Someone said we ought to do lunch sometime. So we did. Ethel Bent Walsh was one of the main movers behind this. So we got together for lunch, and decided to get organized.

As you know, it's one thing to be the senior woman in an organization. It's another thing to know that there are others who are also the first women in these kinds of jobs. So we decided to get organized, to interchange ideas and to network. That was the first top level women's network in the federal government. We called ourselves the Executive Women in Government. Again, Ethel Bent Walsh was a prime mover behind it. Of course, Barbara, Virginia Allan, Virginia Knauer, Catherine Bedell and others . . . were active.

I don't know why, but I was elected as the first chairman. It was the beginning of a wonderful network that still stays in touch. This oral history project . . . I believe is an outgrowth of that same network.

Following her retirement, General Jeanne Holm was a special assistant on women to President Ford and a policy consultant for President Carter. She died in 2010.

State Commissions and the International Women's Year

American governmental participation in international women's meetings represented an important educational and cultural opportunity for women appointees. At a time when women's aspirations were rising and the justice of those aspirations was just beginning to be broadly recognized across the nation, meetings with international peers both solidified women's determination to match strides with those countries that were in some ways more advanced and brought attention to the many situations where women still faced grievous discrimination and injustices. Many American women, however, had had their first exposure to these issues through the work of the state commissions established in the 1960s.

Virginia Allan (1917–1999) was a businesswoman whose interest in women's issues developed through her work as president of the National Federation of Business and Professional Women. Drawing on her experience on Michigan's commission on the status of women,[5] she initiated the idea of linking the state commissions into a national network. In 1969, she was named chair of President Nixon's Task Force on Women's Rights and Responsibilities. In 1972, President Nixon named her deputy assistant secretary of state for public affairs.

FIGURE 89
Virginia Allan after being sworn in as deputy assistant secretary of state for public affairs by Secretary William Rogers at the State Department, 1972. A Few Good Women Oral History Collection, Penn State University Archives.

I think the Task Force [on Women's Rights and Responsibilities in 1969] was instrumental in getting things set up across the nation in various states, and then . . . the states had to think internationally as well as state-wise. . . .

[The federal level and the state level] worked together and that made a difference. I mean, the states had somebody to look to. On the other hand, the states were very energetic and so they prompted the nation to pay attention. . . .

[Now, at the State Department I took the lead on the U.S. observance of International Women's Year.[6]] We had briefings, periodic briefings on the issues as they came out from the U.N. We worked very closely with the U.N. and what messages they wanted to get across. . . . And I knew that many non-governmental organizations, even though they were international . . . were so wrapped up with what was going on in the United States, that many of them didn't get across what was important in terms of women and the international viewpoint.

In fact, we followed what the United Nations had set up in terms of issues and we brought the people in for briefings on those issues. And for the most part, the leadership carried it across the country, our American leadership.

[Earlier I was involved in setting up the state commissions on the status of women]. They were a great outreach. . . . We had information for them that was distributed across the country . . . although most of them were mainly interested in what was going on within their city and their countryside and the state, and nationally with the women's issue. This took it one step more to the international. I found that the response was very heartwarming.

[I represented the United States at Mexico City and was the only person who was a delegate to three international women's conferences]. . . . The very fact that they were held and information got out within various countries on women's issues, women came together on the country and state issues. And so I felt that it was very productive.

[Of the issues we dealt with], I mean, certainly wage levels and how they compare with men's and whether or not women were promoted, given a chance to rise up in their professions. We dealt with health issues. We dealt with social issues. We went across the board really in terms of what affected people.

When we had these conferences, the countries felt the responsibility of having people representing their country, of women representing their country. I think it did a great deal to help women achieve and to be recognized and the leadership within countries to realize that women were taking action worldwide and they better get with it.[7]

Virginia Allan was the government's liaison with nongovernmental organizations for the International Women's Year conference in Mexico City in 1975. She also attended world conferences in Copenhagen in 1980 and Nairobi in 1985. In 1983, she helped to inaugurate the United States Committee of the United Nations Development Fund for Women, a nonprofit organization created to support projects to promote the political, economic, and social empowerment of women around the world. Beginning in 1977, she also served as director of the Graduate School of Women's Studies at George Washington University. She died in 1999.

❋

Pat Hutar was a member of the Task Force on Women's Rights and Responsibilities in 1969. Later she was appointed by President Ford to serve as U.S. representative to the U.N. Commission on the Status of Women, and in that capacity was chair of the U.S. delegation to the 1975 International Women's Year Conference in Mexico City.

> [I was a member of the National Commission on the Observance of International Women's Year,[8] and] I was the United States representative to the United Nations Commission on the Status of Women, and that was a presidential appointment without Senate confirmation.... We took all that we had been learning and going through with women's issues in our country, and ... those were the issues that we could talk about and exchange ideas with women from other delegations....
>
> [The more political women's groups] were not necessarily completely antagonistic toward us, but it was, I think, true of many women who felt that ... the fact that we had a delegation that was a government delegation, and then we had hundreds and hundreds of women in non-governmental organizations, some of a more radical nature, some more conservative, some moderate groups—and it took them a while to understand what was going on, because nobody

was familiar with a lot of the things that we were doing. They weren't familiar with U.N. and U.S. commissions,[9] particularly, and how they operated. We opened up the U.S. State Department, and the State Department was a little bit timid at first about having diversified organizations meeting there. We wanted women representatives from all over the country to come in for the national commission to testify on issues as well as for the preparation of the delegation to IWY [International Women's Year]. There was a great opening up of the system, which was good for the State Department, as it was good for all of us, because that's where you had a very rich exchange. . . .

There were a lot of tensions that would crop up, because everybody felt these things very intensely. So that you didn't always have smooth sailing. And I think nowhere was that more apparent than when we got to Mexico City. . . . we had this great confrontation—it was a stunning example of the fact that these outbursts can be handled, because women would listen to one another. . . .

We had a meeting of the U.S. delegation to Mexico City with the women from the non-governmental organizations who were going to be meeting in the Tribune, in another building, with a separate agenda.

But when they came over to the American Embassy for this first meeting, we had decided we're not going to do this with any head table. We're just going to have our chairs in a circle, because we're all one here, and this will be U.S. people who are on the official delegation, and those who will be attending the Tribune. It was extremely interesting, because everything started out fairly calmly, and then things began to heat up. And I can remember—I opened the meeting as the head of the delegation from the United States. . . .

Then it became a struggle as to who was going to control the microphone—us or them. And I hung on to that microphone for dear life. . . . They're very outstanding women, and there was no animosity among us—it was just, you know, everybody had their viewpoint. I had women on either side of me, squeezing me as I'm hanging onto this microphone. They kept complaining bitterly, and there was chanting and all. So they were complaining, again, because they felt "why aren't we on the official delegation? Who are these women and men who are saying they represent the women of the United States and women in general?" So I said, "Well, why don't we let them speak for themselves?" And they did. . . .

We brought them up—I think Jewel [Lafontant] . . . got up first, and of course, they started to give her a hard time. And she just put her hands on her hips and said I was in the Civil Rights movement before you were born. And she got them quiet and then each person got up and told about themselves.

It was absolutely fascinating. We went right straight through the whole delegation, it took three and a half hours, because needless to say, there were interruptions, there were questions, there were not insults, but very strong feelings hurled around by the women as each of these persons spoke. But by the end of that time, they were quiet and they were listening to one another really intently. And then as the thing broke up, people would get together and talk with one another. . . .

From then on, we had absolutely open sesame, because they couldn't get anything on the floor, for example, at the official meeting. That had to be done by the official delegation members. And if there were something that was worthwhile, certainly that could be worked into maybe a resolution or whatever. At least they knew we were listening to them, and we felt their viewpoints were important, because we were all in the same boat, really, we were just over on the government side as official delegates, and they were on the other side as part of the Tribune. . . .

There were things that we didn't always probably feel as strongly about, but we were bound either to work within the government issues, or if you didn't want to put up with that, you could simply get off. But don't try to represent the government, and then not be somewhat cooperative. . . .

The other wonderful thing about International Women's Year is that we had a meeting in every single one of the states and territories, so to speak, after International Women's Year was ended, and we had the "World Plan of Action," which was the seminal document to come out of IWY. . . .

So that started generating a lot of changes in the states, because now they had not only the [state] women's commission, but they had this special state IWY conference to look at how to implement the World Plan of Action. The plan dealt with issues that had to be taken up at the state level, too, in our case, because we're not just a national government—we have this federal system. Absolutely fascinating process. And not only was it fascinating, it was effective.[10]

Pat Hutar became the founding president of the United Nations Development Fund for Women (UNIFEM). She later served as the director of the Office of International Medicine for the American Medical Association from 1978 to 1996. She was also a member of the Washington Roundtable of the Center for Strategic and International Studies and a founding member and chair of the board of the International Foundation for Election Systems.

Perceptions of President Nixon

In his 1972 reelection landslide, President Nixon won 62 percent of women's votes, compared with 59 percent of men's votes. Yet he was continuously castigated by women's movement activists for moving too slowly and making only token gestures toward the advancement of their agenda. The record shows that the Nixon administration made significant progress on women's issues, despite the conventional wisdom. Appointees to the administration had a variety of opportunities to witness the president's interest and concern.

Margita E. White (1937–2002) was a staff assistant to White House Communications Director Herb Klein. In 1973, she became the assistant director for public information for the U.S. Information Agency.

> I can only speculate [about the president's motives for the women's initiative], but I believe that he was quite sincere in seeing the need for opportunities for women in government, both in human terms and political terms. He had two daughters, no sons, and while I can't imagine that he would envision his wife, Patricia, in a long-term career situation, although she was a teacher initially, as I recall. In terms of government . . . I think that he was sincere in pursuing it. It was still very early-on, in terms of public opinion. But he was always very good at anticipating issues. And I think that he saw that this was an important one.[11]

Margita White later served in communications in the Ford White House and was a member of the Federal Communications Commission.

※

After serving in the state legislature, Catherine May Bedell became the first woman elected to Congress from the state of Washington. After serving six terms in the House of Representatives, she was appointed by President Nixon to the U.S. Tariff Commission in 1971.

> When you talked to Richard Nixon about the importance and how many women . . . in Congress, as well as groups out there in the country, were getting interested in finding, seeking out qualified women that had proven themselves, bright and capable of making good decisions on behalf of lots of people, their communities, you got an enthusiastic reaction. And I often thought it may have been because one thing—we each had daughters. And my daughter, Melinda, was Julie's age. . . . And the two of them [Julie and Tricia] knew Melinda . . . and the President had met Melinda. . . . So after that . . . when I did meet with him . . . he'd say "how is your daughter?" And we would sometimes have just a few minutes to talk about what their plans were for education. He was very interested. You could tell he talked to them a lot about it, and what they wanted to do. And so . . . he was close to his girls, and loved them very much. And I don't know if they've ever written about this or talked about it, but there was obviously a good relationship between Richard Nixon and the two girls. So that he had a great interest in their future, which then had to encompass the future of American women in this country, and what they were doing, and his girls were getting lots of experience through their very position as his daughters in public life. Maybe they had some ideas themselves that they talked about at the dinner table. But he was the most sympathetic in his reaction, and he carried it out by showing, by making appointments of women to public office.[12]

After Bedell completed her term on the Tariff Commission in 1981, she served on President Reagan's Task Force on Legal Equity for Women, the "fifty-state project" that examined state laws for discriminatory language. She died in 2004.

✳

Julie Nixon Eisenhower graduated from Smith College in 1970 and received a master's degree in education from Catholic University. She was an active participant in both of her father's presidential campaigns.

> I knew all these women [on] the task force, I was . . . just a believer in it. . . . One thing that's interesting [about my] campaign

FIGURE 90
*Julie Nixon Eisenhower. A Few Good Women
Oral History Collection, Penn State University
Archives.*

role . . . I was even more active in 1972, and one of the issues that I talked about in 1972 was the fact that there was for the first time in history a presidential assistant who was trying to make sure that if a woman was qualified, she was considered. I talked about that during the campaign. . . .

My father, I don't think he's noted for being particularly for women. But really if you look at the administrations, I think he was more for women than any others [before] because of his appointment of Barbara Franklin but also because of his attitude. I mean, he thought these women were terrific. There was no question but that they were, you know, Helen Bentley, what a feisty, talented woman. He was proud that she was associated with his administration. Elizabeth Dole, Virginia Knauer, he loved Anne Armstrong. He thought she was the best kind of representative for the party because she was always a lady and always so charming, but she was smart and articulate and this is exactly what we need today for women. I don't think you need to sacrifice being the lady who can bring all those wonderful graces into a job as well as the brains and the drive. He really felt that Anne Armstrong was a wonderful role model for the Republican party, and he was very conscious of the women's vote. Very conscious of it. And it's one reason why he always referred to my mother—and she was indeed—[as] his partner, why she traveled with him, why she went abroad with him from the beginning of their campaigns. The whole women's issue was very important. . . .

My father never underestimated the women, and I'm sure that's one reason he wanted to see the Barbara Franklin project succeed. . . . The women's movement was a serious movement. It struck the right chord. The time had come. Instead of letting it disintegrate into angry people, the thing to do was to harness it for good.[13]

From 1973 to 1975, Julie Eisenhower served as assistant managing editor of the *Saturday Evening Post* and helped establish a book division for Curtis Publishing Company, the *Post*'s parent corporation. Since that time, she has written or edited several books, including *Pat Nixon: The Untold Story*, a biography of her mother, and most recently *Going Home to Glory: A Memoir of Life with Dwight D. Eisenhower, 1961–1969*, written with her husband David Eisenhower. In addition to an extensive record of community service in the Philadelphia area, Julie Nixon Eisenhower has devoted much of her volunteer time since 1988 to Jobs for America's Graduates, a nationwide program in twenty-six states that serves at-risk youth. She has served as chair and vice-chair of the organization. From 2002 to 2006, she chaired the President's Commission of White House Fellowships.

Impact and Significance of the Women's Program

Virginia Knauer was director of the White House Office on Consumer Affairs and a mentor to many younger women working in the White House, including Elizabeth Hanford Dole.

Well, I think it was very important [to have Barbara Franklin there]. First of all, it was a headline position. [For example,] we established, and Nixon appointed prominent men and women to the "Presidential Committee on Consumer Affairs" to advise me. I recommended outstanding citizens including Dr. Jean Mayer, who had put together the first U.S. Conference on Food, Nutrition and Health. He later became President of Tufts University and a lifelong friend.

But Jean said, "Virginia, you must do something. Hot dogs are too fat. There's too much fat in hot dogs. It's about 50 percent. We should set a level," and I said, "What do you think the level should be?" He said, "No more than 30 percent." So figuring he was an expert, I went campaigning. The then Secretary of Agriculture blew his gaskets, and he was demanding I be fired, among other things, and I got a call—I was doing an interview with *The New York Times*, sitting beside my desk, and my secretary comes in. Her eyes are staring. She said, "Virginia, the President [Nixon] is on the phone." So instead of excusing himself and leaving, the reporter was sitting there. I took the call at my desk. I wasn't sure whether I was going to be fired or what, but the President got on and he's laughing. He said, "Virginia, you're absolutely right. I can't eat hot dogs anymore. They have too much fat." He said, "That's why I'm eating cottage cheese and what have you," and I said, "Well, I'm sorry I've upset the Secretary of Agriculture." He said, "Oh, don't worry about him. I'll take care of him, but keep on with it." But that's what I mean; Nixon was so sensitive and supportive.[14]

Virginia Knauer continued in her consumer affairs adviser role in the Ford and Reagan administrations. She also served on the Cost of Living Council and a number of other White House domestic policy committees.

✳

Constance Cornell Stuart graduated from the University of Maryland in 1960. She began her service in the federal government in 1969 when she was appointed staff director and press secretary to First Lady Pat Nixon.

I can't say I had any involvement in recruiting. Of course, those people [Barbara] recruited, I often came to work with or know or call upon for their knowledge if Mrs. Nixon had an interest in something they were doing. She did a wonderful job. I think the President listened to Vera [Glaser] that day and said maybe I'd better be doing something about this, found there was a lack and, indeed, for his time he appointed a lot of women . . . when a lot of men were not too keen on all that.

Barbara, of course was the instrument by which he did that. She did a terrific job identifying people and bringing them in. As you know, she has that wonderful enthusiasm about her that just "mows down everything in its wake."[15]

Connie Stuart continued on the First Lady's staff until 1973, when she was named director of the International Visitor's Program at the U.S. Department of State and remained there until 1977. In 1981 she was appointed press secretary at the U.S. Department of Energy, and in 1985 she became staff assistant to the assistant secretary for international affairs at the Department of Energy. She left the federal government in 1989. From 1980 to 1988, she served on the Board of Regents of the University of Maryland system, where she was chair of the Education Policy Committee and vice-chair of the Board. Connie Stuart became president of the University of Maryland Alumni Association and chair of its Board of Trustees. She currently manages the operations of Rose Hill Farm and is the president of Agathon Development Company.

❊

Susan Porter Rose was a one-time congressional staffer but spent much of her early career as an administrator in women's education as assistant dean at the George School and assistant director of admissions at Mount Holyoke College. In 1971, she became assistant director of correspondence for Mrs. Nixon and worked for almost eighteen years in the East Wing of the White House in the Nixon, Ford, Reagan, and Bush administrations.

Of course, Mrs. Nixon was a working woman herself. She had a stellar college record graduating magna cum laude from the University of Southern California, and then she taught for a number of years. She brought having been a working woman, a mom, and a great interest in education, in government and in volunteerism to her position as First Lady. Think how far we have come in terms of working women and women in senior positions! It's really amazing. The public demand for this was happening during those years, but this Nixon White House initiative helped nudge things along in a concrete way. . . .

This day and age it is not unusual to have a lot of very top women in an administration. But this fact, which we now take for granted, was achieved step by step. Better educational opportunities for women, day care availability and parental leave have helped enormously.

Barbara Franklin's office during the Nixon years went to work and effected some very positive results which grew. It was far from the only effort underway, but its accomplishments mattered.

Presidents and administrations now seek not only more women but also a very broad diversity generally. It is not just politically correct. It is expected. And the world is now a different place.[16]

During the Carter administration, Susan Porter Rose worked in the Justice Department as a special assistant to two assistant attorneys general. She returned to the White House in the 1980s as chief of staff to Barbara Bush, wife of the vice president, while also serving on the vice president's staff. In January of 1989, she became chief of staff for the then-First Lady Barbara Bush and deputy assistant to the president. Over her years in the East Wing, she saw a great deal of change and far more extensive cooperation between the staffs of the president and the First Lady.

✳

Major General Jeanne Holm served as director of women in the air force from 1965 to 1973.

The White House was very supportive. Certainly we got support in the late 1960s during the effort to remove the promotion restrictions on military women. Also written in the 1948 law that established the peacetime components was a two percent ceiling on the total numbers [of women] who could serve in the regular Army, Navy, Air Force and Marine Corps. It had very little practical effect since the services were not recruiting many women because they were able to draft all the men they needed. . . .

So with a great deal of lobbying, a great deal of effort, Congress passed the law [to remove promotion restrictions], after numerous hearings, and President Johnson signed it in the White House in November 1967 with a great fanfare and wonderful photographs. This was a major breakthrough. Included in that law was something that was rather minor, the repeal of the two percent ceiling on military women. . . . The total numbers of women on active duty at that point was less than one percent, not the two percent authorized by law.

So repeal of the ceilings had very little practical effect until 1972 when President Nixon decided to eliminate the draft and go for an all-volunteer force. With that decision, the handwriting was on the wall. Without the draft, the services would need other resources. And women were a very important resource for the Armed Forces that . . . had not [been] tapped at all since the Korean War.

But in 1972, the elimination of the two percent ceiling (on women) became an important factor because the numbers of women that had to be recruited for the all-volunteer force far exceeded anything anyone had ever envisioned before. And in fact, had that decision *not* been made by the Nixon Administration to expand the use of women, the all-volunteer force would have failed. Women saved the all-volunteer force during the ensuing year.

[Barbara Franklin's office was helpful], but not in this sense [of promoting women officers]. . . . The recognition that women really could hold higher level positions was seen as a commitment by the Administration. Her job was to go out and recruit civilian women with remarkable qualifications that sent a message about women that resonated throughout the government.

Not only did she have to go out and find them but then she had to find appropriate positions for them to be appointed. She had to convince the agencies['] heads to accept them. That was a selling job that she did very well. She was very good at it. She has a manner that I think was indispensable to her achievements in that area. Some of the positions were within the Department of Defense and I think that sent a message to the military as well.

By then, women in the military were becoming brigadier generals. So that we became part of that package. When President Nixon was preparing for his 1972 election, he had wanted to show off what he was doing for the military under his stewardship. So he invited the female generals over to the Oval Office for a meeting and photo op. There were five of us. . . .

I think [the era] was a watershed, a turning point for our society as a whole. Certainly, it was for the military. When I meet with young women today and tell them the way life was before and after 1972 they are astonished. They're so used to things as they are today they take it all for granted. They even complain about the fact that things don't change fast enough and there aren't enough women doing this and there aren't enough women doing that. They don't comprehend how far we have come.

The women who are in government today and who are in big positions in industry or wherever, all are there because the course was set back then. No longer can people easily dig in their heels or try to move the clock back, even though there are those who would like to. There are men and women who would like to move the clock back, but it can't be done anymore. The changes are part of our culture. And I believe it springs largely from the events of the late '60s and early '70s.[17]

After her retirement, Jeanne M. Holm served as a special assistant on women for President Ford and as a policy consultant for the Carter administration. She served on the boards of several nonprofit organizations and wrote two books on women in the military. She died in 2010.

*

Sallyanne Payton worked on the Domestic Policy Council, often focusing on District of Columbia affairs.

> [Barbara] was running her own operation, of course, but she could call on me. I must say that Bud [Krogh] and I put women on the DC City Council, too, the first chance we got. Appointing Marjorie Holloman Parker was part of our strategy of showcasing the best of the District's civic leadership. Of course, I was active in the DC Women's Political Caucus and the National Women's Political Caucus. This was all because of Barbara and Bobbie Kilberg, who asked me to go to Houston as part of the Republican delegation to the first convention of the National Women's Political Caucus. I am African American, you understand, so I am thinking race rather than gender most of the time. It was Barbara who introduced me to the gender issues and persuaded me of the rightness of the Equal Rights Act and the importance of promoting women. So I owe all of that to Barbara.[18]

Sallyanne Payton joined the Urban Mass Transportation Administration in the Department of Transportation as chief counsel in 1973. She has been a member of the faculty of the University of Michigan Law School since 1976.

*

Anne Armstrong (1928–2008) was born in New Orleans, graduated from Vassar in 1949, but became a Texan after her marriage to rancher Tobin Armstrong. She became prominent in state Republican circles and eventually became cochair of the Republican National Committee. She was named a counselor to the president in 1972 with cabinet rank, the first woman to hold that position, and established the first Office of Women's Programs in the White House.

> I think it was a coalescing. I can't say that at the federal level that we were the only beacon. I think it was happening also at the

To my very good friend, Anne Armstrong, in appreciation of your dedicated and effective public service. Warmest best wishes.
Jerry Ford

FIGURE 91
Anne Armstrong with President and Mrs. Ford and Secretary of State Henry Kissinger. White House photograph, A Few Good Women Oral History Collection, Penn State University Archives.

local level. For instance, in my home state now, every major city either has or has had by now a woman mayor. There were none when I was up here. But I'm not sure that's because of federal leadership. I think the time had come. Women were educated, number one. I mean, how rare it was 50 years ago to have a woman college graduate much less a woman Ph.D.; all the labor saving devices, the new attitude towards marriage and women's careers. There were social forces at work and then there were the political forces that abetted them. But certainly as a symbol to other women, something they could graphically see, the advancement of women in positions in government was probably the most inspiring thing for women. The whole nation could see it. There were women mayors and council members but you didn't hear about them. When it happened in high government positions, all women could see it and take heart.[19]

In 1976, Anne Armstrong was the first woman to be named American ambassador to Great Britain. She was awarded the Presidential Medal of Freedom in 1987. While she retired to her ranch in the late 1970s, she still found time to serve her community as a county commissioner. She died in 2008.

✳

Rita E. Hauser, an international lawyer, chaired the 1968 campaign for Richard Nixon in New York and in 1969 served as a consultant to the Task Force on Women's Rights and Responsibilities. She was appointed U.S. representative to the U.N. Commission on Human Rights and served on commissions affiliated with the U.S. Department of State. In 1972, she cochaired the president's national campaign.

[That period], I would say it was the real beginning, you know, the break through. I know everybody always used to cite numbers, whether the Republicans had appointed more than the Democrats. But, you know, the fact that it was there, that they were conscious of it, that the President couldn't go out before a woman's audience without having something in his speech that said and I have appointed 12 women, more than anybody else. You know, it was a given that he was going to have to say that.

Some of it was conscious-raising. It was making these men of another generation realize this was a sensitive issue and a hot political issue. When we came down to the campaign, again, campaigns had always been organized. There was a women's division of the campaign. And you did things with women. And I fought very hard with Haldeman and others and said that's not right anymore.

You've got to have—sure you've got to do something for the traditional women, no doubt. But you have to have a campaign staff that's got men and women. And you've got to send men out to talk to women and women to talk to men. And it was hard pushing that.

But the argument I could make effectively there was just looking at the data because more women voted in presidential elections than men for some significant time. And it was clear to me that while they didn't vote only on women's issues, they had agendas. They were interested in certain subjects. And you had to approach them on those subjects. They were less bellicose than men. They were more interested in peace than men. And they still are. All the data shows that.

So you have to nuance what you're going to do and do it effectively. And this, of course, was unfortunately in the full blow of the Vietnam War. And there were endless protests and demonstrations and all that stuff. So that was part of the background here.

[There was a need for women to work together]. We were so few that you felt a certain obligation to try to promote others, to find them, to identify them, to give them support. I don't know how strong that is today because there are so many women in so many places that I'm not sure it's as major as it was then. But, you know, when the numbers are so tiny, you feel kind of alone. And let's say a woman was in a job and she made a mistake or faux pas, said something she shouldn't have said, she had to look somewhere for some support. So the women tended to support each other in that measure. And I think that was terrific. That was the early system.

[The women of that period], apart from being well-trained and educated, which was already a big difference from prior generations, I think there was a real determination on the part of all of these women. We're going to make something of ourselves. We are going to overcome the difficulties.

And the difficulties were major, right out. Just getting a job, a real job, you know, whatever it was you trained for that you wanted to be, was very, very tough. Most women were rebuffed. And you had to learn how to take that and come back again and say I'm still here, knock on the door. It was a very different time. So I think determination was essential.[20]

Rita Hauser continues in an international law practice and has been chair or director of a wide variety of organizations devoted to international conflict resolution, security, and individual rights. From 2001 to 2004, she served as a member of the President's Foreign Intelligence Advisory Board.

※

Betty Southard Murphy was appointed by President Nixon to be general counsel of the National Labor Relations Board (NLRB) in 1972, the first of seven presidential appointments she received. In 1974 she became administrator of the Wage and Hour Division of the Department of Labor, a position she held until 1975, whereupon she was appointed chair of the NLRB.

> [Were] we in the Nixon-Ford Administrations "different"? I think President Nixon and President Ford were the first Presidents to realize the potential of all women, not just some of their close friends. President Nixon put Barbara in an important position in the White House and she ran with it.
>
> When I became National Labor Relations Board Chairman, there were no women chief counsels. There were five Board Members who each had their own Chief Counsel, and no women had ever been in that super-position. I appointed the first woman Chief Counsel. One member had *never* hired a *single* woman lawyer. There were no women or minority Regional Directors. My first year, we appointed two women Regional Directors, one minority male Director, and one woman Regional Attorney.
>
> I had told all my male colleagues at the NLRB about a Health and Human Services study that showed that men who had intelligent mothers or intelligent wives gave women opportunities and those who did not, did not. No one wanted to think that his mother or his wife was not intelligent, so they all began hiring women lawyers at the NLRB, even the member who had been there for 15 years and had *never* hired a woman lawyer before. He hired several women my first year as Chairman. When an opening came up in the Executive Secretary's office—where women only held secretarial positions—I asked the Executive Secretary who was a terrific person, to find a qualified woman or let me know why he could not. He found one of course. . . .
>
> On reflection . . . I think we might have been a little "different." In addition to two presidents pushing women—and Barbara was the first woman to hold that job in the White House—there were two things that made us different: we had a unique attitude and a unique belief. Our unique attitude was that we thought we were very well qualified for success, and our unique belief was that we *would* succeed.[21]

In 1979, Betty Murphy left the NLRB and reentered private practice. She served on several presidential commissions afterward.

Breaking Barriers and Opening the Floodgates

"It's part of a continuum of marching ahead for more equality for women, and we're not done."[1] That was the simple way Barbara Hackman Franklin summed up her work in the White House.

This initiative broke many barriers, and as a result, it opened many doors. In a 1998 interview, she expanded on that theme:

> It was a watershed in terms of advancement for women. It be-gan with the Federal Government being in the lead, and I believe that the efforts of President Nixon to appoint more women and [to] pay attention to equality in a serious way brought a bra-burning, left-leaning movement right into society's mainstream. This made women's equality legitimate. That's probably the biggest thing that happened. But then, if you just look at the numbers of women ap-pointed and the breakthroughs that were made, this really was quite a special era, and I believe it opened the floodgates. Once that hap-pened, there was no turning back in terms of equality for women, and even though the ERA, which President Nixon supported, failed to be ratified in the states, by that time it didn't make any difference. We were on the way. There was nothing that was going to stop this movement. I think that's quite remarkable, actually, and when we now realize that it's 25 years ago, there has been so much change in those 25 years. It happened faster than I might have imagined.
>
> [In a] press interview [of that time], I was quoted as saying that this White House job, and what needs to be done in terms of appoint-ing women, is bigger than I ever would have thought, and the more you get into it, the bigger it gets and the more you see how much more there is to do. We're still not finished, but we've come a long way in [all these] years.
>
> Again, one of the great things about this country . . . is the fact that we have so much mobility. . . . We're not a rigid society, locked

into either classes or tracks, and it's one of the reasons I think this change happened as fast as it did. This is America.[2]

There is no question that this effort broke a logjam. Previous presidents had very gradually increased the numbers of women appointed to higher-level positions. President Nixon's initial assignment to Barbara Franklin was to double the previous record of such appointments, which she accomplished and then went on to triple and then nearly quadruple it. Just as significantly, as Vera Glaser and other advocates of the time recognized, the previous administrations had done little to change the "guts" of the system. The overwhelming majority of women working in the civil service were in the lowest range of pay grades, making the least amount of money. The majority of job classifications were officially closed to women. This all began to change in the Nixon administration as rules and practices were reformed, and agencies were directed to begin to hire and promote women at the middle grades and to set up training programs for those below so that they, too, might later on advance as far as their capabilities would carry them.

It is extraordinary how quickly the changes came once the floodgates were opened. The sense that women had to occupy a separate, and usually unequal, segment of the bureaucracy, or, for that matter, the party machinery, changed for good. Very quickly, the idea that a woman could play almost any role became not just official policy but, more and more, actual practice. The women who speak in this book were professionals of various types, alumnae of colleges, graduate, and professional schools. They came into the government and demonstrated that they could do the things they had been trained for and were already experienced at doing, and they did them extremely well. The success of this program is even more emphatically shown by how many of these women continued to learn and develop leadership and managerial skills and kept advancing to the highest ranks of government to become cabinet secretaries, general officers in the military, and judges of the highest courts in the land.

Connie Stuart, Mrs. Nixon's staff director and press secretary, talked about the remarkable fact that in answering Vera Glaser's question, President Nixon decided to do something about appointing more women, and she said, "Barbara, of course was the instrument by which he did that." All of these women share similar sentiments about Barbara Franklin's enthusiasm, drive, determination, good humor, and ability to move people along (who often didn't really want to move at all), and they believe it was those character traits and hard work that made this program thrive. She was a successful

FIGURE 92

Lawyer and leading feminist Marguerite Rawalt greets Barbara Franklin at a General Federation of Women's Clubs meeting. Barbara Hackman Franklin Papers, Penn State University Archives.

recruiter of new talent, but she was also a successful saleswoman of the need for innovation. She demonstrated the value of taking just that first step to change, and then a second, and a third, until suddenly the administration was steadily moving ahead. Through the departmental action plans, she gradually persuaded and cajoled the departments and agencies into adding more women and then promoting them to more responsible positions as they demonstrated their capabilities.

But Barbara Franklin played another equally important role in the White House. She became visible—far more so than others at her grade and station—and traveled the country making speeches about the program and the need to advance women's rights. Franklin confidently sent memos forward to encourage the president to speak out for women's rights and about the program she was implementing for him. She quietly insisted it was a priority for the administration to take a position in support of the Equal Rights Amendment, even when there was little enthusiasm among the male staff. She urged the party and the Committee to Re-Elect the President to have more women participate at higher levels and to mount a vigorous

FIGURE 93
Barbara Franklin at her formal swearing-in as twenty-ninth secretary of commerce, March 23, 1992. Left to right: Justice Sandra Day O'Connor, Barbara Bush, President George H. W. Bush, Wallace Barnes, Barbara Franklin. Barbara Hackman Franklin Papers, Penn State University Archives.

campaign to win the women's vote at a time when the president was not attracting much fervor from women. She was, for all intents and purposes, the liaison of the White House to the women's movement. Barbara Franklin developed the role that Anne Armstrong would fill after the 1972 election, when Armstrong was named a counselor to the president and head of a new Office of Women's Programs.

Feeling confident that the women's program was moving forward, Franklin then stepped into a new role as an original commissioner of the U.S. Consumer Product Safety Commission and became one of those pioneering women in government herself. Upon leaving the commission in 1979, she joined the faculty of the Wharton School, formed her first consulting business, joined the boards of seven large corporations, and then became secretary of commerce in the administration of President George H. W. Bush. As commerce secretary she led a special mission to China in 1992 to normalize commercial relations and was the first cabinet officer to go to China following the events of June 1989 at Tiananmen Square. Interestingly, before she left for China, former President Nixon called her to encourage and support what she had been sent to do. Twenty years after his pathbreaking trip to China in 1972, she was continuing the work he had begun. Today she is president of her own international business consulting firm, in Washington, D.C., has served on the boards of directors of fourteen public companies, is chair of the National Association of Corporate Directors and chair emerita of the Economic Club of New York, and participates in numerous other national and international organizations.

Perhaps a key point is that all of the effort expended toward these goals created changes that were not and, soon, could not be rolled back. The program of appointing women to high-level positions continued under President Ford and thereafter. Although there might have been somewhat less enthusiasm about the entire range of women's issues in later times, since other events had overtaken America's conversation about women's rights, major appointments of women to top positions did not diminish. President Ford appointed Carla Hills to be secretary of housing and urban development in 1975, and President Carter appointed three women to his cabinet: Juanita M. Kreps as secretary of commerce in 1977, Patricia Roberts Harris first as secretary of housing and urban development in 1977 and then as secretary of health and human services in 1979, and Shirley M. Hufstedler as secretary of education in 1979.

President Reagan appointed Sandra Day O'Connor to the Supreme Court in 1981, and his cabinet included Elizabeth H. Dole as secretary of transportation, Margaret M. Heckler as secretary of health and human services (both appointed in 1983), and Ann McLaughlin Korologos as secretary of labor (appointed in 1987). President Bush appointed Elizabeth Dole in 1989 and her successor Lynne Martin in 1991 as secretaries of labor and Barbara Franklin as secretary of commerce in 1992.

President Clinton appointed Ruth Bader Ginsburg to the Supreme Court in 1993; he also appointed Madeleine Albright (1997), Hazel O'Leary (1993), and Janet Reno (1993), the first female secretaries of state and energy and attorney general, respectively, as well as Donna Shalala as secretary of health and human services in 1993 and Alexis Herman as secretary of labor in 1997. President George W. Bush appointed Gale Norton and Ann Veneman, both in 2001, as the first female secretaries of interior and agriculture, respectively; Elaine Chao as secretary of labor in 2001; Condoleezza

Rice as secretary of state and Margaret Spellings as secretary of education, both in 2005; and Mary Peters as secretary of transportation in 2006. President Barack Obama has appointed Sonia Sotomayor in 2009 and Elena Kagan in 2010 to the Supreme Court, and four women as cabinet secretaries so far, including Janet Napolitano as the first female secretary of homeland security, Hillary Clinton for State, Hilda Solis for Labor, and Kathleen Sibelius for Health and Human Services, all in 2009.[3]

These have become among the most prominent women in government, and we have also increasingly seen more women in the House and Senate, as governors, state legislators, and state officials, and in local government positions as well. The primary sources—both the interviews and the documents of the Nixon administration—recount the hopes and expectations of these women and that they were determined that such progress would eventually happen.

The women's movement, despite its best efforts, has never presented a united front. But all the organizations and activists contributed to forward movement, whether they worked from within the system or raised issues from the outside. In these interviews, almost entirely of Republican women, it is apparent that they perceived themselves to be somewhat different from the strident feminists and "women's libbers." Initially, they were reluctant to call themselves feminists, as were most American women. A Republican sensibility that government could not do everything, or solve every problem, was present among them to one degree or another. However, changing the government to enable women to participate in it more equitably, and to the best of their abilities, by banishing sexist customs, regulations, and laws, was very much on their agenda. Just as important was the example government could set for the rest of the country's businesses and institutions, and these women worked diligently for that example to be seen and repeated.

The landmark acts of the Kennedy and Johnson administrations—the Equal Pay Act of 1963, which prohibited discrimination by gender in pay for employees covered under the Fair Labor Standards Act as well as executives and professionals; along with Title VII of the Civil Rights Act of 1964—brought women's rights further along the path to gender equity.

However, one other very significant piece of legislation has not been mentioned so far. The Education Amendments, signed by President Nixon on June 23, 1972, included the famous Title IX. Its simple sentence was another major victory for women in the fight for equal rights. When the final regulations were issued in 1975, Title IX covered women and girls, students and employees alike, protecting them from discrimination, including sexual

---

TITLE IX, EDUCATION AMENDMENTS OF 1972

No person in the United States shall, on the basis of sex, be excluded from
participation in, be denied the benefits of, or be subject to discrimination
under any educational programs or activity receiving federal financial
assistance.

---

harassment, in admissions and every other aspect of education, from kinder-
garten to graduate school, in every institution receiving federal assistance.
Today, Title IX has become almost synonymous with women's participation
in athletics—which is sometimes the most controversial aspect of it—but its
impact has been far broader. Title IX grew out of the 1967 change to Executive Order 11246 (i.e., Executive Order 11375 of October 13, 1967), barring
sex discrimination by federal contractors. Women legislators like Martha
Griffiths and Edith Green (D-OH) quickly began to advocate for broader
measures in education to ban discrimination against women, and the legislation slowly began to take form.

❋

The women's movement has continued to evolve over the last thirty years,
and controversies over family planning, abortion rights, and social issues
have redrawn the political landscape for women. The civil rights that women
achieved in the 1970s and since have not been reversed, and the economic
power of women has never been stronger. This book has attempted to present the achievements of Barbara Hackman Franklin and the memories of "a
few good women" in the hope that their role in that continuum of women's
history will not be forgotten or overlooked in the future. In memory of all
those women who worked so hard to change the federal government, and by
extension the rest of the country some forty years ago, it seems fitting to
close with a quotation from former National Labor Relations Board chair
Betty Southard Murphy: "I cannot really 'pay back,' but I can try. So I guess
that I think that everybody should just keep building. Everybody should contribute something for those yet to come."[4]

by Barbara Hackman Franklin

As you have read, forty years ago I was an assistant vice president at Citibank in New York, thoroughly enjoying my job when Fred Malek called. He said that President Nixon was initiating an effort to advance women in the federal government and asked me to consider joining the White House staff to create a new position charged with recruiting women for high-level jobs in government. I agreed to consider this, but some friends advised me not to go to Washington. They thought the Nixon administration wasn't really interested in advancing women and that being part of a fruitless effort would damage my career.

At that time, the women's movement was in full swing and had greatly elevated the issue of equality for women. I believed in that cause then and still do today. So, despite the advice of those naysayers, I took a leave of absence from the bank and joined the White House staff in April of 1971. There I spent the next two years working day and night to identify and recruit women for executive positions in the federal government, work with women's groups, and build connections between the administration and American women. At the time, I never dreamed that this would turn out to be a watershed period of women's history.

My experience in the White House nearly forty years ago left a deep and lasting impression. I saw firsthand the results of inequality in the workplace. I received so many letters and résumés from women who really needed a job. They were divorced or widowed, not financially secure, and simply did not have the training or skills needed for the workplace. Then, too, there were the stereotypes about what women should and should not do. Women in leadership positions were rare, and American society had not fully accepted the idea of women having both families and careers.

When I left my White House position two years later, I had mixed emotions. I felt good about what we had accomplished for women but knew there was still so much more to do. But I believed our society would change to make things fairer for women, though it would take longer than we might wish.

FIGURE 94
*Barbara Hackman Franklin, U.S. secretary of
commerce, February 27, 1992–January 20,
1993. Barbara Hackman Franklin Papers,
Penn State University Archives.*

As the years went by, change did come—faster than I had originally
thought. In the late 1980s, nearly two decades later, I, along with Margita
White, who had also served in the Nixon White House, and Jean Rainey,
began to look at what had been accomplished in the early 1970s to push
women toward fuller participation in the federal government. We believed
those actions opened new doors for women and prompted a ripple through
our society. This chapter of progress had been forgotten, overwhelmed by
such things as President Nixon's opening to China and the Watergate scandal.
We believed there was importance in telling the story of those times and the
difficulties that were faced and overcome. We wanted to bring this chapter to
life but didn't know how.

In 1992, I returned to government to serve as secretary of commerce
for President George H. W. Bush. After this, my governmental papers—those
I was free to take copies of—went to the archives at the Pennsylvania State
University, my alma mater. Lee Stout, the university archivist, catalogued my
papers. Upon perusing the White House material, which was quite frankly a
mess since it had been in boxes in the basement for twenty years, he was
impressed by what he saw. "This effort to advance women was real," he said,
"It wasn't just public relations. You should do something with this. How
about oral history?"

That was the genesis of the idea for an oral history project, which we
started on a wing and a prayer in my company's Washington office in 1996
with the Penn State University Libraries as our partner. Margita White came up
with the name for the project—"A Few Good Women"—and then we added
"Advancing the Cause of Women in Government, 1969–74." Fortunately for

the project, Jean Rainey agreed to become its first administrator. She was the ideal choice. Jean was herself a pioneer who had her own public relations firm in the 1970s while raising three children, and she knew and had befriended many of the women in Washington at that time. After being trained in oral history technique, Jean conducted nearly all of the fifty-some interviews that are part of this collection. She did an extraordinary job, and we are tremendously grateful to her.

Before we began, we formulated a budget, and I raised the initial funding for the project, mainly from corporate foundations. I single out the Aetna Foundation, the major foundation supporter, and its then-president, Marilda Gandara, who believed in the project from the beginning and gave us inspiration every inch of the way. We established a small advisory board, which I still chair, to oversee the project. We had our meetings around the conference table in my offices and relived many experiences, both good and bad, from those early days. In addition to Margita, Jean, and Marilda, several other members of that initial advisory board gave great support and advice: Helen Delich Bentley, Charlie Clapp, Pat Hutar, and Jewel Lafontant. Special thanks must also go to Dean Nancy Eaton, then the newly appointed dean of Penn State Libraries. She joined our advisory board and was an invaluable participant and supporter from that time forward. We would not be where we are today were it not for her leadership of the Penn State side of our partnership.

As the project began, the first task was to locate the women—and the men—who had made these advances possible and secure their agreement to be interviewed. We worked from the list of appointees that had been in my papers. Locating some of these people turned out to be quite difficult, a real sleuthing job. And unfortunately, some of the most important were no longer with us—President Nixon, Mrs. Nixon, and Robert Finch, former HEW secretary and counselor to the president.

Special mention must be made of Bob Finch because I believe that the Nixon women initiative, which was in a formative state, really began to move when he joined the White House staff as counselor to the president. Bob understood the politics around the drumbeat for women's equality, but he also believed that furthering equality was the right thing to do. And while I was several layers down in the White House hierarchy, in Presidential Personnel led by Fred Malek, I always thought there was someone higher in the chain of command who had the president's ear.

Jean Rainey began the interview process—these are audio interviews—and the material she collected is fascinating and so are the personal stories of these women pioneers. The Penn State Special Collections Library holds the

FIGURE 95
Reunion of "A Few Good Women" at the invitation of President George W. Bush. Photographed in the Indian Treaty Room, Eisenhower Executive Office Building, March 27, 2003. Front row, seated, left to right: Tricia Nixon Cox, Helen Delich Bentley, Vera Glaser, Virginia Knauer, Vera Hirschberg. Back row, left to right: Margaret Gaynor, Pat Hutar, Betty Athanasakos, Connie Stuart, Judy Cole, Ruth Davis, Barbara Franklin, Georgiana Sheldon Sharp, Betty Murphy, Julie Nixon Eisenhower, Bret Sturtevant, Bobbie Kilberg, Fred Malek, Lucy Winchester Breathitt, Maria Downs, Charlie Clapp, and Nancy Steorts. Reflections Photography, Barbara Hackman Franklin Papers, Penn State University Archives.

histories as well as additional papers some of the interviewees have donated. Penn State created a website and produced a brochure to describe the project. When Jean completed the first phase of the project—some twenty-five interviews—we had the project peer-reviewed by an oral history professional, since there are standards to be met if a project is to stand up academically. Our project passed with flying colors.

Then, in 2003, the White House of President George W. Bush hosted a reception to honor "A Few Good Women," and we invited everyone on our interview list, current women cabinet members, and other well-known women. The reception happened to fall on the very day the Iraq war began, and there were additional security checkpoints to pass through to get into the Eisenhower Office Building. I remember being very concerned that some of our older interviewees would have difficulty navigating all of this and that things would be worse if it rained (it didn't). The gathering instantly took off—many of the former appointees had not seen each other in years. Vera Glaser, the reporter whose question at the Nixon news conference triggered a series of events, was front and center. President Nixon's daughters, Tricia Nixon Cox and Julie Nixon Eisenhower, were there. Elizabeth Dole, who had been interviewed and was then in the U.S. Senate, attended. The enthusiasm of that event moved us into phase two of the project, during which another twenty-two interviews were completed.

During this time, we began to discuss ways to put a more public face on the project to illuminate what happened back then and to tell the stories of that remarkable group of women appointees. The idea of a book emerged, and it seems fitting that the author is Lee Stout, the man who came up with the idea of the oral history project in the first place. We appreciate his work.

There is one other man I want to single out for appreciation, and that is my husband, Wally Barnes, the retired chairman and CEO of Barnes Group, Inc, in Bristol, Connecticut. He has been enormously supportive of me and my career throughout our marriage and has been an enthusiastic supporter and believer in this project.

And so here we are. We want young people today to know what the world was like back then and to understand that a lot of pioneering work was done to create the opportunities that women have in this century. We want them to know that one individual—or "a few"—with the courage of their convictions can absolutely make a difference. But we also recognize that there are barriers still to be broken if women are to enjoy true equality. We need more women in our political leadership posts, and I am confident that one day Americans will elect a woman president of the United States. I made speeches to that effect forty years ago to young women, saying that I hoped to see in my lifetime a woman elected president. "Maybe it will be one of you," I would tell them. I do think this will happen, and thanks to the efforts of "A Few Good Women" and many others who worked for this cause over the years, that day is closer than ever.

Washington, D.C., and Bristol, Connecticut
June 2011

The "A Few Good Women" Oral History Project

Interviewees, status of their interview transcript, and brief description of their role or position during the Nixon administration.

ALLAN, VIRGINIA — *Interview open.* Chair of the Task Force on Women's Rights and Responsibilities, deputy assistant secretary of state for public affairs, and worked with the International Women's Year conference in Mexico City in 1975.

ANDERSON, STANTON D. — *Interview open.* Member of the White House Personnel Office and deputy secretary of state for congressional relations.

ARMSTRONG, ANNE L. — *Interview open.* Cochair of the Republican National Committee in 1971 and counselor to the president in 1972.

ATHANASAKOS, BETTY — *Interview open.* A Florida municipal judge, she was a member of the Task Force on Women's Rights and Responsibilities, chaired the Secretary's Advisory Committee on the Rights and Responsibilities of Women for the Department of Health, Education, and Welfare from 1972 to 1976, and was also a member of the National Commission on the Observance of International Women's Year from 1975 to 1978.

BAÑUELOS, ROMANA — *Interview closed.* California businesswoman, she served as treasurer of the United States from 1971 to 1974.

BEDELL, CATHERINE — *Interview open.* Member of the U.S. House of Representatives from Washington (1959–1971), appointed to the United States International Trade Commission and served 1971 to 1981.

BENTLEY, HELEN DELICH — *Interview open.* Baltimore journalist, she chaired the Federal Maritime Commission from 1969 to 1975.

CLAPP, CHARLES L. — *Interview open.* Special assistant to the president, responsible for the seventeen presidential task forces developed in the domestic area, and a member of the Domestic Council staff.

COLE, JUDY — *Interview closed.* Secretary to the president's political adviser, then staff assistant to the president in the Office of Personnel, later serving as a staff assistant to the director of the Arms Control Disarmament Agency, and as deputy assistant administrator for legislative affairs for the National Aeronautics and Space Administration.

CUNNINGHAM, EVELYN — *Interview open*. African American journalist and former assistant to New York Governor Rockefeller, she was a member of the Task Force on Women's Rights and Responsibilities in 1969.

DAVIS, RUTH M. — *Interview open*. Pioneering computer scientist, she held many scientific positions in the federal government, including deputy undersecretary of defense for research and advanced technology.

DOLE, ELIZABETH — *Interview open*. From 1969 to 1973, she served as deputy assistant to President Nixon for consumer affairs.

EISENHOWER, JULIE NIXON — *Interview open*. Graduated from Smith College in 1970 and received a master's degree in elementary education from Catholic University in 1971; she was active in both of her father's presidential campaigns and was a frequent spokesperson for him.

FRANKLIN, BARBARA HACKMAN — *Interview open*. Staff assistant to President Richard M. Nixon from 1971 to 1973 to recruit talented women into leadership positions in the federal government, appointed as commissioner and vice-chair of the Consumer Product Safety Commission in 1973.

GLASER, VERA — *Interview open*. Washington journalist and a member of the Task Force on Women's Rights and Responsibilities.

HALL, CYNTHIA HOLCOMB — *Interview open*. Lawyer and former Treasury official, she was appointed a judge in the United States Tax Court in 1972.

HAUSER, RITA — *Interview open*. An international lawyer, she served as a consultant to the Task Force on Women's Rights and Responsibilities and was appointed U.S. representative to the U.N. Commission on Human Rights.

HERRINGER, FRANK — *Interview open*. A member of the White House Personnel Office liaison staff, he became urban mass transit administrator in 1973.

HILLS, CARLA — *Interview open*. Formerly assistant U.S. attorney in Los Angeles, she became assistant U.S. attorney general in 1973.

HIRSCHBERG, VERA — *Interview restricted*. A journalist, she was a presidential speechwriter from 1972 to 1974.

HITT, PAT — *Interview open*. National cochair of the Nixon-Agnew campaign in 1968. In January 1969, she was named assistant secretary for community and field services, in the Department of Health, Education, and Welfare, where she served until 1975.

HOLM, JEANNE M. — *Interview open*. An army veteran of World War II, she was director of Women in the Air Force from 1965 to 1973. She was the first woman brigadier general in the air force and first woman major general in the U.S. Armed Forces.

HUTAR, PATRICIA — *Interview open*. Cochair of the Republican National Committee. She was a member of the Task Force on Women's Rights and Responsibilities. She was later appointed U.S. representative to the U.N. Commission on the Status of Women and chaired the U.S. delegations to the International Women's Year Conference in Mexico City in 1975.

JAMES, E. PENDLETON — *Interview open.* From 1970 to 1972, he served as deputy special assistant to the president with primary responsibility for recruiting leading figures to fill presidential appointment positions.

JONES, JERRY — *Interview closed.* Joined the White House Personnel Office in 1970. From April to November 1972, he worked on Nixon's reelection campaign and then returned to the Personnel Office, of which he became director in January 1973. In the spring of 1974, he became staff secretary to the president.

KAUPINEN, ALLEN G. — *Interview open.* Joined the White House in 1969 to recruit candidates for public advisory boards and commissions. In 1970, his role expanded to include recruiting for cabinet-level departments and agencies. He served on the president's campaign committee starting in November 1971. Following the reelection, he resumed recruiting presidential appointees. In 1973, he became assistant administrator of the U.S. General Services Administration.

KILBERG, BOBBIE — *Interview open.* In 1969, she was named a White House fellow and served first on the staff of the Domestic Policy Council in the Nixon White House and then as a staff assistant to the president through 1971.

KINGSLEY, DANIEL — *Interview open.* During the Nixon administration, he served as special assistant to the president and director of presidential personnel in the White House. He was also commissioner of the General Services Administration and was responsible for oversight of the Strategic and Critical Materials Reserve.

KNAUER, VIRGINIA — *Interview open.* In April 1969, she became special adviser to the president and director of the Office for Consumer Affairs. She also served on the Cost of Living Council and a number of other White House domestic policy committees.

KOROLOGOS, ANN M. — *Interview restricted.* Worked on the reelection campaign from October 1971 and then became public affairs director at the Environmental Protection Agency after the election and stayed until the late summer of 1973, when she returned to the private sector.

LAIRD, MELVIN — *Interview open.* After nine terms representing Wisconsin in the House, he served as secretary of defense from 1968 to 1973 and as counselor to the president for domestic affairs from 1973 to 1974.

LAWTON, ESTHER — *Interview open.* An expert in position classification, she was a longtime staff member of the Treasury Department, becoming assistant director in 1961 and deputy director of personnel for the department in 1972. She was an internationally recognized expert in personnel work and a major supporter of Barbara Franklin's work in the White House.

MALEK, FREDERICK V. — *Interview open.* Appointed deputy undersecretary of the Department of Health, Education, and Welfare in 1969. Then in 1970 he became special assistant to President Nixon, heading the White House Personnel Office. He later served as deputy director of the Office of Management and Budget and then as a member of the White House Domestic Council, before leaving government service in 1975.

MARSHALL, CAROL M. — *Interview open.* After almost eight years as a legislative staff member on the Hill, she was appointed congressional relations director for the Office of Economic Opportunity in 1971. She remained with OEO in various roles until 1973, when she left government to attend law school.

MURPHY, BETTY SOUTHARD — *Interview open.* A lawyer and adjunct professor of law, in 1974 she was appointed administrator of the Wage and Hour Division of the Department of Labor, and in 1975, she was appointed chair of the National Labor Relations Board.

NEWMAN, CONSTANCE BERRY — *Interview open.* From 1969 to 1971, she was special assistant to the secretary and deputy undersecretary of the U.S. Department of Health, Education, and Welfare. In 1971, she was appointed director of Volunteers in Service to America, in which capacity she served until 1973. She was named a commissioner of the Consumer Product Safety Commission from 1973, serving in 1976 as vice-chair as well.

PAYTON, SALLYANNE — *Interview open.* In 1971, she began work on the White House Domestic Council staff. In 1973, she became chief counsel of the Urban Mass Transportation Administration in the Department of Transportation. She left in 1976 to join the faculty of the University of Michigan Law School.

ROSE, SUSAN PORTER — *Interview restricted.* A former congressional staff assistant and educator, she served from 1971 to 1972 as assistant director of correspondence and from 1972 to 1974 as director of scheduling for First Lady Pat Nixon.

SHARP, GEORGINA SHELDON — *Interview restricted.* A former assistant to Representative Rogers B. Morton, she became a special recruiter for the Peace Corps in 1969 and from 1969 to 1975 was deputy director of the Defense Civil Preparedness Agency.

STUART, CONSTANCE C. — *Interview open.* In 1969, she was appointed staff director and press secretary to First Lady Pat Nixon. She held this position until 1973, whereupon she became director of the International Visitor's Program at the U.S. Department of State, where she remained until 1977.

STURTEVANT, BRET — *Interview open.* An experienced patent attorney, in 1971 she was appointed examiner-in-chief for the U.S. Patent and Trademark Office Board of Appeals. She remained in office through four administrations, retiring in 1988.

TENNANT, PAULA ADAMS — *Interview open.* A former assistant U.S. attorney for the Territory of Alaska and a California district attorney, she was appointed, in 1970, to the U.S. Board of Parole, where she played a significant role over a number of years in reforming the federal parole process.

TOOTE, GLORIA — *Interview closed.* An attorney and entrepreneur, she was named assistant director of ACTION (1971–1973). From 1973 to 1975, she served as assistant secretary of the U.S. Department of Housing and Urban Development.

UCCELLO, ANN — *Interview open.* After a career as a retailing executive and election as council member and mayor of Hartford, Connecticut, she was named director of the Office of Consumer Affairs in the Department of Transportation in 1971.

She continued to serve in Washington until 1979, when she returned to her family business.

WALKER, CHARLS — *Interview closed*. Having served as a Federal Reserve economist and adviser to the secretary of the treasury in the Eisenhower administration, he was deputy secretary of the treasury during the first Nixon administration. He also chaired President Nixon's Committee on Minority Enterprise before forming his own consulting firm in 1973.

WHITE, MARGITA — *Interview open*. After working on the 1968 Nixon campaign, she joined the White House as an assistant to Communications Director Herbert G. Klein. In 1973, she was named assistant director for public information at the U.S. Information Agency and in 1975 returned to the White House as, first, assistant press secretary and, then, director of the restored Office of Communications for President Ford.

WHITMAN, MARINA — *Interview open*. A professor of economics at the University of Pittsburgh, she served, in 1972, as a member of the Price Commission and then as a member of the Council of Economic Advisers until 1973, when she returned to Pitt.

PREFACE

1. Robert V. Daniels, *The Fourth Revolution: Transformations in American Society from the Sixties to the Present* (New York: Routledge, 2006), 144.

2. From "Declaration of Sentiments," on the website of the Women's Rights National Historical Park, Seneca Falls, N.Y., http://www.nps.gov/wori/historyculture/declaration-of-sentiments.htm (accessed May 2, 2011). Originally published in Elizabeth Cady Stanton, *A History of Woman Suffrage*, vol. 1 (Rochester, N.Y.: Fowler and Wells, 1889), 70–71.

3. Betty Friedan, *The Feminine Mystique* (New York: Norton, 1963), 18.

INTRODUCTION

1. *Public Papers of the Presidents, Richard Nixon . . . 1969* (Washington, D.C.: Government Printing Office, 1971), 75–76.

2. Paul Healy, "Capitol Stuff," *Washington Daily News*, February 7, 1969. Clipping in folder 16.27, Catherine East Papers, Schlesinger Library, Radcliffe Institute for Advanced Study, Harvard University. Hereafter cited as CEP.

3. *Public Papers of the Presidents*, 75–76.

4. Vera Glaser, interview by Jean Rainey, August 19, 1997, transcript, "A Few Good Women" Oral History Collection, Penn State University Archives, Special Collections Library, University Libraries, 32. All interview transcripts from this collection hereafter cited as AFGWOHC.

5. Glaser, Speech to CACSW, February 7, 1970, folder 16.26, CEP.

CHAPTER ONE

A variety of sources were drawn on for this chapter, including, in particular, Susan B. Carter et al., eds., *Historical Statistics of the United States: Earliest Times to the Present*, 5 vols. (New York: Cambridge University Press, 2006); Gail Collins, *When Everything Changed: The Amazing Journey of American Women from 1960 to the Present* (New York: Little, Brown, 2009); Stephanie Coontz, *The Way We Never Were: American Families and the Nostalgia Trap* (New York: Basic Books, 1992); David M. Kennedy, *Freedom from Fear: The American People in Depression and War, 1929–1945* (New York: Oxford University Press, 1999); and James T. Patterson,

Grand Expectations: The United States, 1945–1974 (New York: Oxford University Press, 1996).

1. "Legal Contender: Victoria C. Woodhull, First Woman to Run for President; a Brief Historical Sketch by Susan Kullmann." Originally published in *The Women's Quarterly* (Fall 1988). Available from http://feministgeek.com/teaching-learning /woodhull/ (accessed July 29, 2010).

2. James T. Patterson, *Grand Expectations: The United States, 1945–1974* (New York: Oxford University Press, 1996), 719.

CHAPTER TWO

1. White House Central Files (hereafter WHCF), Subject Files HU 2–5, Box 22, folder 2, Nixon Presidential Library. Hereafter cited as NPL.

2. Memo from Cole to Burns and Anderson, February 18, 1969, WHCF, Staff Member and Office Files (hereafter SMOF), Garment Files, Box 170, folder 6, NPL.

3. Dwyer to the president, February 26, 1969, WHCF, Subject Files HU 2–5, Box 22, folder 2, NPL. See also Burns to Dwyer, April 11, 1969, WHCF, SMOF, Garment Files, Alpha-Subject Files, Box 170, folder Women's Affairs: Women's Rights /Miscellaneous, NPL.

4. East to Glaser, February 7, 1969, folder 17.3, CEP.

5. Vera Glaser, interview by Jean Rainey, August 19, 1997, transcript, AFGWOHC, 6.

6. Glaser to Ziegler, March 27, 1969, folder 17.3, CEP.

7. Richard M. Nixon, "Remarks at the Swearing in of Virginia H. Knauer as Special Assistant to the President for Consumer Affairs," April 19, 1969, American Presidency Project. Available from http://www.presidency.ucsb.edu/ws/index.php?pid= 2007 (accessed December 20, 2009).

8. Virginia Knauer, interview by Jean Rainey, April 14, 1998, transcript, AFGWOHC, 7–8.

9. Charles B. Wilkinson to Nola F. Smith, April 29, 1969, WHCF, Subject Files HU 2–5, Box 21, folder 1, Women [beginning December 31, 1969], NPL.

10. Glaser to East, April 18, 1969; Glaser to Pat Nixon, May 9, 1969, both in folder 17.3, CEP.

11. Notes on *Washington Post* story of May 8, 1969, WHCF, Subject Files HU 2–5, Box 21, folder 1, Women [beginning December 31, 1969], NPL.

12. Transcript of Burns's remarks, attached to letter, Glaser to Burns, May 23, 1969, folder 17.3, CEP.

13. Glaser interview, 8.

14. Glaser, notes of telephone conversation with Burns, May 26, 1969, folder 17.3, CEP.

15. Cole to Burns, June 2, 1969, WHCF, SMOF, Garment Files, Box 87, Alpha-Subject Files, folder 3, NPL.

16. Glaser to Burns, May 23, 1969, folder 17.3, CEP.

17. Glaser, "conf with dr Arthur burns . . ." June 4, 1969, folder 17.3, CEP.

18. Cole to Burns, June 3, 1969, WHCF, SMOF Garment Files, Box 170, folder 6, NPL.

19. Baldrige to Flanigan, June 19, 1969, and Flanigan to Baldrige, June 25, 1969, both in WHCF, Subject Files HU 2–5, Box 21, folder 2, Women [beginning June 30, 1969], NPL.

20. Representative Dwyer to the President, July 8, 1969, folder 15.22, CEP.

21. Glaser to John Mitchell, August 23, 1969, folder 9.6, CEP; which also includes responses from eleven agencies, a number of which are annotated by East with the word "sad."

22. Vera Glaser, "The Cabinet's Done Nothing," *Miami Herald*, October 9, 1969, 1G, WHCF, SMOF, Clapp files, Box 39, Task Force Files, folder 2, Women's Rights and Responsibilities [1 of 2], July–October 1969, NPL.

23. Moynihan to Nixon, August 20, 1969, WHCF, Subject Files HU 2–5, Box 21, folder 1, Women [beginning June 30, 1969], NPL.

24. Ehrlichman to Nixon, September 29, 1969, WHCF, Subject Files HU 2–5, Box 21, folder 1 [beginning December 31, 1969], NPL.

25. Melvin Laird, interview by Jean Rainey, October 11, 2004, transcript, AFGWOHC, 11.

26. Glaser interview, 10.

27. Charles Clapp, interview by Jean Rainey, November 17, 1997, transcript, AFGWOHC, 3.

28. Ibid., 5–6.

29. Ibid., 7.

30. Ibid., 7–8.

31. Virginia Allan, interview by Jean Rainey, August 30, 1998, transcript, AFGWOHC, 6–7.

32. Ibid., 27–29.

33. Ibid., 14–15.

34. Clapp interview, 6–7, 8–9.

35. Ibid., 10–11.

36. Ibid.

37. Ibid.

38. Ibid.

39. Patricia Hutar, interview by Jean Rainey, December 2, 1997, transcript, AFGWOHC, 4.

40. Burns to Allan, September 12, 1969, WHCF, SMOF, Clapp files, Box 39, Task Force Files, folder 2, Women's Rights and Responsibilities [1 of 2], July–October 1969, NPL.

41. Hutar interview, 5.

42. Rita E. Hauser, interview by Jean Rainey, July 1, 1998, transcript, AFGWOHC, 7–8.

43. Hutar interview, 9.

44. Evelyn Cunningham, interview by Jean Rainey, February 27, 1998, transcript, AFGWOHC, 17–18.

45. Allan interview, 21. Charles Clapp was present for part of the interview.

46. Hutar interview, 6.

47. The President's Task Force on Women's Rights and Responsibilities, *A Matter of Simple Justice* (Washington, D.C.: Government Printing Office, 1970), pp. iv–vi. Available from http://www.afgw.libraries.psu.edu/AMatterofSimpleJustice.pdf (accessed October 7, 2009).

48. "State of the Union Address, Richard Nixon, January 22, 1970." Available from http://teachingamericanhistory.org/library/index.asp?document=1385 (accessed October 7, 2009).

49. Cunningham interview, 18–19.

50. Ted Lewis, *New York Daily News*, April 24, 1970, photocopy in WHCF, SMOF, Clapp Files, Box 39, folder WRR, Correspondence [1 of 2], August 1969–April 1970, NPL.

51. Hutar interview, 36–37.

52. At that time, the only way women could attend Harvard Business School (HBS) was to complete the first year in the Harvard-Radcliffe Program in Business Administration (HRPBA). The program's forerunner was begun by Radcliffe College in 1937 as an offering in business education. In 1956, it changed to follow a curriculum similar to that taught during the first year of HBS. It was taught by HBS professors on the Radcliffe campus "on the other side of the river" in Cambridge. Franklin, therefore, had to begin her first-year MBA studies in this program. Her second-year studies were at the HBS campus, which is on the Boston side of the Charles River, with the male students. When she accepted the offer to attend HBS and received the combination financial package, it was assumed that she would go on to the second year to complete the MBA degree. Following the 1962–1963 school year, the HRPBA was discontinued, and from then on female students matriculated directly into the HBS's first year on campus. *A "Daring Experiment": Harvard and Business Education for Women, 1937–1970* (Boston: President and Fellows of Harvard College, 2008).

53. Barbara Hackman Franklin, interview by Jean Rainey, November 10, 1998, transcript, AFGWOHC, 3.

54. Ibid., 4.

55. Ibid., 45.

CHAPTER THREE

1. Quoted by Paul Healy, "Capitol Stuff," *Washington Daily News*, February 28, 1969. Clipping in folder 16.27, CEP.

2. Patricia Hitt, interview by Jean Rainey, September 23, 1997, transcript, AFGWOHC, 38.

3. Ibid., 34.

4. Ibid., 35.

5. Healy, "Capitol Stuff."

6. Hitt interview, 17–18. Hitt also mentioned Clair Booth Luce and Faith Baldwin as members.

7. Glaser, notes from Louise Gore Party, March 2, 1969, folder 17.3, CEP. Louise Gore was "the grande dame of Maryland Republican politics," a state legislator, unsuccessful gubernatorial candidate, and Nixon appointee as U.S. ambassador to UNESCO.

8. Virginia Allan, interview by Jean Rainey, August 30, 1998, transcript, AFGWOHC, 3–4.

9. List of suggestions for discussion by the task force, October 6, 1969, WHCF, SMOF, Clapp files, Box 39, Task Force Files, folder Women's Rights and Responsibilities [1 of 2], July–October 1969, NPL.

10. Evelyn Cunningham, interview by Jean Rainey, February 27, 1998, transcript, AFGWOHC, 21.

11. BPW press release, "25 Million Women Ask for White House Representation," September 25, 1970, folder 16.33, CEP. The other fourteen organizations were American Association of University Women, American Home Economics Association, American Medical Women's Association, Association of American Women Dentists, B'nai B'rith Women, Church Women United, National Association of Women Deans and Counselors, National Council of Administrative Women in Education, National Council of Catholic Women, National Home Fashions League, National League for Nursing, Ninety-Nines, Quota International, and Soroptimist.

12. Glaser, "Nixon Silent on Women's Rights," *Miami Herald*, January 23, 1970, folder 16.29, CEP.

13. Nixon's letter to Dwyer quoted in a press release from Dwyer's office, January 29, 1970, folder 16.34, CEP.

14. Helen Delich Bentley, interview by Jean Rainey, February 18, 1998, transcript, AFGWOHC, 20–21.

15. Catherine May Bedell, interview by Jean Rainey, September 29, 1997, transcript, AFGWOHC, 5–6.

16. Richard M. Nixon, "Statement on Announcing the Nomination of Mrs. Helen D. Bentley as a Member of the Federal Maritime Commission." August 9, 1969, American Presidency Project, Document 325. Available from http://www.presidency.ucsb.edu/ws/index.php?pid=2192 (accessed December 10, 2009).

17. Janet M. Martin, *The Presidency and Women: Promise, Performance, and Illusion* (College Station: Texas A&M Press, 2003), 132.

18. Colson was clearly involved in planning for the meeting, and documents in the file show that he knew they wanted to talk about the report in a confidential,

off-the-record meeting. WHCF, Subject Files HU 2–5, Box 22, folder Women's Rights 1/1/70–12/31/70, NPL.

19. Glaser, draft story on the meeting, and "Mrs. Lucille H. Shriver's statement" attached, folder 16.27, CEP.

20. Glaser, text of speech for the Citizens' Advisory Council on the Status of Women, February 7, 1970, folder 16.27, CEP.

21. "Summary of Meeting, February 6–7, 1970, 2d Meeting of the Citizens' Advisory Council on the Status of Women," and memo, Shultz to Nixon, February 13, 1970, both in folder 13.43, CEP.

22. Blackham to Clapp, February 24, 1970, and Clapp's response, March 2, 1970, WHCF, SMOF, Clapp Files, Box 39, Task Force Files, Women's Rights and Responsibilities, Correspondence [1 of 2], August 1969–April 1970, NPL.

23. Memos from Garment to these recipients, April 6, 1970, WHCF, SMOF, Finch Files, Box 29, folder Women's Rights [1 of 2], NPL. A budgetary review of the recommendations had already been done soon after the recommendations were submitted: General Government Management Division to the Director, Bureau of the Budget, December 19, 1969, WHCF, SMOF, Finch Files, Box 29, folder Women's Rights [1 of 2], NPL. In the same folder, at the bottom of an April 10 memo from Clapp to Garment, suggesting a strategy for responding to Republican women who were anxious for the release of the report, Clapp penciled, "You get all the easy areas! Ha! Charlie."

24. Glaser, notes of conversation with "Bruce Rabb, Bradley Patterson (in Garment's office), June 11, 1970," folder 16.33, CEP.

25. Colson to Garment, April 22, 1970, WHCF, SMOF, Finch Files, Box 30, folder Women's Rights [1 of 3], NPL.

26. Note attached to Colson's April 22, 1970, memo to Garment; also attached was a photocopy of the April 22 story from the *Miami Herald* on the report. There was no reporter named, but the story came from the Knight Newspapers' Washington Bureau, which was Glaser's place of employment.

27. Partial transcript of May 4, 1970, press conference held by Constance Stuart concerning Mrs. Nixon's activities, WHCF, SMOF, Finch Files, Box 30, folder Women's Rights [2 of 2], NPL.

28. Glaser, "Bayh Nicks Nixon on Women's Report," *Miami Herald*, May 8, 1970, folder 16.29, CEP.

29. Quoted in memo from Garment to Ken Cole, May 27, 1970, WHCF, SMOF, Finch Files, Box 30, folder Women's Rights Amendment [1 of 4], NPL.

30. Garment to Ken Cole, June 3, 1970, WHCF, SMOF, Clapp Files, Box 39, folder Women's Rights and Responsibilities [2 of 2], November 1969–June 1970, NPL.

31. Department of Justice press release, July 20, 1970, *United States v. Libby-Owens Ford and the United Glass and Ceramic Workers of North America and Its*

Local 9, WHCF, SMOF, Clapp Files, Box 39, Women's Rights and Responsibilities Correspondence [2 of 2], May–December 1970, NPL.

32. Robert B. Semple Jr., "Tighter Rules on Job Prejudice against Women Issued by U.S.," *New York Times*, June 10, 1970.

33. August 26, 1970, was also the date of the Women's Strike for Equality, when 20,000 women demonstrated for social, economic, and political rights in New York City and other sites around the country. Sponsored by NOW, it was the largest protest to date on behalf of women.

34. Colson to David Parker, May 4, 1971, concerning Hauser's "emergent feminism" memorandum, WHCF, Subject Files HU 2–5, Box 21, folder 1/1/1971– 12/31/1971, NPL.

35. Glaser, "as of September 22, 1970 . . . status of recommendations in task force report," folder 16.33, CEP.

36. Glaser, notes of conversation with Harry Fleming, September 28, 1970, folder 16.33, CEP.

37. BPW press release, September 25, 1970, and letter from Leonard Garment to Lucille H. Shriver, October 6, 1970, both in folder 16.33, CEP.

38. Haldeman to Finch, September 9, 1970, WHCF, SMOF, Finch files, Box 28, folder Women and the Administration [1 of 2], NPL. Although there can be no certain connection, it may not be a coincidence that Pat Hitt said "it would certainly take the ball away from the Democrats" when she advocated for a presidential message supporting the ERA in an April 15, 1970, memo to Bob Haldeman, quoted in Martin, *The Presidency and Women*, 132.

39. Glaser notes of conversation with Catherine East, October 20, 1970, folder 16.33, CEP.

40. Glaser notes of conversation with Helen Bentley, October 22, 1970, folder 16.33, CEP.

41. Finch to Office of the Staff Secretary, draft October 29, 1970, WHCF, SMOF, Finch Files, Box 28, folder Women and the Administration [1 of 2], NPL.

42. Glaser notes of conversation with Catherine East, October 20, 1970.

43. Glaser notes of conversation with Helen Bentley, October 22, 1970.

44. Pendleton James, interview by Jean Rainey, October 6, 2000, transcript, AFGWOHC, 3–4.

45. Frederick V. Malek, oral history interview by Martha Joynt Kumar, November 23, 1999, transcript, Office of Presidential Libraries, National Archives and Records Administration; White House Interview Program, White House Transition Project. Available from http://www.archives.gov/presidential-libraries/research/transition -interviews/pdf/malek.pdf (accessed December 21, 2009), 12.

46. Ibid., 4.

47. Helen Delich Bentley, memorandum to the president, "Women in Government and the Nixon Administration," cover memo dated October 22, 1970, p. 11.

Barbara Hackman Franklin Papers, Penn State University Archives, Special Collections Library, University Libraries, Box AM06.02, folder "Program Documents on Women's Recruiting, 1970." Hereafter cited as BHFP.

48. Colson, memo to Bell, October 24, 1970, BHFP.

49. Bentley, memorandum to the president.

50. Malek oral history interview, 2.

51. Richard M. Ferry, memo to Frederick V. Malek, November 20, 1970, "Agenda for Meeting with Mesdames Catherine May, Helen Bentley, and Patricia Hitt. Friday, November 20, 1970," BHFP.

52. Glaser, notes of interview with Bob Finch, November 27, 1970, CEP.

53. Jack Anderson, "Ladies Irate over Nixon Quote," December 7, 1970, folder 15.22, "CACSW, CEP."

54. Glaser, notes of interview with Bob Finch.

55. This procedure is described in an interview with Jon M. Huntsman Sr., the staff secretary to the president. Jon M. Huntsman Sr., oral history interview by Martha Joynt Kumar, February 25, 2000, transcript, Office of Presidential Libraries, National Archives and Records Administration; White House Interview Program, White House Transition Project. Available from http://www.archives.gov/presidential-libraries/research/transition-interviews/pdf/huntsman.pdf (accessed December 21, 2009), 2–6.

56. Robert H. Finch, memorandum to Office of Staff Secretary, December 4, 1970, "Women and the Administration," BHFP.

57. Glaser, interview with Malek, January 6, 1971, folder 16.33, CEP.

58. Glaser, news story (teletype), February 16, 1971, folder 16.33, CEP.

59. Garnett D. Horner, "Nixon Plans Women's Appointments," *Washington Evening Star*, March 10, 1971, E-12, folder 16.33, CEP.

60. Glaser, interview with Hitt, March 10, 1971, folder 16.33, CEP.

61. Glaser, "Women Are a Political Issue in D.C. Circles," *Long Island Press*, March 28, 1971, folder 16.33, CEP.

CHAPTER FOUR

1. Glaser, news story (teletype), April 9, 1971, folder 27.40, CEP.

2. Ibid. Franklin later recalled how such stereotyping frequently appeared in the press and was a constant irritant to her. "Would we ever talk about the 'diminutive, Dresden-doll-like' Henry Kissinger? I used that line. I don't think Henry appreciated this very much." Barbara Hackman Franklin, interview by Jean Rainey, November 10, 1998, transcript, AFGWOHC, 51.

3. Glaser, news story (teletype), April 9, 1971, folder 27.40, CEP.

4. Frederick V. Malek, interview by Jean Rainey, January 14, 1999, transcript, AFGWOHC, 7.

5. Franklin interview, 9.

6. White House press release, April 22, 1971, BHFP, Box AM06.02, folder BHF Biographical/Press Releases, 1971–73.

7. Glaser, interview with Margita White, April 23, 1971, folder 16.32, CEP.

8. Margita White, interview by Jean Rainey, August 16, 2000, transcript, AFGWOHC, 11.

9. Franklin interview, 15.

10. Policy-making positions for purposes of President Nixon's efforts to advance women in the federal government were defined as GS-16 and above. Policy-making jobs fell into two pay categories, the GS or General Schedule and the ES or Executive Schedule. The General Schedule, established by statute, is the predominant pay scale within the U.S. civil service. It includes the majority of professional, technical, administrative, and clerical positions, which fall within GS grades 1 through 15. The top grades, GS-16, 17, and 18, were considered policy-making positions.

Above the General Schedule is the Executive Schedule, which governs the highest-ranked appointive positions. The president appoints individuals to these positions, and most require confirmation by the U.S. Senate. All of these positions are considered policy making and include Cabinet officers, sub-Cabinet officers, the chairman of the Board of Governors of the Federal Reserve System, and certain others.

In the 1970s, the pay for a GS-16 position was $28,000. The top Executive Schedule position paid $60,000. In today's dollars, the equivalent of a GS-16 position pays approximately $120,000; and the highest Executive Schedule positions pay $199,700.

11. "Plan for Recruitment and Placement of Women," ca. February 8, 1971, BHFP, folder Program Documents on Women's Recruiting, February–May, 1971.

12. Malek to Finch and Rumsfeld, memo, March 31, 1971, BHFP, folder Program Documents on Women's Recruiting, February–May, 1971.

13. Finch to the President, memo (Draft), April 14, 1971, BHFP, folder Program Documents on Women's Recruiting, February–May, 1971.

14. Malek to Finch and Rumsfeld, memo with attachments, May 11, 1971, BHFP, folder Program Documents on Women's Recruiting, February–May, 1971.

15. Publicity timetable developed by Malek and Franklin, April 1971, WHCF, SMOF, Finch Files, Box 28, folder Women in Government [1 of 2], NPL.

16. Malek to the President, memo, April 28, 1971, BHFP, folder Program Documents on Women's Recruiting, February–May, 1971.

17. Franklin interview, 12–13.

18. Franklin, "Discussion Draft 1," ca. July 15, 1971, BHFP, folder Program Documents on Women's Recruiting, June–December, 1971.

19. Franklin interview, 16.

20. Ibid., 17.

21. Franklin, e-mail to the author, September 14, 2010.

22. Ibid.

23. Ibid.

24. "Detailed Recruiting Plan for Women—1971," BHFP, folder Program Documents on Women's Recruiting, June–December, 1971.

25. Franklin to Dorothy Allen, December 14, 1971, WHCF, Subject Files HU 2–5, Box 21, 1/1/71–12/31/71, NPL.

26. Pendleton James, interview by Jean Rainey, October 6, 2000, transcript, AFGWOHC, 8.

27. After service on the Committee to Re-elect the President, Jones was chosen to manage the Personnel Office after Malek left to become deputy director of the Office of Management and Budget in early February 1973.

28. Jerry Jones, interview by Lee Stout, December 8, 2008, transcript, AFGWOHC, 9.

29. Stanton D. Anderson, interview by Lee Stout, 8 December 2006, transcript, AFGWOHC, 7.

30. Frank C. Herringer, interview by Lee Stout, April 21, 2008, transcript, AFGWOHC, 5.

31. Jones interview, 10–11.

32. Allan G. Kaupinen, interview by Jean Rainey, June 22, 2006, transcript, AFGWOHC, 20.

33. Anderson interview, 7.

34. Jones interview, 14–15.

35. James interview, 7–8.

36. Esther Lawton, interview by Jean Rainey, January 18, 1998, transcript, AFGWOHC, 22.

37. Franklin interview, 44.

38. Judy Kaufman to Fred Fielding, October 11, 1972, seeking advice on how to handle the donations for the statue, WHCF, Subject Files HU 2–5, Box 21, folder 4/1/1972–12/31/1972, NPL.

39. Franklin interview, 91.

40. Ibid., 44–45.

41. Ibid., 19–20.

42. William P. Rogers to the President, memo, May 18, 1971, "Plans for Improving the Status of Women," BHFP, folder Departmental Plans.

43. "Summary—Departmental Vacancies Targeted for Women," BHFP, folder Program Documents on Women's Recruiting, February–May, 1971.

44. Charls E. Walker, interview by Jean Rainey, December 5, 2005, transcript, AFGWOHC, 24.

45. Franklin interview, 36.

46. Franklin to Malek, memo, June 26, 1971, BHFP, folder Program Documents on Women's Recruiting, June–December, 1971. Franklin began the memo, "Bleeding slightly, but otherwise undaunted, I emerged from the FEW meeting today."

47. Franklin interview, 36–37.

48. Herringer interview, 13–14.

49. Ibid., 28–29.

CHAPTER FIVE

1. Franklin, through Malek, to Finch and Rumsfeld, memo, October 11, 1971, "Progress Report on Women's Program," BHFP, folder Program Documents on Women's Recruiting, June–December 1971.

2. Barbara Hackman Franklin, interview by Jean Rainey, November 10, 1998, transcript, AFGWOHC, 41.

3. "Justice Lillic Remembered for Hard Work, Long Years of Service," *Los Angeles Metropolitan News-Enterprise*, October 31, 2002. Available from http://www.metnews.com/articles/lill103102.htm (accessed January 29, 2010).

4. Julie Nixon Eisenhower, interview by Jean Rainey, March 9, 1999, transcript, AFGWOHC, 14.

5. Malek to Haldeman, memo, October 22, 1971, BHFP, folder Program Documents on Women's Recruiting, June–December 1971.

6. Richard M. Nixon, "Remarks at the Convention of the National Federation of Republican Women," October 22, 1971. American Presidency Project, Document 338. Available from http://www.presidency.ucsb.edu/ws/index.php?pid=3197&st=woman&st1=women (accessed February 12, 2010).

7. Hauser to the president, copied to Mitchell, Ehrlichman, Garment, Price, and Safire, April 12, 1971, WHCF, SMOF, Finch files, Box 29, folder Women in Government [2 of 3], NPL.

8. Garment to Haldeman, April 19, 1971, WHCF, SMOF, Finch files, Box 29, folder Women in Government [2 of 3], NPL.

9. Colson to David Parker, May 4, 1971, mentioning the views of several staffers, WHCF, Subject Files HU 2–5, Box 21, folder 1/1/1971–12/31/1971, NPL.

10. "The Women's Vote," October 1971, WHCF, SMOF, Finch files, Box 28, folder Women—Memos, NPL.

11. Franklin interview, 45–46.

12. Richard M. Nixon, "Address on the State of the Union Delivered Before a Joint Session of the Congress," January 20, 1972. American Presidency Project, Document 14. Available from http://www.presidency.ucsb.edu/ws/index.php?pid=3396 (accessed February 1, 2010).

13. Richard M. Nixon, "Annual Message to the Congress on the State of the Union," January 20, 1972. American Presidency Project, Document 15. Available from http://www.presidency.ucsb.edu/ws/index.php?pid=3407&st=&st1= (accessed February 1, 2010).

14. Ibid.

15. Franklin interview, 35.

16. Garment's documents and reactions to them are found in WHCF, SMOF, Garment files, Box 86, Alpha-Subject Files, folder Equal Rights for Women Amendment

[4 folders], NPL. Franklin has a number of memos to Finch that forward women's letters about the ERA in WHCF, SMOF, Finch files, Box 28, folder Barbara Franklin, NPL. Her answers to many women's inquiries about the president's position are in WHCF, Subject Files HU 2–5, folder 10/1/1971–12/31/1971, NPL. Joan Hoff, in her book *Nixon Reconsidered* (New York: Basic Books, 1994), spends considerable space analyzing the White House's gyrations over the ERA in this period (pp. 105–109).

17. President Nixon's note of congratulations, May 10, 1972, WHCF, Subject Files HU 2–5, Box 21, folder 4/1/1972–12/31/1972, NPL.

18. See WHCF, Subject Files HU 2–5, folder 10/1/1971–12/31/1971, NPL, for examples.

19. Anna May Hayes, U.S. Army (1970), Elizabeth P. Hoisington, U.S. Army (1970), Jeanne M. Holm, U.S. Air Force (1971), Mildred Inez C. Bailey, U.S. Army (1971, who replaced Gen. Hoisington on her retirement), Alene B. Duerk, U.S. Navy (1972), and E. Ann Hoefly, U.S. Air Force (1972).

20. Melvin Laird, interview by Jean Rainey, October 11, 2004, transcript, AFG-WOHC, 8.

21. White House press releases, April 28, 1972, "Statement by the President, Status of Women in the Administration," and "Fact Sheet, Women in the Federal Government," with cover letter from Barbara Franklin, same date. BHFP, folder Program Documents on Women's Recruiting, 1972.

22. Hoff, *Nixon Reconsidered*, 113.

23. Wilma Scott Heide to Richard M. Nixon, letter, April 1, 1972, folder 17.2, CACSW. Women—1972 [Vera Glaser files], CEP.

24. Wilma Scott Heide to Barbara Franklin, letter, May 5, 1972, folder 17.2, CACSW. Women—1972 [Vera Glaser files], CEP.

25. Barbara Franklin, "Plan—to Reach Women," April 4, 1972, BHFP, folder Program Documents on Women's Recruiting, 1972.

26. Franklin interview, 39–40.

27. Franklin, conversation with author, February 12, 2010.

28. Biographical sketch, Ray, Dixy Lee (1914–1994), Essay 601, Online Encyclopedia of Washington State History. Available from http://www.historylink.org/index.cfm?DisplayPage=output.cfm&File_Id=601 (accessed February 2, 2010).

29. Franklin interview, 23–24.

30. "The Administration: Help Wanted (Female)," *Newsweek*, August 21, 1972, 16–17. Available from BHFP, folder Press/Magazine clippings, 1971–1973.

31. Barbara Franklin, "Women's Surrogate Program," as annotated by Clark MacGregor, August 19, 1972, BHFP, folder Program Documents on Women's Recruiting, 1972.

32. James T. Patterson, *Grand Expectations: The United States, 1945–1974* (New York: Oxford University Press, 1996), 762.

33. Franklin, conversation with author.

34. Richard M. Nixon, "Remarks on Plans for the Second Term," November 27, 1972. American Presidency Project, Document 421. Available from http://www.presidency.ucsb.edu/ws/index.php?pid=3710&st=woman&st1=women (accessed February 12, 2010).

35. Ibid.

36. Stanton D. Anderson, interview by Lee Stout, 8 December 2006, transcript, AFGWOHC.

37. Ibid., 3.

38. Jerry Jones, interview by Lee Stout, December 8, 2008, transcript, AFGWOHC, 4–5.

39. Frank C. Herringer, interview by Lee Stout, April 21, 2008, transcript, AFGWOHC, 19.

40. Franklin, conversation with author.

41. Copies of those lists are found in BHFP, folder Compiled Lists of Candidates.

42. She would be sworn in on February 3, along with Fred Malek, who became deputy director of the Office of Management and Budget, and Frank Herringer, who became urban mass transit administrator in the Department of Transportation.

43. Franklin to Malek, memo, December 18, 1972, BHFP, folder Program Documents on Women's Recruiting, 1972.

44. Franklin to Ehrlichman, note, December 12, 1972, BHFP, folder Program Documents on Women's Recruiting, 1972.

45. Ibid.; Marlene Cimons, "First Woman Counselor to President," *Los Angeles Times*, n.d., clipping in folder 1.16, Anne Armstrong, 1972–73, CEP.

46. Anne Armstrong, interview by Jean Rainey, March 24, 1998, transcript, AFGWOHC, 7–8.

47. Anne Armstrong, letter to "Republican Legislators," January 20, 1973, and Anne Armstrong, memo to "Republican Officials in States Where Ratification of the ERA Is Pending," January 19, 1973, both in folder 1.16, Anne Armstrong, 1972–73, CEP.

48. Richard M. Nixon, "Remarks to Recipients of the Federal Woman's Award," March 7, 1973. American Presidency Project, Document 72. Available from http://www.presidency.ucsb.edu/ws/index.php?pid=4133&st=&st1= (accessed February 6, 2010).

49. "About the CPSC." Available from http://www.cpsc.gov/about/about.html (accessed February 6, 2010).

50. Jones interview, 26.

51. "President to Name a Woman Counselor," *New York Times*, December 18, 1972.

52. Franklin, conversation with author.

53. Franklin interview, 57.

54. Franklin to Jones, memo, May 9, 1973, BHFP, folder Program Documents on Women's Recruiting, 1973.

55. Harriet Yedlowski, executive secretary in the Office of Women's Programs, referred a job seeker to Nola Smith and Jerry Jones, head of the White House Personnel Office. See letter dated April 9, 1974, WHCF, Subject Files HU 2–5, Box 23, folder 1/1/1974–8/9/1974, NPL.

CHAPTER SIX

1. Helen Delich Bentley, interview by Jean Rainey, February 18, 1998, transcript, AFGWOHC, 11–12.

2. Catherine May Bedell, interview by Jean Rainey, February 8, 1998, transcript, AFGWOHC, 49–51.

3. Margita White, interview by Jean Rainey, August 16, 2000, transcript, AFGWOHC, 1–4.

4. Patricia Hitt, interview by Jean Rainey, September 23, 1997, transcript, AFGWOHC, 1–2.

5. Marina von Neumann Whitman, interview by Jean Rainey, May 19, 2004, transcript, AFGWOHC, 1–2.

6. Cynthia Holcomb Hall, interview by Jean Rainey, April 10, 1998, transcript, AFGWOHC, 2–3, 33–34.

7. Elizabeth Dole, interview by Jean Rainey, November 5, 2007, transcript, AFGWOHC, 1–2.

8. Carol Mayer Marshall, interview by Jean Rainey, November 17, 2003, transcript, AFGWOHC, 1–2.

9. Corydon Ireland, "O'Connor Marks Women's Progress in Legal Profession, but Warns in Radcliffe Talk of 'Victorian Echoes,'" *Harvard Gazette Online*, June 11, 2009. Available from http://news.harvard.edu/gazette/story/2009/06/0%E2%80%99connor-marks-women%E2%80%99s-progress-in-legal-profession/ (accessed October 2, 2010).

10. Quoted by Elena Kagan in "Women and the Legal Profession—A Status Report. The Leslie H. Arps Memorial Lecture," *The Record* 61:1 (2006): 39. Available from http://www.law.yale.edu/documents/pdf/women_and_the_legal_profession_a_status_report.pdf (accessed September 30, 2010).

11. Fred Strebeigh, *Equal: Women Reshape American Law* (New York: Norton, 2009), x.

12. Rita E. Hauser, interview by Jean Rainey, July 1, 1998, transcript, AFGWOHC, 1–3.

13. Gloria Toote, interview by Jean Rainey, November 20, 2003, transcript, AFGWOHC, 6–7.

14. Paula Adams Tennant, interview by Jean Rainey, August 3, 2000, transcript, AFGWOHC, 35–36, 3–4.

15. Brererton Sturtevant, interview by Jean Rainey, January 10, 2004, transcript, AFGWOHC, 3–6.

16. Carla Hills, interview by Lee Stout, December 8, 2006, transcript, AFGWOHC, 1–3, 22.

17. Sallyanne Payton, interview by Jean Rainey, May 20, 2004, transcript, AFGWOHC, 7–9.

18. Bobbie Greene Kilberg, interview by Jean Rainey, April 4, 2005, transcript, AFGWOHC, 3–5.

19. Betty Southard Murphy, interview by Jean Rainey, March 21, 2005, transcript, AFGWOHC, 2–4.

20. "Legends in the Law: A Conversation with Betty Southard Murphy," originally published in *Bar Report*, October/November 1996. Available from http://www .dcbar.org/for_lawyers/resources/legends_in_the_law/murphy.cfm (accessed June 27, 2010).

CHAPTER SEVEN

1. Fred Strebeigh, *Equal: Women Reshape American Law* (New York: Norton, 2009), x.

2. Marina von Neumann Whitman, interview by Jean Rainey, May 19, 2004, transcript, AFGWOHC, 4–6.

3. Ruth M. Davis, interview by Jean Rainey, May 24, 2006, transcript, AFGWOHC, 22–24.

4. Evelyn Cunningham, interview by Jean Rainey, February 27, 1998, transcript, AFGWOHC, 1–4.

5. "Jeanne Holm," member of the National Women's Hall of Fame, Seneca Falls, N.Y. Available from http://www.greatwomen.org/component/fabrik/details/2/77 (accessed May 7, 2011).

6. Major General Jeanne Holm, interview by Jean Rainey, November 11, 1997, transcript, AFGWOHC, 6, 8–11.

7. Catherine May Bedell, interview by Jean Rainey, February 8, 1998, transcript, AFGWOHC, 35, 33–34.

8. Ann Korologos, interview by Lee Stout, September 1, 2006, transcript, AFGWOHC, 7.

9. Barbara Franklin recalls that she and Stan Anderson asked the Treasury official to make the contact with John Hall as a strategy for recruiting Cynthia Hall.

10. "Expected salaries: his[,] $36,000, hers, $42,500," according to James F. Clarity, "Notes on People: 2 New Tax Brackets," *New York Times*, August 12, 1972, 24.

11. Cynthia Holcomb Hall, interview by Jean Rainey, April 10, 1998, transcript, AFGWOHC, 14–15, 6–11.

12. Constance Newman, interview by Jean Rainey, June 21, 2006, transcript, AFGWOHC, 4–5.

13. Carol Mayer Marshall, interview by Jean Rainey, November 17, 2003, transcript, AFGWOHC, 18–19.

14. Sallyanne Payton, interview by Jean Rainey, May 20, 2004, transcript, AFGWOHC, 10–17.

15. Virginia Knauer, interview by Jean Rainey, April 14, 1998, transcript, AFGWOHC, 2–3, 30.

16. Patricia Hutar, interview by Jean Rainey, December 2, 1997, transcript, AFGWOHC, 52–53.

17. Patricia Hitt, interview by Jean Rainey, September 23, 1997, transcript, AFGWOHC, 43–45.

CHAPTER EIGHT

1. Elizabeth Dole, interview by Jean Rainey, November 5, 2007, transcript, AFGWOHC, 14.

2. Paula Adams Tennant, interview by Jean Rainey, August 3, 2000, transcript, AFGWOHC, 11, 13, 39–40.

3. Sallyanne Payton, interview by Jean Rainey, May 20, 2004, transcript, AFGWOHC, 27.

4. Brereton Sturtevant, interview by Jean Rainey, January 10, 2004, transcript, AFGWOHC, 15–16, 19.

5. State women's commissions resulted from the President's Commission on the Status of Women (PCSW). It was created through executive order by President Kennedy in December 1961 and issued its report in October 1963. The national commission subsequently encouraged states and localities (cities, colleges, universities, etc.) to begin studying women's socio-legal status. All fifty states had women's commissions in operation by 1967. The Citizens' Advisory Council on the Status of Women, administered through the Women's Bureau of the Department of Labor, was the successor organization to the PCSW.

6. The International Women's Year of 1975 was proclaimed by the United Nations General Assembly in 1972. It was planned as an endeavor to promote the equality of women in all societies. The international conference in Mexico City, from June 19 to July 2, was the high point of the year. A ten-year program entitled "World Plan of Action" and a declaration on women's rights were the primary outcomes. In late 1975, the International Women's Year expanded into the International Women's Decade. The United Nations sponsored conferences around the world to discuss women's issues, and the International Women's Decade concluded in 1985.

7. Virginia Allan, interview by Jean Rainey, August 30, 1998, transcript, AFGWOHC, 33, 36, 42–45.

8. The National Commission on the Observance of International Women's Year was created through Executive Order 11832, signed by President Ford on January 9, 1975. It was intended to investigate and suggest solutions to "those inequities that still linger as barriers to the full participation of women in our Nation's life." It coordinated activities in the United States and each state had its own Coordinating

Committee, which raised funds and served as an outreach point to the community. In 1976, the commission issued a report titled " . . . *To Form a More Perfect Union . . .*": *Justice for American Women.* The commission was disbanded after the National Women's Conference in November 1977.

9. The United Nations Commission on the Status of Women was established in 1946 to secure equal political rights, economic rights, and educational opportunities for women throughout the world. It is a functional commission of the U.N. Economic and Social Council. It allows both states and nongovernmental organizations to participate in its sessions. "Every year, representatives of Member States gather at United Nations Headquarters in New York to evaluate progress on gender equality, identify challenges, set global standards and formulate concrete policies to promote gender equality and advancement of women worldwide."

10. Patricia Hutar, interview by Jean Rainey, December 2, 1997, transcript, AFGWOHC, 25, 13, 31–35, 41–42.

11. Margita White, interview by Jean Rainey, August 16, 2000, transcript, AFGWOHC, 23–24.

12. Catherine May Bedell, interview by Jean Rainey, February 8, 1998, transcript, AFGWOHC, 66–67.

13. Julie Nixon Eisenhower, interview by Jean Rainey, March 9, 1999, transcript, AFGWOHC, 5–6, 8.

14. Virginia Knauer, interview by Jean Rainey, April 14, 1998, transcript, AFGWOHC, 17–18.

15. Constance Cornell Stuart, interview by Jean Rainey, October 18, 2005, transcript, AFGWOHC, 25–26.

16. Susan Porter Rose, interview by Jean Rainey, September 15, 2006, transcript, AFGWOHC, 13–14, 12.

17. Major General Jeanne Holm, interview by Jean Rainey, November 11, 1997, transcript, AFGWOHC, 18, 20–22, 38–39.

18. Sallyanne Payton, interview by Jean Rainey, May 20, 2004, transcript, AFGWOHC, 30.

19. Anne Armstrong, interview by Jean Rainey, March 24, 1998, transcript, AFGWOHC, 14–15.

20. Rita E. Hauser, interview by Jean Rainey, July 1, 1998, transcript AFGWOHC, 16–19.

21. Betty Southard Murphy, interview by Jean Rainey, March 21, 2005, transcript, AFGWOHC, 17–19.

CONCLUSION

1. Barbara Hackman Franklin, interview by Lee Stout, December 16, 2009, transcript, AFGWOHC, 20.

2. Barbara Hackman Franklin, interview by Jean Rainey, November 10, 1998, transcript, AFGWOHC, 86–87.

3. Women cabinet secretaries are listed in tabular form on Wikipedia at http://en.wikipedia.org/wiki/List_of_female_United_States_Cabinet_Secretaries (accessed May 9, 2011). Another list on the U.S. House of Representatives website lists former women members of Congress who have served on the cabinet and as U.S. Diplomats: http://womenincongress.house.gov/historical-data/cabinet-members-diplomats.html (accessed May 9, 2011).

4. Betty Southard Murphy, interview by Jean Rainey, March 21, 2005, transcript, AFGWOHC, 19.

BIBLIOGRAPHY

Archives and Manuscripts

East, Catherine. Papers, 1941–1995. MC 477. Arthur and Elizabeth Schlesinger Library on the History of Women in America, Radcliffe Institute for Advanced Study, Harvard University, Cambridge, Mass.

"A Few Good Women" Oral History Collection, 1938–2000. MGN 984. Penn State University Archives, Special Collections Library, The Pennsylvania State University Libraries, University Park.

Franklin, Barbara Hackman. Papers, 1953–1995. MGN 281. Penn State University Archives, Special Collections Library, The Pennsylvania State University Libraries, University Park.

Marshall, Alice K., Women's History Collection. Posters, Ephemera, and Graphics Series. Special Collections, Penn State Harrisburg Library, Middletown.

Presidential Papers of Richard M. Nixon, White House Central Files (WHCF), Richard Nixon Presidential Library (NPL) and Museum, Yorba Linda, Calif.

Staff Member & Office Files, Charles L. Clapp, Administrative Files, Task Force Files, in WHCF, NPL.

Staff Member & Office Files, Robert H. Finch, Women's Rights Files, in WHCF, NPL.

Staff Member & Office Files, Leonard Garment Files, Alpha-Subject Files, in WHCF, NPL.

Subject Files, HU (Human Rights) 2–5 (Equality—Women), in WHCF, NPL.

Books and Articles

American Women: A Library of Congress Guide for the Study of Women's History and Culture in the United States. Edited by Sheridan Harvey et al. Washington, D.C.: Library of Congress, 2001.

Burns, Arthur F. *Inside the Nixon Administration: The Secret Diary of Arthur Burns, 1969–1974.* Edited by Robert H. Ferrell. Lawrence: University Press of Kansas, 2010.

Collins, Gail. *America's Women: Four Hundred Years of Dolls, Drudges, Help-mates, and Heroines.* New York: HarperCollins, 2003.

———. *When Everything Changed: The Amazing Journey of American Women from 1960 to the Present.* New York: Little, Brown, 2009.

Coontz, Stephanie. The *Way We Never Were: American Families and the Nostalgia Trap.* New York: Basic Books, 1992.

A *"Daring Experiment": Harvard and Business Education for Women, 1937–1970.* Boston: President and Fellows of Harvard College, 2008.

Drew, Elizabeth. *Richard M. Nixon.* New York: Times Books, 2007.

Hoff, Joan. *Nixon Reconsidered.* New York: Basic Books, 1994.

Kennedy, David M. *Freedom from Fear: The American People in Depression and War, 1929–1945.* New York: Oxford University Press, 1999.

Martin, Janet. *The Presidency and Women: Promise, Performance, and Illusion.* College Station: Texas A&M Press, 2003.

Nixon, Richard M. *RN: The Memoirs of Richard Nixon.* New York: Grosset & Dunlap, 1978.

The Other Elites: Women, Politics, and Power in the Executive Branch. Edited by MaryAnne Borrelli and Janet M. Martin. Boulder, Colo.: Lynne Reiner Publishers, 1997.

Patterson, James T. *Grand Expectations: The United States, 1945–1974.* New York: Oxford University Press, 1996.

"President to Name a Woman Counselor." *New York Times,* December 18, 1972.

Small, Melvin. *The Presidency of Richard Nixon.* Lawrence: University Press of Kansas, 1999.

Strebeigh, Fred. *Equal: Women Reshape American Law.* New York: Norton, 2009.

Strober, Deborah H., and Gerald S. Strober. *The Nixon Presidency: An Oral History of the Era.* Rev. ed. Washington, D.C.: Brassey's, 2003.

Websites

"About the CPSC." U.S. Consumer Product Safety Commission. http://www.cpsc .gov/about/about.html (accessed February 6, 2010).

"'A Few Good Women . . .': Advancing the Cause of Women in Government, 1969–74." Penn State University Archives, Special Collections Library, Penn State University Libraries. http://www.afgw.libraries.psu.edu/ (accessed June 1, 2011).

"'A Few Good Women . . .': Advancing the Cause of Women in Government, 1969–74. A Curriculum for Grades 6–12." AFGW Project, Pennsylvania Center for the Book, Penn State University Libraries. http://www.pabook .libraries.psu.edu/afgwcur/home.html (accessed June 1, 2011).

Huntsman, Jon M., Sr. Oral history interview by Martha Joynt Kumar, February 25, 2000, transcript, Office of Presidential Libraries, National Archives and Records Administration; White House Interview Program, White House Transition Project. http://www.archives.gov/presidential-libraries/research /transition-interviews/pdf/huntsman.pdf (accessed December 21, 2009).

Ireland, Corydon. "O'Connor Marks Women's Progress in Legal Profession, but Warns in Radcliffe Talk of 'Victorian Echoes.' " *Harvard Gazette Online*, June 11, 2009. http://news.harvard.edu/gazette/story/2009/06/o%E2%80% 99connor-marks-women%E2%80%99s-progress-in-legal-profession/ (accessed October 2, 2010).

"Jeanne Holm," member of the National Women's Hall of Fame, Seneca Falls, N.Y. http://www.greatwomen.org/component/fabrik/details/2/77 (accessed May 7, 2011).

"Justice Lillie Remembered for Hard Work, Long Years of Service," *Los Angeles Metropolitan News-Enterprise*, October 31, 2002. http://www.metnews .com/articles/lill103102.htm (accessed January 29, 2010).

Kagan, Elena. "Women and the Legal Profession—A Status Report. The Leslie H. Arps Memorial Lecture," *The Record*, 61:1 (2006). http://www.law.yale .edu/documents/pdf/women_and_the_legal_profession_a_status_report.pdf (accessed September 30, 2010).

"Legal Contender: Victoria C. Woodhull, First Woman to Run for President; a Brief Historical Sketch by Susan Kullmann." Originally published in *The Women's Quarterly*, Fall 1988. http://feministgeek.com/teaching-learning /woodhull/ (accessed July 29, 2010).

"Legends in the Law: A Conversation with Betty Southard Murphy," originally published in *Bar Report*, October/November 1996. http://www.dcbar.org/for _lawyers/resources/legends_in_the_law/murphy.cfm (accessed June 27, 2010).

"List of Female United States Cabinet Secretaries." http://en.wikipedia.org/wiki/List _of_female_United_States_Cabinet_Secretaries (accessed May 9, 2011).

Malek, Frederick V. Oral history interview by Martha Joynt Kumar, November 23, 1999, transcript, Office of Presidential Libraries, National Archives and Records Administration; White House Interview Program, White House Transition Project. http://www.archives.gov/presidential-libraries/research /transition-interviews/pdf/malek.pdf (accessed December 21, 2009).

"A Matter of Simple Justice. The Report of the President's Task Force on Women's Rights and Responsibilities, April 1970." http://www.afgw.libraries.psu.edu /AMatterofSimpleJustice.pdf (accessed October 7, 2009).

Nixon, Richard M. "Address on the State of the Union Delivered Before a Joint Session of the Congress." January 20, 1972. American Presidency Project, Document 14. http://www.presidency.ucsb.edu/ws/index.php?pid=3396 (accessed February 1, 2010).

————. "Annual Message to the Congress on the State of the Union." January 20, 1972. American Presidency Project, Document 15. http://www.presidency .ucsb.edu/ws/index.php?pid=3407&st=&st1= (accessed February 1, 2010).

————. "Remarks at the Convention of the National Federation of Republican Women." October 22, 1971. American Presidency Project, Document 338. http://www.presidency.ucsb.edu/ws/index.php?pid=3197&st=woman&st1 =women (accessed February 12, 2010).

————. "Remarks at the Swearing in of Virginia H. Knauer as Special Assistant to the President for Consumer Affairs." April 19, 1969. American Presidency Project. http://www.presidency.ucsb.edu/ws/index.php?pid=2007 (accessed December 20, 2009).

————. "Remarks on Plans for the Second Term." November 27, 1972. American Presidency Project, Document 421. http://www.presidency.ucsb.edu/ws /index.php?pid=3710&st=woman&st1=women (accessed February 12, 2010).

————. "Statement on Announcing the Nomination of Mrs. Helen D. Bentley as a Member of the Federal Maritime Commission." August 9, 1969. American Presidency Project, Document 325. http://www.presidency.ucsb.edu/ws /index.php?pid=2192 (accessed December 10, 2009).

————. "State of the Union Address, January 22, 1970." http://teachingamerican history.org/library/index.asp?document=1385 (accessed October 7, 2009).

"Ray, Dixy Lee (1914–1994), Biographical Sketch, Essay 601." The Online Encyclopedia of Washington State History. http://www.historylink.org/index.cfm ?DisplayPage=output.cfm&File_Id=601 (accessed February 2, 2010).

"Women Members Who Became Cabinet Members and United States Diplomats." Women in Congress. http://womenincongress.house.gov/historical-data /cabinet-members-diplomats.html (accessed May 9, 2011).

INDEX

Note: Italicized page numbers denote illustrations.

ACTION, 119
affirmative action, 12, 54
Albright, Madeleine, 185
Allan, Virginia, 26, 90, *163*
    and BPW, 24
    and EWG, 90, 162
    influence of, 30
    and Labor Department, 41
    oral history interview, 163–65
    and political balance, 27
    and President's Task Force, 25–26,
        27, 28, 30, 163–64
    and State Department, 73
    and talent banks, 37
Ancker-Johnson, Betsy, 96
Anderson, Jack, 53
Anderson, Marty, 26
Anderson, Stanton (Stan), 69, 70, 87,
    90, 93–94
Anthony, Daniel R., 9
Anthony, Susan B., bronze bust, 72–73
Armstrong, Anne, 95, 99, *177*
    appointment of, 94–95, 98, 170
    on ERA, 95–96
    and Franklin, 57, 62–64
    as Nixon's favorite, 170
    and Office of Women's Programs,
        95, 176, 184
    oral history interview, 176–80
    as spokesperson, 87
    and Tower, 99

Armstrong, Tobin, 176
Athanasakos, Elizabeth (Betty), 25, 27,
    28, 88, 99, *192*

Baldrige, Letitia, 20
Bañuelos, Romana, 77, *78, 78*
Barnes, Wallace, *184*
Bedell, Catherine May, *12, 40, 88, 105*
    and Amtrak, 53
    as congresswoman, 168
    and Equal Pay Act, 12
    and ERA, 84
    and EWG, 162
    and fifty-state project, 106–7,
        169
    as Franklin supporter, 68
    and Malek, 52
    and Nixon, 39–40
    oral history interview, 104–7,
        141–42
    on presidential action for women,
        38, 39–40
    and Tariff Commission, 53, 61,
        65, 105, 106, 141, 169
    as White House adviser, 55
Bell, George, 51
Bentley, Helen Delich, 39, *51*, 90, *192*
    described, 170
    and ERA, 55, 84
    and Federal Maritime
        Commission, 38–40, 103

Bentley, Helen Delich (*continued*)
    and female presidential
        appointees, 90
    and Finch, 48, 55
    and Franklin, 68, 92
    and Nixon, 49, 50–52, 84, 170
    oral history interview, 103–4
    recruitment of, 92
    as spokesperson, 87
birth control, 6, 7, 41
Black, Hugo, 78
Blackham, Ann, 27, 42
Blackmun, Harry, 38, 78
Bloomberg, Michael, 137
Boersma, Dee, 27
BPW. *See* National Federation of
        Business and Professional
        Women
Breathitt, Lucy Winchester, *192*
Browne-Mayers, Charlotte, 34
Burns, Arthur, 19–20, 23, 24, 28
Bush, Barbara, *184*
Bush, George H. W., 116, 119, 128,
        143–44, *184*, 185
Bush, George W., 185

Carpenter, Liz, 37, 78
Carswell, G. Harrold, 38, 78
Carter, Jimmy, 100, 123, 140, 163,
        186
Castro, Fidel, 137
Chao, Elaine, 185
Citibank. *See* First National City Bank
Citizens' Advisory Council on the Status
        of Women, *21*
    and East, 16, 21
    and Finch, 53, 68, 72
    and Franklin, 68, 72
    and Glaser, xxi, 41
civil rights
    for African Americans, 8, 83
    news coverage of, 135

Nixon on, 82, 153
    for women, 3, 9, 10, 30, 83, 85,
        183
Civil Rights Act (1964), 8, 30, 46, 54,
        186
Clapp, Charles, *192*
    and Allan, 30
    and Blackham, 42
    and Glaser, 23
    and President's Task Force, 26, 27,
        30, 31, 42
    White House role, 23–24
Clark, John, 59
Clinton, Bill, 127, 185
Clinton, Hillary, 186
Cole, Judy, 66, 67, *192*
Cole, Kenneth, 127
Cole, Tom, 14, 19, 20
Colson, Charles W. (Chuck)
    and Bentley, 51
    on Franklin, 72
    and President's Task Force,
        43–44, 46
    on women's movement, 82
    and women's organizations, 40–41
Cook, Bethel O., 77
Council of Economic Advisers, 75, 111,
        112, 134
Cox, Archibald, 98, 123
Cox, Tricia Nixon, 87, *88*, 169, *192*,
        193
Cunningham, Evelyn
    oral history interview, 135–37
    and President's Task Force, 27,
        29–30, 31, 136
    on talent banks, 37
Curtis, Charles, 9

Davis, Ruth M., *134*, 134–35, *192*
day care, 6, 55, 173
Dean, John, 80
Diggs, Charles, 153

discrimination in employment
BPW on, 25
Dwyer on, 14
Executive Order 10925, 12
Executive Order 11246, 8, 42, 54
Executive Order 11375, 41, 45, 187
at First National City Bank, 33
President's Task Force on, 30
suit filed, 46
and Title VII, 8
Whitman on, 132–34
District of Columbia home rule, 150–52
divorce rate, 6–7
Dole, Elizabeth Hanford, 51, 90, 115
appointments of, 162, 170, 185
and Knauer, 17, 171
oral history interview, 113–15,
159–60
Dole, Robert, 115
Domestic Policy Council, 127, 150
Downs, Maria, 192
Dwyer, Florence
on discrimination in employment,
14
on presidential action for women,
19, 20, 38, 83–85
support for Bentley, 39

East, Catherine, 16
and BPW, 26
and Burns, 19–20
and Citizens' Advisory Council,
21
and President's Task Force, 28
on women's political choices, 49
on women's rights, 16
EEOC. See Equal Employment
Opportunity Commission
Ehrlich, Bob, 104
Ehrlichman, John, 40, 72, 151
and Armstrong, 95
and Kilberg, 127

and Payton, 126, 150
on women in government, 23
Eisenhower, David, 171
Eisenhower, Dwight D., 11
Eisenhower, Julie Nixon, 80, 87, 88,
169–71, 170, 192, 193
Environmental Protection Agency (EPA),
142
Eppley, Evelyn, 90
Equal Credit Opportunity Act (1974),
100
Equal Employment Opportunity
Commission (EEOC), 8
Equal Pay Act (1963), 12, 186
Equal Rights Amendment (ERA)
campaign button, 13
Franklin on, 72
Hitt on, 207 n. 38
introduction of, 9
Nixon on, 44–45, 55–56, 83–84
political support for, 10, 44–45,
53, 55, 84, 181
ERA. See Equal Rights Amendment
EWG. See Executive Women in
Government
Executive Order 10925. See under
discrimination in
employment
Executive Order 11246. See under
discrimination in
employment
Executive Order 11375. See under
discrimination in
employment
Executive Women in Government
(EWG), 159, 160, 161, 162

Fair Labor Standards Act, 186
Federally Employed Women, 74, 75
Federal Maritime Commission, 38, 103
Federal Trade Commission, 66, 115, 159
Federal Women's Program, 20

"Female Revolt, The" (Glaser), 15
female suffrage. *See* voting
Feminine Mystique, The (Friedan), 6, 8
feminism
    See also women's movement
    emergent, 81–82
    vs. homemakers, 83
    and labor movement, 11
    peak of, 12–13
    and voting, 82
    vs. women's movement, 186
Ferraro, Geraldine, 4
Ferry, Richard, 52, 59
Fielding, Fred, 62
Fifteenth Amendment, 10
Fifth Amendment, 30
Finch, Robert H. (Bob), 36, 49, 62
    and Franklin, 61–62, 77, 97
    Glaser interview, 52–53
    and Hitt, 35, 37
    on women in administration, 56,
      61
    and women's issues, 48–49, 51,
      53, 55
First National City Bank, 33–34
Flanigan, Peter M., 19, 20, 20, 23,
    39–40
Fleming, Harry, 17, 47
Ford, Betty, 100, *177*
Ford, Gerald, 100, 109, 123, 140,
    151–52, 155, 157, 163, 165,
    172, 177, 180, 185
Fortas, Abe, 38, 78
Fourteenth Amendment, 10, 30, 38
Franklin, Barbara Hackman, 33, *51*,
    57–76, *58*, *59*, *60*, 65, 69,
    75, *79*, 90, 127, *133*, *183*,
    184, *190*, 192
    appointments of, 57–60, 64, 96,
      98
    education, 32–33, 59, 204 n. 52
    and EWG, 159
    and Finch, 61–62, 77, 97
    at First National City Bank, 33–34
    and Korologos, 143
    and Malek, 57–58, 60–61, 62,
      66, 77
    and Newman, 147–48
    on press, 78, 208 n. 2
    on recruiting women, xxii–xxiii,
      34, 38, 57, 60–61, 64–65,
      72–76, 83, 90, 91–91, 98,
      141, 147, 173
    on request for resignations, 94
    staff of, 66
    and talent bank, 60–61, 68–69,
      77, 80, 98
    thesis, 108
    White House role, 182–85
    on women in judiciary, 78–80, 90
    on women's equality, 96, 181–82
    and women's movement, 184
    on women's vote, 82
Friday, Herschel, 79
Friedan, Betty, 6–7, 8
Furness, Betty, 114

Gannon, Ann Ida, 27
Garment, Leonard (Len), 43
    and BPW, 47
    on President's Task Force report,
      43–44, 46
    on women in administration,
      52, 82
Gaynor, Margaret, *192*
gender and workforce, 3, 4–5, 127, 159
G.I. Bill of Rights, 5
Ginsburg, Ruth Bader, 116, 117, 185
Glaser, Vera, 15, 192
    appointment of, 23
    and Burns, 19
    Finch interview, 52–53
    and Fleming, 47
    on Franklin, 57

and Hitt, 37, 56
and Nixon administration, 18–19,
    21, 46, 54–55, 172, 182
at Nixon press conference,
    xxi–xxii, 14, 15, 182
and President's Task Force, 27, 30
on women's issues, 41–42
Going Home to Glory (Eisenhower
    Nixon), 171
Graham, Mary, 151
Green, Edith, 187
Grier, Mary Lou, 61
Griffin, Robert, 115
Griffiths, Martha, 8, 42, *105*, 187
Griswold v. Connecticut, 7

Hackman, Barbara. *See* Franklin,
    Barbara Hackman
Haener, Dorothy, 27
Haldeman, H. R. (Bob), 47
    and Franklin, 72
    and Garment, 82
    and Harlow, 23
    and Hauser, 178
    and Malek, 80
    on women in White House, 47
Hall, Cynthia Holcomb, 89–90, 112–13,
    144, 144–48
Hall, John, 89–90, 144, 145–46
Hampton, Robert, 20, 64
Hanford, Elizabeth. *See* Dole, Elizabeth
    Hanford
Hanks, Nancy, *51*
Harlan, John M., 78, 79
Harlow, Bryce, 18, 23, 35
Harvard Business School, 33, 58, 159,
    204 n. 52
Harvard-Radcliffe Program in Business
    Administration, 204 n. 52
Hauser, Rita, 28–29, 29, 81–82, 117–18,
    178–79
Hayes, Anna, *105*

Haynsworth, Clement, 38, 78
Heckler, Margaret (Peg), 38, 39, 185
Herman, Alexis, 185
Herringer, Frank, 70, 75–76, 93–94, 94
HEW. *See* U.S. Department of Health,
    Education, and Welfare)
Higby, Larry, 93
Hills, Carla Anderson, 92, *123*, 123–25,
    145, 185, 186
Hirschberg, Vera, 88, *192*
Hitt, Bob, 158
Hitt, Patricia Reilly (Pat), *15, 36, 64,*
    109, 157
    appointment of, 14, 35, 110
    on ERA, 207 n. 38
    oral history interview, 109–10,
        157–58
    on women in administration,
        35–37, 56
Hobby, Oveta Culp, 11
Hoisington, Elizabeth, *105*
Holm, Jeanne M., *85, 99, 138*
    and Air Force, 137, 140, 162, 174
    oral history interview, 137–41,
        162–63, 174–76
Home Rule Act (1973), 152
HRPBA. *See* Harvard-Radcliffe Program
    in Business Administration
Hutar, Laddie, 156, *156*
Hutar, Patricia, *156, 192*
    oral history interview, 156–57,
        165–68
    and President's Task Force, 27, 28,
        29, 32, 156, 165

International Women's Day, 100
International Women's Decade, 216 n. 6
International Women's Year
    National Commission on the
        Observance of, 216–17 n. 8
    and state commissions, 163–68,
        216 n. 6

Payton, Sallyanne, *51*, *65*, 90, 125–27, *127*, 149–53, 176
PCSW. *See* President's Commission on the Status of Women
Peace Corps, 119
Pennsylvania State University, 32
Percy, Charles, 115
Peters, Mary, 186
policy-making positions, 209 n. 10
popular culture, 7
Powell, Lewis, 79, 81
Pregnancy Discrimination Act (1981), 100
President's Commission on the Status of Women (PCSW), 11–12, 216 n. 5
President's Task Force on Women's Rights and Responsibilities, 23–32
   and Allan, 25–26, 28, 30, 163
   and Athanasakos, 28, 88
   and Clapp, 26–28, 30
   and Cunningham, 27, 29–30, 31, 136
   and Finch, 53
   and Glaser, 27, 30
   and Hauser, 29, 147, 178
   and Hutar, 27, 28, 29, 32, 156, 165
   and Julie Eisenhower, 169
   members, 25, 26–27
   report of, 30–31, 41–45, 50–51, 54–55, 65, 83
press
   improved coverage, 77–78
   stereotyping in, 208 n. 2

Rainey, Jean, 190–91
Raulinaitis, Valerija, 64, *65*
Rawalt, Marguerite, *183*
Ray, Dixy Lee, 88–89, *89*
Reagan, Ronald, 48, 81, 115, 119, 123, 142, 143, 155, 160, 172, 185

recruiting
   of minority men, 74
   of women, xxii–xxiii, 34, 38, 57, 60–61, 64–65, 72–76, 83
Rehnquist, William, 79, 81, 84
Reid, Charlotte, 38, 61
Reno, Janet, 185
Rice, Condoleezza, 185–86
Richardson, Elliott, 98, 123, 147
Roberts, Carlene, 35
Robinson, Jackie, 136
Rockefeller, Nelson, 118, 136
Roe v. Wade, 38
Rogers, William, *163*
Roosevelt, Eleanor, 11
Roosevelt, Franklin D., 11
Roosevelt, Theodore, 13
Rose, Susan Porter, 173–74
Rosie the Riveter, 4
Ruckelshaus, Jill, 95
Ruckelshaus, William, 142
Rumsfeld, Donald, *43*, *54*, *55*, *148*
   and Franklin, 61, 77
   and Marshall, 149
   on women in administration, 53, 61
Russell, Charles, 103, 104

Sanger, Margaret, 6
Saxbe, William B., 123–24
Schlesinger, James, 89
Schultz, George, 42, *133*
Schweiker, Richard, 115
Scrugham, James G. (Jim), 103, 104
Servicemen's Readjustment Act (1944). *See* G.I. Bill of Rights
sex discrimination. *See* discrimination in employment
sexual behavior, 7
Shafer, Raymond, 154
Shalala, Donna, 185
Sharp, Georgiana Sheldon, 85, 90, *192*
Shay, Sharon, 66

Shriver, Lucille, 41
Sibelius, Kathleen, 186
Simpson, Alan, 27
Smith, Howard W., 8
Smith, Nola, 98, 99
Solis, Hilda, 186
Sotomayor, Sonia, 186
Spain, Jayne, 61, 64, 65, 65, 90
Spellings, Margaret, 186
Stans, Maurice, 122
Stanton, Elizabeth Cady, 9
Stein, Herbert, 133
Steorts, Nancy, 192
stereotyping
    in press, 208 n. 2
    in workforce, 5
Stuart, Constance (Connie), 44, 45,
    172–73, 182–83, 192
Sturtevant, Brereton (Bret), 77, 90,
    121–23, 122, 161, 192
suffrage. See voting

Taft, Robert, Sr., 116
talent banks
    and BPW, 37–38, 47, 67
    and Franklin, 60–61, 68–69, 77,
    80, 98
Task Force on Women's Rights and
    Responsibilities. *See*
    President's Task Force
    on Women's Rights and
    Responsibilities
Tennant, Paula Adams, 90, 119–21, 121
Thomas, Helen, 59
Title IX, Education Amendments,
    186–87
Title VII. *See* Civil Rights Act (1964)
"Tomorrow's Woman" (Glaser), 41
Toote, Gloria, 90, 118–19
Tower, John, 17, 98
Train, Russell, 41
Truman, Harry, 11

Uccello, Ann, 61, 61
United Nations
    Commission on Human Rights,
        118, 178
    Commission on the Status of
        Women, 165, 217 n. 9
Urban Mass Transportation Act (1974),
    152
Urban Mass Transportation
    Administration, 126, 153,
    160–61, 176
U.S. Air Force, 85, 137, 140, 162, 174
U.S. Board of Parole, 120–21, 160
U.S. Civil Service Commission, 11–12,
    60, 65, 68, 182, 209 n. 10
U.S. Department of Defense, 77, 85,
    175
U.S. Department of Health, Education,
    and Welfare (HEW), 35, 54,
    77, 88, 110, 147, 157
U.S. Department of Interior, 77
U.S. Department of Justice, 54, 79, 124,
    125, 174
U.S. Department of Labor, 45, 180, 185,
    187
U.S. Department of State, 73, 77, 118,
    163, 164, 166, 178
U.S. Department of Treasury, 72, 73–74,
    77, 112, 144
U.S. Information Agency, 108, 168
U.S. Patent and Trademark Office Board
    of Appeals, 121, 161
U.S. Supreme Court, 78–81, 92
U.S. Tariff Commission, 53, 61, 65, 105,
    106, 141
U.S. Tax Court, 89, 112, 113, 144, 145,
    147

Veneman, Ann, 185
VISTA, 97, 116, 147
Volunteers in Service to America.
    See VISTA

voting
>patterns, 82
>right to, 10
Voting Rights Act (1965), 8

Walker, Charls, 73–74, 74
Walsh, Ethel Bent, 46, 46, 51, 90, 92,
>92, 162
Watergate scandal, 91, 97, 98–99, 123
White, Margita E., 59, 107, 107–9, 168
White House Domestic Council, 64, 98,
>125, 150, 160
White House Office of Consumer
>Affairs, 17, 114, 154, 155,
>159, 171
White House Office of Women's
>Programs, 95, 176, 184
Whitlow, Evelyn, 27
Whitman, Marina von Neumann, 75,
>75, 110–12, 111, 132–34,
>133
Wilkinson, Charles B., 17, 43
Womanpower Talent Bank, 37
women
>civil rights for, 3, 9, 10, 30, 85,
>183
>education levels, 5, 7
>in law, 116–17, 132, 180
>in military, 3–4, 4, 85, 100,
>138–40
>proper role of, 7
>supportive husbands of, 154–58
>in workforce, 3, 4–6, 127, 159

Women Airforce Service Pilots, 3–4
"Women in Government and the Nixon
>Administration" (Bentley),
>50–52
Women in the Military (Holm), 141
Women's Bureau (Department of
>Labor), 45
women's movement
>*See also* feminism
>as catalyst of change, xxi, 7, 72,
>171
>and civil rights, 3
>on equality, 99–100
>evolution of, 187
>and Franklin, 184
>and Nixon, 82, 86, 90–91, 168
>and PCSW, 12
>peak of, 12–13
>and workforce, 127, 159, 182
Women's Rights Convention, 9–10
Women's Strike for Equality, 207 n. 33
Women's Surrogate Program, 91
"Women's Vote, The" (Franklin), 82
Woodhull, Victoria, 10, 10
Woods, Rose Mary, 52, 52, 67, 90
workforce
>federal pay categories, 68, 209
>n. 10
>women in, 3, 4–5, 11, 54–55, 127,
>135, 159
Wriston, Walter, 34, 97

Ziegler, Ron, 16